WITHDRAWAL

QUOTATIONS
IN
BLACK

QUOTATIONS IN BLACK

Compiled and Edited by

ANITA KING

GREENWOOD PRESS
Westport, Connecticut • London, England

Library of Congress Cataloging in Publication Data
Main entry under title:

Quotations in black.

Includes indexes.
1. Quotations, Black. 2. Proverbs, Black.
I. King, Anita, 1931-
PN6081.3.067   081   80-1794
ISBN 0-313-22128-6 (lib. bdg.)

Library of Congress Catalog Card Number: 80-1794
ISBN: 0-313-22128-6

First published in 1981

Greenwood Press
A division of Congressional Information Service, Inc.
88 Post Road West, Westport, Connecticut 06881

Printed in the United States of America

10 9 8 7 6 5 4 3 2 1

Copyright Acknowledgments

Grateful acknowledgment is given for permission to reprint materials in this book.

Quotes 4, 5, 6, and 7 are from "Hymn to the Sun," "The Whole Creation," and "Watering
the Earth in Egypt and Abroad." Reprinted by permission of Charles Scribner's Sons from

IN MEMORY OF
MY MOTHER AND FATHER

CONTENTS

PREFACE

Several years ago a free-lance assignment took me in search of short sayings by black people. I was surprised to find that although there are several books of quotations in print, the representation of black persons in them is negligible. I was forced to read quantities of material in order to find the relatively small number of sayings required for the assignment.

Realizing that a collection under one cover would save others considerable time and effort, I set out to compile a book of quotations representative of blacks from all over the world and from the past and the present. *Quotations in Black* is the result. Over eleven hundred quotations from more than two hundred men and women are included, along with over four hundred anonymous proverbs attributable to blacks.

The individuals quoted in the first part of the book represent some thirty-seven countries and ten languages. Although contemporary authors account for part of the collection, this first edition concentrates on figures of the past, many of whom have been bypassed in general historical works and textbooks. An effort has been made to include people from all walks of life—politicians, writers, ministers, abolitionists, musicians—whose opinions are as diverse as their professions.

The collection of proverbs which forms the second part of the book presents material from thirty-four nations on the African continent (thirty tribal languages), Democratic Republic of Madagascar, the Cape Verde Islands, six Caribbean countries, South America, and the United States. The specific cultural matrix (that is, language, social customs, religion) distinguishes the proverbs of one group from those of another, yet they all possess a nuance, style, and pattern of phrasing that make them remarkably alike and unmistakably black.

Regardless of nationality, the racial identity of the authors collected here is based on American cultural attitudes and racial concepts according to which all persons with discernible admixtures of Negro ancestry are considered to be Negroes. The following excerpt from *White Over Black: American Attitudes Toward the Negro, 1550-1812* by Winthrop Jordan (Baltimore: Penguin Books, 1968), pp. 167-68, explores this issue:

As far as the continental colonies were concerned, it is easy to detect a pattern which has since become so familiar to Americans that they rarely pause to think about it or to question its logic and inevitability. The word *mulatto* is not frequently used in the United States. It is customarily reserved for biological contexts, and for social purposes a mulatto is termed a *Negro*. Americans lump together both socially and legally all persons with perceptible admixture of Negro ancestry, thus making social definition without regard to genetic logic; white blood becomes socially advantageous only in overwhelming proportion. This peculiar bifurcation seems to have existed almost from the beginning of English contact with Negroes. . . . From the first, every English continental colony lumped mulattoes with Negroes in their slave codes and statutes governing the conduct of free Negroes: the law was clear that mulattoes and Negroes were not to be distinguished for different treatment.

The common link among the individuals represented in *Quotations in Black*, then, is the presence or probability of African ancestors.

Quotations in Black is one writer's selection of black expression. It is intended to reflect the culture, concerns, and compassion of a people during the times and in the places in which they lived. You are invited to share in this selection and to contribute your own favorite extracts and sayings of black people, which will be gratefully acknowledged by this compiler if sent to her in care of the publisher.

Special acknowledgment is extended to the Schomburg Center for Research in Black Culture in New York City, where most of the research for *Quotations in Black* was done.

HOW TO USE
QUOTATIONS IN BLACK

The authors are arranged in chronological sequence according to date of birth. The place of birth is also given, when known. As some persons included in *Quotations in Black* may be unfamiliar to some readers, a short biographical note precedes each author's quotations. For ease of access through indexing, all quotations, including the proverbs, are numbered sequentially throughout the volume. Each author's quotations are arranged chronologically, the sources they come from are identified, and the dates are given whenever possible.

(Example 1)

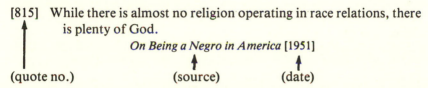

[815]   While there is almost no religion operating in race relations, there
       is plenty of God.
On Being a Negro in America [1951]

(quote no.)   (source)   (date)

In some cases only certain lines of a source have been used. These are indicated by abbreviations: line (1.), lines (11.), stanza(s).

(Example 2)

[569]   Life is half insanity
      As we choose to make it.
Life (s. 2, 11. 3-4) [1910]

The proverbs are organized according to regions, countries, and languages. The countries are arranged alphabetically within the regions, and the languages are arranged alphabetically within the countries. Where a language is spoken in more than one country, the countries that have the largest estimated number of speakers are listed.

Two indexes follow the numbered entries. The first is an alphabetical index of authors, which includes the author's life dates and the first page of the section on that author.

In the second index, sayings are entered by their first lines, which are sometimes abbreviated to conform to space limitations. The quotations are organized under alphabetized subject and key word headings (entry words) rather than initial words. The subject headings are for the convenience of readers seeking quotable material on particular subjects rather than specific quotations. The key words provide an aid in finding specific sayings. Example 3 illustrates the selection of key words from a quotation (no. 689) by Jean Toomer:

(Example 3)

　Fear is a *noose* that *binds* until it *strangles*.

The italicized words all appear as entry words in the index. Subject and key entries appear in the same alphabetical progression.

Following each index item is the author's last name, and the entry number of the quotation. Proverbs are designated by (P) in place of an author's name (see examples 4 and 5).

The entry word is not spelled out in the entry itself; instead, it is indicated by its initial letter, capitalized:

(Example 4)

FAME, notoriety is often mistaken for F (Aesop) - [15]

However, if the entry word has been repeated more than once within the index line, it is spelled out after the first repeat:

(Example 5)

MAN, one M, no man (P) - [1413]

QUOTATIONS IN BLACK

QUOTATIONS

PTAH-HOTEP

Fifth Dynasty (c. 2500 - c. 2340 B.C.)   Egypt

Ptah-hotep was a priest of the pyramids of Aser. A collection of his precepts was found in the Prisse Papyrus, the world's oldest book. A translation from the Egyptian of Ptah-hotep's sayings appears in Hardwicke Rawnsley's Notes for the Nile (1892).

[1]   Happy the sons whom fathers educate,
      There is no error in their being's plan;
      Train thou thy son to be a docile man,
      Whose wisdom is agreeable to the great;
      Let him direct his mouth by what is said,
      Docility his wisdom doth discover;
      Conduct in him grows perfect day by day,
      While error casts the unteachable away;
      The ignorant and fool will be thrown over,
      But knowledge shall lift up the scholar's head.
                    On Home Education [c. 2400 B.C.]

[2]   As for the man who lacks experience
      And listens not, he nothing good can do.
      Knowledge he seems to see in ignorance,
      Profit in loss—to mischief he will go,
      And running in the error of his ways,
      Chooses the opposite of what men praise;
      And so on what is perishing he lives,
      With evil words his belly he doth fill,
      Yea, thereat is astonied, and he thrives
      On what great men think vain, shortlived, and ill,
      And daily from things profitable flies,
      Misled by errors' multiplicities.
                    On the Unteachable and Fools [c. 2400 B.C.]

[3]   Do as your master bids you, how much rather
      Know thou, my son, the precepts of thy father,

Get his commands by heart, to please, his will,
Beyond the letter of his word, fulfill,
Truly the gift of God is a good son
Who doth more than was ordered to be done.
He strives to satisfy his master's heart,
With all his might doth choose the better part.
So shall thy body healthful be, thy king
Will be content with thee in everything.
Upon thee many days the sun shall shine,
And length of years without default be thine.
Wisdom has caused me, in high place, to live
Long on the earth, a hundred years and ten,
I found the favour that a king can give,
First, for life's labour, honoured amongst men.

On Obedience to Fathers—His Last Word [c. 2400 B.C.]

AKHENATON

(c. 1385 - c. 1355 B.C.)   Egypt

Akhenaton, one of the most familiar of ancient Egyptian pharaohs, lived during the Eighteenth Dynasty. His religious hymns, translated from the Egyptian, appear in a reprint of James H. Breasted's Development of Religion and Thought in Ancient Egypt *(1970).*

[4]   The dawning is beautiful in the horizon of heaven,
       O living Aton, beginning of life!
       When thou risest in the eastern horizon,
       Thou fillest every land with thy beauty.
       Thou art beautiful, great, glittering high
           above every land,
       Thy rays they encompass the lands, even all
           thou has made.
       Thou art Ra, and thou carriest them away captive;
       Thou bindest them by thy love.
       Though thou art afar, thy rays are upon the earth;
       Though thou art high, thy footprints are the day.

Hymn to the Sun [c. 1360 B.C.]

[5]   How manifold are thy works!

The Whole Creation [c. 1360 B.C.]

[6] Thou settest every man into his place,
Thou suppliest their necessities.
Everyone has his possessions,
And his days are reckoned.
The tongues are diverse in speech,
Their forms likewise and their skins are distinguished.
The Whole Creation [c. 1360 B.C.]

[7] How excellent are thy designs, O lord of eternity!
Watering the Earth in Egypt and Abroad [c. 1360 B.C.]

[8] By thee man liveth.
Hymn to Aton [c. 1360 B.C.]

AESOP

(c. 620 - 560 B.C.)   Cotieum, Phrygia Major (Turkey)

Aesop is world renowned for his classic fables. They were transmitted by oral tradition before reaching written form about 300 B.C. Aesop's Fables are available translated from the Greek in several contemporary editions.

[9] Necessity is the mother of invention.
The Crow and the Pitcher

[10] Union is strength.
The Lion and the Three Bulls

[11] Self-help is the best help.
Hercules and the Wagoner

[12] Whatever you do, do with all your might.
The Boy and the Nettles

[13] Equals make the best friends.
The Two Pots

[14] Everyone is more-or-less the master of his own fate.
The Traveler and Fortune

[15] Notoriety is often mistaken for fame.
The Mischievous Dog

[16]   If words suffice not, blows must follow.
                         The Farmer and the Cranes

[17]   Look before you leap.
                         The Fox and the Goats

PUBLIUS TERENTIUS AFER (Terence)

(192 - 157 B.C.)   Carthage, North Africa (Tunisia)

*The slave of a Roman senator, Terence was freed because of his extra-
ordinary talent. He became one of Rome's outstanding playwrights and his
works were widely studied in the schools of the time. An edition of* The
Comedies of Terence, *translated from the Latin, was published in 1962.*

[18]   . . . love, you know, is strangely whimsical, containing affronts,
jars, parleys, wars, then peace again. Now for you to ask advice to
        love by, is all one as if you ask advice to run mad by.
                         The Eunuch, act I [167 B.C.]

[19]   . . . every dog has his day; there is a time for all things.
                         The Eunuch, act II [167 B.C.]

[20]   Necessity has no law.
                         The Eunuch, act V [167 B.C.]

[21]   So many men, so many minds.
                         Tricks of Phormio, act III [166 B.C.]

[22]   Among men all things are common.
                         The Brothers, act III [165 B.C.]

[23]   Love is a mere caterwaul where scratching begets kissing.
                         The Fair Andrian, act I [162 B.C.]

[24]   Never buy wit, when you can have it at another man's cost.
                         The Self-Tormentor, act I [161 B.C.]

[25]   Too much liberty corrupts an angel.
                         The Self-Tormentor, act III [161 B.C.]

[26]   Diligence outdoes the devil.
>   *The Self-Tormentor*, act III [161 B.C.]   ·

[27]   Pray learn first what 'tis to live; when you have tried that and don't
>   like it, then die if you will.
>   *The Self-Tormentor*, act V [161 B.C.]

QUINTUS SEPTIMIUS FLORENS TERTULLIANUS
(Tertullian)

(c. 160 - c. 230)   Carthage, North Africa (Tunisia)

*Tertullian was an outstanding theologian, writer and philosopher prior to
Saint Augustine. He left the church in 213 to form his own sect known as the
Tertullianists. Tertullian's writings, translated from the Latin, are collected
in* Tertullian, Disciplinary, Moral and Ascetical Works *(1959).*

[28]   . . . men remain in ignorance as long as they hate, and they hate
>   unjustly as long as they remain in ignorance.
>   *Apology* [197]

[29]   Men praise what they know and find fault with what they don't
>   know.
>   *Apology* [197]

[30]   We must . . . consider not only by whom all things were created but
>   also by whom they were perverted.
>   *Spectacles* [c. 198]

[31]   When a thing is abundant it is always cheap.
>   *The Apparel of Women* [c. 200]

[32]   The harder we work to conceal our age, the more we reveal it.
>   *The Apparel of Women*, II [c. 200]

[33]   Although anyone may become evil, not everyone can persevere in
>   good.
>   *Patience* [c. 202]

ORIGINES ADAMANTIUS (Origen)

(c. 185 - 255)   Alexandria, Egypt

Christian philosopher, teacher and scholar, Origen won wide acclaim for his lectures and interpretations of the scriptures. Among his surviving works in modern editions are Prayer: Exhortation to Martydom *(1954) and* The Song of Songs; Commentaries and Homilies *(1954). The following quotations have been translated from the Latin.*

[34]   It is better to be wise than to seem wise.
Against Celsus, Book 3 [c. 215]

[35]   People, in their rashness and ignorance, like to condemn things that are difficult and obscure, rather than . . . learn their meaning by diligent painstaking.
De Principiis, Book 3 [c. 221]

[36]   We do not pray not to be tempted, but not to be conquered when we are tempted.
Concerning Prayer [c. 233]

[37]   Unity comes about by love and truth and good purpose.
Origen on Jeremiah (Fragments) [c. 240]

[38]   When the devil speaks the truth, even his truth does damage.
Origen on Jeremiah (Fragments) [c. 240]

THACIUS CAECILLUS CYPRIANUS (Saint Cyprian)

(200 - 258)   Carthage, North Africa (Tunisia)

A disciple of Tertullian, Cyprian became one of Africa's most powerful bishops and an influential leader in the universal Church. Contemporary editions of Cyprian's works translated from the Latin include his Treatises *(1958) and* Letters *(1964).*

[39]   Every age is reminded by what it hears, that what has been done can be done again. Transgressions never die from the passage of age; crime is never erased by time; vice is never buried in oblivion.
To Donatus [246]

[40]   Arbitrary power exacts usury; the more abundant are the dignities, the more severe the interest on their loan.

To Donatus [246]

[41]   The torments of a few are examples for all.

The Lapsed [251]

[42]   It nothing profits to show virtue in words and destroy truth in deeds.

On Morality [252]

[43]   You who judge others, at sometime be also a judge of yourself. Look into the recesses of your own conscience.

Address to Demetrian [252]

[44]   What a plague of one's thoughts, how great a rust of the heart, to be jealous of another.

On Jealousy and Envy [256]

AURELIUS AUGUSTINUS (Saint Augustine)

(354 - 430)   Tagaste, Numidia (Algeria)

Theologian, scholar, author, and bishop of Hippo (396-430), Saint Augustine exerted an important influence on the development of Western Christianity through his philosophy and thought. A fourteen-volume edition of Saint Augustine's writings, translated from the Latin, was reprinted in 1956.

[45]   For knowledge about all the things that we understand, we do not apply to somebody speaking audible words outside us, but to the truth which governs the mind itself inside us. . . .

The Teacher Within [389]

[46]   . . . many people profit by a preliminary dose of fear or force, which makes it possible for them to be taught something, or to put into practice what had previously been only words to them.

Appeal to the Secular Arm [c. 409]

[47]   . . . while the best men are well guided by love, most men need to be goaded by fear.

Appeal to the Secular Arm [c. 409]

[48] To conquer truly is to overcome all the contrivances of your enemy.
On the Birth of Saint Vincent (Sermon) [Date Unknown]

[49] Those who are agitated must be chastened, the faint-hearted must
be consoled, the feeble must be sustained, the argumentative
must be refuted, the treacherous must be guarded against, the
untutored must be taught, the indolent must be goaded, the
conscientious must be restrained, the proud must be held in
check, the quarrelsome must be placated, the impoverished must
be aided, the oppressed must be delivered, the good must be
commended, the evil must be endured, and all must be loved.
On the Anniversary of His Ordination [Date Unknown]

ANTARAH IBN SHADDAD (Antar)

(c. 650 - c. 715)   Arabia (United Arab Republic)

*Antar was a legendary warrior-poet, celebrated in his own day as a tribal
chief and hero. Tales of his adventures are a part of traditional Arabian
folklore. A four-volume edition of Antar's adventures,* Antarah ibn
Shaddad: Antar, a Bedoueen Romance *was published, translated from the
Arabic, in 1820.*

[50] 'Twas then her beauties first enslaved my heart—
Those glittering pearls and ruby lips, whose kiss
Was sweeter far than honey to the taste.
As when a merchant opes a precious box
Of perfume, such an odor from her breath
Came toward thee, harbinger of her approach;
Or like an untouched meadow, where the rain
Hath fallen freshly on the fragrant herbs
That carpet all its pure untrodden soil:
A meadow where the frequent raindrops fall
Like coins of silver in the quiet pools,
And irrigate it with perpetual streams;
A meadow where the sportive insects hum
Like listless topers singing o'er their cups.

. . . .

But if my valour needeth warranty,
Go ask the hero horsemen of thy tribe,

Ask them how fares it, when I once bestride
My steed, whom every lance by turns assails,
Now rushing singly to defy the host,
Now plunging headlong where the bowmen crowd.
Each glad survivor of the fierce affray
Will tell thee truly how I love the fight,
How little care I have to share the spoils.

from *Ode* [c. 685]

ABU 'UTHMAN AMR IBN BAHR AL-JAHIZ

(c. 778 - 869)   Basra, Asia Minor (Iraq)

Scholar, philosopher and author, al-Jahiz is considered one of the great writers in Arabic literature. Among his major works (all written in Arabic) are The Book of Animals, The Book of Eloquence and Rhetoric, *and numerous essays and treatises.*

[51]   Man indeed hates the one whom he knows, turns against the one
        whom he sees, opposes the one whom he resembles, and
        becomes observant of the faults of those with whom he mingles;
        the greater the love and intimacy, the greater the hatred and
        estrangement.

A Risala [published c. 1012]

[52]   . . . the reward of the work is to come, whereas, the endurance of
        the labor is immediate.

*The Exploits of the Turks and the Army of the Khalifate in
General*, Letter I to al-Fath ibn Khaqan [Date Unknown]

[53]   The man who is an hereditary defender of his rights beats a
        newcomer to them.

*The Exploits of the Turks and the Army of the Khalifate in
General*, Letter I to al-Fath ibn Khaqan [Date Unknown]

[54]   . . . the well-informed, but dishonest in their hostility and malice,
        often succeed in passing off lies as truth and in clothing deception
        in the guise of wisdom.

*The Exploits of the Turks and the Army of the Khalifate in
General*, Letter II to al-Fath ibn Khaqan [Date Unknown]

[55]   . . . a little that makes for concord is better than a great deal that makes for division.

The Exploits of the Turks and the Army of the Khalifate in General, Letter III to al-Fath ibn Khaqan [Date Unknown]

ALI IBN MUSA IBN SA'ID

(1210 - 1280)   Alcalá la Real, Spain

Ibn Sa'id, born of a well-to-do family and educated in Seville, traveled extensively in the Islamic countries. He wrote several books and compiled an anthology, Moorish Poetry *(1243). An English translation from the Arabic was published in 1953.*

[56]   The sun, that bright swan, stoops
       Serenely to the west
       And, slowly sinking, droops
       Its wing on the sea's breast.

Sunlight on the Sea [c. 1230]

[57]   The stars are foam-flecks, white
       Upon the sea of night;
       The moon, frigate proud,
       Tosses on a cloud.

Sea of Night [c. 1231]

JUAN LATINO

(c. 1516 - c. 1599)   Barbary Coast, West Africa

Juan Latino was a famed Latin scholar and leading poet of the Spanish Renaissance. The following excerpts, translated from the Latin, are taken from a biography of Latino, Juan Latino, Slave and Humanist, *written by V. B. Spratlin (1938).*

[58]   Three hundred long ships with strident beaks completed the great
       line, cleaving the surface of the water—as many as powerful
       Bizantium had previously seen in port—which ships seething

Bosphorus sent to the narrow sea. Pines arose to the heavens, a forest dense with trees was seen on the shining surface to traverse the waves. It was opposite the Spanish fleet, for the commands of the Tyrant urged the Turks to seek the Spaniards far and wide. They are heard shouting to each other as far as the distant pillars of Hercules.

from *The Astriad* [1573]

[59]   Tethys herself stretched out the waves for her Achilles; she tempered the foamy surface for the fleet Austria. Azure Triton sings the doom of the Turkish nation to the future victor with the song of a shell, the untoward fates of the Turkish leaders in the ship of the Tyrant, the Parcae cutting off the spun threads of Bassan, the three sisters devoted to the honor of Austria, the victor. And the three pray the marine gods to uncover Syrtis in order that Austria might perforce avoid the rocks concealed in the sea, for whom Scylla laughed and Charybdis stood implacable. The dolphins leap, sweeping the waters with their tails. Old Nereus called his daughters with a loud voice; the Nereids hasten happy to the trumpet calls of Austria.

from *The Austriad* [1573]

SOR JUANA INES DE LA CRUZ

(1651 - 1695)   San Miguel Neplantla, Mexico

Sor Juana Ines de la Cruz, a child prodigy, took the Holy Orders at Mexico City's Convent of St. Jerome. Her library was one of the largest in New Spain, and she is considered among the best early Mexican poets. Her poems appear, translated from the Spanish, in the anthology, Some Spanish American Poets, *reprinted in 1968.*

[60]   *Charges with inconsistency the appetite and the condemnation of men, who blame in women that of which they themselves are the cause.*

Foolish men, who accuse woman without reason, without seeing that you are yourselves the cause of the very thing that you blame!
    If with unparalleled longing you importune her when she scorns you, why do you wish that women should do well if you incite them to evil?

You combat their resistance, and soon you gravely declare
to be light-mindedness that which your own diligent efforts
have brought about.

The audacity of your mad opinion is like the child who
sets up a bugbear and presently is afraid of it.

With foolish presumption you wish to find her whom
you seek Thaïs when you attempt her and Lucretia when
you possess her.

What humor can be more extraordinary than that, lacking
good counsel, the same person should tarnish the mirror
and regret that it is not clear?

You blame women alike whether they favor or scorn you,
complaining of them if they treat you ill, mocking
them if they love you dearly.

No woman wins your good opinion, since the most prudent
is ungrateful if she does not yield to you, and light-minded
if she does.

You always proceed so foolishly that with unequal
measure you blame one for being cruel and another for
being too easy.

Your amorous pains cast off restraint, and after making
women bad, you wish to find them very good.

Who is the more in fault in an erring passion, she who
falls through entreaty, or he who entreats her to fall?

Or which is the more to blame, although both do ill, she
who sins for pay or he who pays for sinning?

                    Roundels [c. 1670]

[61]   Stay, shade of my shy treasure! Oh, remain,
       Thou image of the charmer I love best—
       Fair dream, for which I die with joyful breast,
       Illusion sweet, for which I live in pain!

       Thy winning graces all my heart enchain;
       It follows as the steel the magnet's test;
       But wherefore gain my love and make me blest
       If thou must mock me, fading soon again?

       Yet canst thou never boast, with fullest pride,
       Triumphant o'er me is thy tyranny;
       For though thou from the close embrace dost glide
       That held thy visionary form to me,
       No matter! In my arms thou wilt not bide,
       But fancy builds a prison still for thee!

                    Sonnet [c. 1680]

FRANCIS WILLIAMS

(c. 1700 - c. 1774)   Jamaica

Francis Williams, a protégé of the Duke of Montague, was educated in England and became an accomplished classical and math scholar. He returned to Jamaica and opened a school where he also taught Latin and math. Most of Williams' works, including the excerpt below, were written in Latin.

[62] We live, alas! where the bright God of day,
      Full from the zenith whirls his torrid ray;
      Beneath the rage of his consuming fires,
      All fancy melts, all eloquence expires.
      Yet may you deign accept this humble song
      Tho' wrapt in gloom, and from a faltering tongue;
      Tho' dark the stream on which the tribute flows.
      Not from the *skin*, but from the *heart* it rose.
      To all of humankind benignant heaven
      (Since nought forbids) one common soul has given.
      This rule was 'stablished by th' Eternal Mind;
      Nor virtue's self, nor prudence are confin'd
      To *colour*; none imbues the honest heart;
      To science none belongs, and none to art.
      Oh! *Muse* of blackest tint, why shrinks thy breast,
      Why fears t' approach the *Caesar* of the *West*!
      Dispel thy doubts, with confidence ascend
      The regal dome and hail him for thy friend:
      Nor blush, altho' in garb funereal drest,
      Thy body's white, tho' clad in sable vest
      Manner's unsullied, and the radiant glow
      Of genius, burning with desire to know;
      And learned speech with modest accent worn,
      Shall best the sooty African adorn.
      An heart with wisdom fraught, a patriot flame,
      A love of virtue; these shall lift his name
      Conspicuous, far beyond his kindred race,
      Distinguished from them by the foremost place.
      In this prolific isle I drew my birth,
      And Britain nurs'd, illustrious through the earth;
      This, my lov'd isle, which never more shall grieve,
      Whilst you our common friend, our father live.
      Then this my pray'r—"May earth and heaven survey
      A people ever blest, beneath your sway!"
               from *Ode* [1759]

JUPITER HAMMON
(1711 - 1800)   Queen's Village, New York

*Jupiter Hammon had no formal education and lived his entire life as a
slave. Believed to be the first Afro-American to have his work published in
this country, Hammon's poetry and prose reflected the religious times in
which he lived.* Complete Works of Jupiter Hammon *was published in
1970.*

[63]   God's tender mercy brought thee here;
       Tost o'er the raging main;
       In Christian faith thou has a share,
       Worth all the gold of Spain.
                    Address to Phillis Wheatley, IV (s. 4) [August 4, 1778]

[64]   . . . I do not wish to be free, yet I should be glad if others, especially
       young Negroes were to be free, for many of us who are grown up
       slaves and have always had masters to take care of us should
       hardly know how to take care of ourselves, and it may be of more
       comfort to remain as we are. That liberty is a great thing we may
       know from our own feelings. . . .
                    Address to the Negroes of the State of New York
                    [September 24, 1786]

JACOBUS ELISA JOHANNES CAPITEIN
(1717 - 1747)   Elmina, Ghana

*Taken to Holland at the age of seven, Jacobus Capitein later became a
respected theologian and writer. A graduate of the University of Leyden,
Capitein wrote a book of sermons and several treatises on Christian thought.
His best known work is his doctoral thesis,* Dissertatio politico-theologica,
de servitute, libertati christianae non contraria *(Politico-theological dis-
sertation, that slavery is not contrary to Christian liberty), published in
1742. The following elegy has been translated from the Dutch.*

[65]   Envious Death brandishes its weapons through the whole world,
       And rejoices that someone has succumbed to it.
       Free from fear, it wings its way into Kings' Chambers,
       And bids them lay down the sceptres of power from their hand.

It does not allow leaders long to behold their triumphs won,
But forces them to relinquish their brilliant trophies.
It claims for itself both the treasures of the rich,
And also the cottage of the beggar to distribute them to others.
With ruthless sickle it cuts off old men and young,
With no discrimination, like ears of corn,
It was this bold creature that, clad in black robe,
Dared to upset the portal of Manger's house.
And when the fatal cypress stood in front of the dwelling
High-born Haga gave bent to mournful groans.

Elegy on the Death of Manger [c. 1740]

IGNATIUS SANCHO

(1729 - 1780)   England

Ignatius Sancho was born on a slave ship bound for Cartagena, Colombia and later sent to England. After gaining his freedom, Sancho ran a grocery business and became a respected music critic. Sancho's Letters, *noted for their wit and humor, were published posthumously in 1782 and are available in a reprint edition.*

[66] Vice is a coward; to be truly brave, a man must be truly good.
Letter to Mrs. S. [October 11, 1772]

[67] Time leaves the marks of his rough fingers upon all things.
Letter to Mrs. S. [November 26, 1774]

[68] Philosophy is best practiced . . . by the easy and affluent.
Letter to Miss L. [October 16, 1775]

[69] One ounce of practical religion is worth all that the stoics wrote.
Letter to Miss L. [October 16, 1775]

[70] . . . self-love without principle will inspire even devils with affection.
Letter to Mr. M. [August 14, 1777]

[71] . . . what cannot be cured must be endured.
Letter to Mr. M. [September 16, 1777]

[72] I sincerely believe the Sacred Writ and, of course, look upon war

in all its horrid arrangements as the bitterest curse that can fall
upon a people, and this American one as one of the very worst of
things. That it is just a judgment, I do believe—that the eyes of
our rulers are shut, and their judgments stone-blind.
Letter to Mr. S. [December 20, 1777]

[73]   The grand object of English navigators—indeed of all Christian
navigators—is money, money, money.
Letter to Mr. J. W. E. [1778]

[74]   In the race of fortune, knaves often win the prize, whilst honesty is
outdistanced, but . . . whilst the knave full often meets his
deserved punishment, Honesty yoked with Poverty, hugs Peace
and Content in his bosom.
Letter to Mr. R. [October 16, 1778]

[75]   The man of levity often errs, but it is the man of sense alone who
can gracefully acknowledge it.
Letter to Mr. G. [February, 1779]

[76]   Time tries us all . . . but in the end we shall be an over-match for
Time and leave him, scythe and all in the lurch, when we shall
enjoy blessed eternity.
Letter to Mrs. H. [May 20, 1780]

[77]   . . . among the multitude of public prints, it is hard to say which
lyes the most.
Letter to Mr. I. W. E. [January 5, 1780]

VENTURE SMITH

(1729 - c. 1803)   Dukandarra, Guinea

*Sold into slavery at the age of eight, Venture Smith was resold three times
before he was thirty-one. After earning his own freedom, Smith soon
earned enough to free his family. His autobiographical* Life and Adventures
of Venture, a Native of Africa *was published in 1798.*

[78]   [On acquiring his name]

While we were going to the vessel, our master told us to appear to
the best possible advantage for sale. I was brought on board by

one Robertson Mumford, steward of said vessel, for four gallons
of rum and a piece of calico and called Venture, on account of his
having purchased me with his own private venture.

Life and Adventures of Venture, A Native of Africa [1798]

[79]   Though once straight and tall . . . I am now bowed down with age
and hardship. . . . But amidst all my griefs and pains, I have
many consolations. Meg, the wife of my youth, whom I married
for love, and bought with my money, is still alive. My freedom is
a privilege which nothing else can equal. Notwithstanding all the
losses I have suffered by fire, by the justice of knaves, by the
cruelty and oppression of falsehearted friends, and the perfidy of
my own countrymen whom I have assisted and redeemed from
bondage, I am now possessed of more than one hundred acres of
land, and three hospitable dwelling houses. It gives me joy to
think that I have and that I *deserve* so good a character, especially
for truth and *integrity*.

Life and Adventures of Venture, a Native of Africa [1798]

BENJAMIN BANNEKER

(1731 - 1806)   Ellicott's Mill, Maryland

*Benjamin Banneker, a self-taught astronomer and mathematician, wrote
and published his own almanacs and was also a member of the survey team
that planned the city of Washington, D.C.* The Life of Benjamin Banneker
by Silvio Bedini was published in 1972.

[80]   I heard the discharge from a gun, and in four or five seconds time
the small shot came rattling about me, one or two of which struck
the house, which plainly demonstrates that the velocity of sound
is greater than that of a cannon bullet.

Notes [August 27, 1791]

[81]   . . . the color of the skin is in no ways connected with strength of the
mind or intellectual powers. . . .

Preface, *Banneker's Almanac* [1796]

[82]   When fleecy skies have Cloth'd the ground
With a white mantle all around
Then with a greyhound Snowy fair

In milk white fields we Cours'd a Hare
Just in the midst of a Champaign
We set her up, away she ran,
The Hound I think was from her then
Just thirty leaps or three times ten
Oh it was pleasant for to see
How the Hare did run so timorously
But yet so very Swift that I
Did think she did not run but Fly
When the Dog was almost at her heels
She quickly turn'd, and down the fields
She ran again with full Career
And 'gain she turn'd to the place she were
At every turn she gain'd of ground
As many yards as the greyhound
Could leap at thrice, and She did make,
Just Six, if I do not mistake
Four times She Leap'd for the Dogs three
But two of the Dog's leaps did agree
With three of hers, nor pray declare
How many leaps he took to Catch the Hare.

[Answer]

Just Seventy two I did Suppose,
An Answer false from thence arose,
I Doubled the Sum of Seventy two,
But still I found that would not do,
I mix'd the Numbers of them both,
Which Shew'd so plain that I'll make Oath,
Eight hundred leaps the Dog did make,
And Sixty four, the Hare to take.

```
4 :   72   :  :   48
       48
      ----
      576
      288
    ----
   4)3456
      ----
      864   ans.
```

Puzzle of the Dog and the Hare (Recorded in Banneker's manuscript journal) [c. 1798]

[83]   Evil communications corrupt good manners. I hope to live to hear
       that good communications correct bad manners.
                       Almanac Inscription [c. 1800]

[84]   In the morning part of the day there arose a very dark cloud, fol-
       lowed by snow and hail, a flash of lightning and a loud thunder-
       crash, and then the storm abated until afternoon, when another
       cloud arose at the same point, viz., the northwest with a beautiful
       shower of snow. But what beautified the snow was the brightness
       of the sun, which was near setting at the time.
                       Notes [February 3, 1803]

LUCY TERRY PRINCE

(c. 1731 - c. 1822)   Africa

*Lucy Terry was kidnapped from Africa as a child. She lived in Deerfield,
Massachusetts, and was married to Abijah Prince, a free black. They had
six children. When a local landowner tried to steal part of their property,
Lucy eventually pled the case before the Supreme Court and won.*

[85]   August 'twas the twenty-fifth
       Seventeen hundred forty-six;
       The Indians did in ambush lay,
       Some very valient men to slay,
       The names of whom I'll not leave out.
       Samuel Allen like a hero fout,
       And though he was so brave and bold,
       His face no more shall we behold.
       Eleazer Hawks was killed outright,
       Before he had time to fight,—
       Before he did the Indians see,
       Was shot and killed immediately.
       Oliver Amsden he was slain,
       Which caused his friends much grief and pain.
       Simeon Amsden they found dead,
       Not many rods distant from his head.
       Adonijah Gillett we do hear
       Did lose his life which was so dear.
       John Sadler fled across the water,

And thus escaped the dreadful slaughter.
Eunice Allen see the Indians coming,
And hopes to save herself by running,
And had not her petticoats stopped her,
The awful creatures had not catched her,
Nor tommy hawked her on her head,
And left her on the ground for dead.
Young Samuel Allen, Oh lack-a day!
Was taken and carried to Canada.

Bars Fight—Bars [Date Unknown]

PRINCE HALL

(c. 1735 - 1807)   Bridgetown, Barbados, West Indies

Prince Hall was a prominent figure in the fight for Afro-American equality during the last quarter of the eighteenth century. In 1787 he organized African Lodge Number 459, the first black Masonic lodge in America.

[86]   Nothing is stable.
                        Address, African Lodge, Menotomy, Massachusetts
                        [June 24, 1797]

[87]   O, the patience of the blacks!
                        Address, African Lodge, Menotomy, Massachusetts
                        [June 24, 1797]

FRANÇOIS-DOMINIQUE TOUSSAINT L'OUVERTURE

(1743 - 1803)   Haut du Cap, Haiti

Great revolutionary general and hero, Toussaint L'Ouverture was the leading figure in the Haitian liberation struggle against France. He was subsequently betrayed by the enemy, arrested, and deported to France where he died in prison. L'Ouverture's biography, Toussaint L'Ouverture *(1863), by John R. Beard, was reprinted in 1971. The following quotations have been translated from the French.*

[88]   I have undertaken to avenge you. I want liberty and equality to
       reign throughout Santo Domingo. I am working towards that
       end. Come join me, brothers, and fight by our side for the same
       cause.
                           Proclamation [August 29, 1793]

[89]   One cannot give to a person that which he already possesses.
                           Proclamation [March 1, 1802]

[90]   The colony of Santo Domingo, over which I had command enjoyed
       the greatest tranquility, with a flourishing trade and culture. The
       island had reached a degree of splendor never before witnessed.
       All this, I dare to say, was my own handiwork.
                           Memoirs [published 1853]

OLAUDAH EQUIANO

(1745-1797)   Essaka (Benin), Nigeria

Olaudah Equiano was kidnapped, taken to Virginia, and sold into slavery.
After buying his freedom, Equiano settled in England, joined the abolition-
ist movement, and published his autobiography in 1789.

[91]   [On the Middle Passage]:

       One day we had a smooth sea and moderate wind, two of my
       countrymen were chained together (I was near them at the time),
       preferring death to such a life of misery, somehow made through
       nettings and jumped into the sea: immediately another quite
       dejected fellow, who, on account of his illness, was suffered to be
       out of irons, also followed their example; and I believe many
       more would very soon have done the same if they had not been
       prevented by the ship's crew. . . .
                           The Interesting Narrative of the Life of Olaudah Equiano
                           or Gustavus Vassa, the African [1789]

OTTOBAH CUGOANO

(born c. 1748)   Agimaqua, Mfanti District Central Province, Ghana

Ottobah Cugoano was kidnapped into slavery and taken to England via Grenada. He was a zealous abolitionist, a worker among poor Anglo-Africans and publisher of his own Thoughts and Sentiments on the Evils of Slavery *(1787).*

[92]   . . . the robbers of men, the kidnappers, ensnarers and slaveholders, who take away the common rights and privileges of others to support and enrich themselves are universally those pitiful and detestable wretches; for the ensnaring of others, and taking away their liberty by slavery and oppression is the worst kind of robbery. . . .

Thoughts and Sentiments on the Evils of Slavery [1787]

[93]   A good man will neither speak nor do as a bad man will; but if a man is bad, it makes no difference whether he be a black or white devil.

Thoughts and Sentiments on the Evils of Slavery [1787]

[94]   . . . I must own, to the shame of my own countrymen, that I was first kidnapped and betrayed by some of my own complexion; but if there were no buyers, there would be no sellers.

Thoughts and Sentiments on the Evils of Slavery [1787]

[95]   . . . men of activity and affluence, by whatever way they are possessed of riches, or have acquired greatness of such property, are always preferred to take the lead in matters of government, so that the greatest depredators, warriors, contracting companies of merchants, and rich slaveholders always endeavour to push themselves on to get power and interest in their favor; that whatever crimes any of them commit, they are seldom brought to a just punishment.

Thoughts and Sentiments on the Evils of Slavery [1787]

JEAN JACQUES DESSALINES
(1749 - 1806)   Grand Rivière du Nord, Haiti

Revolutionary and military strategist, Jean Jacques Dessalines served under General Toussaint L'Ouverture in the struggle for Haitian liberation. He became emperor in 1804 but met death by ambush two years later. The following quotations have been translated from the French.

[96]   We have dared to be free; let us dare to be so by ourselves and for ourselves.
>   *Proclamation* [January 1, 1804]

[97]   Let us swear to the entire universe, to posterity, and to ourselves to renounce France forever and die, rather than live under her domination; wage war to the last gasp for independence of our country.
>   *Proclamation* [January 1, 1804]

PHILLIS WHEATLEY
(c. 1753-1784)   Senegal

Phillis Wheatley was the first Afro-American to gain international literary fame. She is best known for her single collection of verse, Poems on Various Subjects, Religious and Moral *(1773).*

[98]   'Twas mercy brought me from my *Pagan* land,
           Taught my benighted soul to understand
           That there's a God, that there's a *Saviour* too.
       Once I redemption neither sought nor knew.
       Some view our sable race with scornful eye,
       "Their colour is a diabolic dye."
       Remember, *Christians*, *Negroes* black as Cain,
       May be refined, and join the angelic train.
>   *On Being Brought from Africa to America* [c. 1768]

[99]   Nor here, nor there; the roving fancy flies,
       Till some lov'd object strikes her wandering eyes.
       Whose silken fetters all the senses bind,
       And soft captivity involves the mind.
>   *On Imagination* [c. 1770]

[100] Attend my lays, ye ever honour'd nine,
           Assist my labours, and my strains refine;
           In smoothest numbers pour the notes along,
       For bright Aurora now demands my song.
           Aurora, hail and all the thousand dyes,
       Which deck thy progress through the vaulted skies;
       The morn awakes, and wide extends her rays,
       On ev'ry leaf the gentle zephyr plays;
       Harmonious lays the feather'd race resume,
       Dart the bright eye, and shake the painted plume.
           Ye shady groves, your verdant gloom display
       To shield your poet from the burning day:
       Calliope, awake the sacred lyre,
       While thy fair sisters fan the pleasing fire:
       The bow'rs, the gales, the variegated skies
       In all their pleasures in my bosom rise.
           See in the east th' illustrious king of day!
       His rising radiance drives the shades away—
       But oh! I feel his fervid leaves too strong,
       And scarce begun, concludes th' abortive song.
                       An Hymn to the Morning [c. 1772]

JOHN MARRANT

(1755 - 1790)   New York, New York

*After receiving a "call to the ministry" at the age of fourteen, John Marrant
worked among the Indians before his formal ordination in England in 1785.
Marrant spent four years preaching in Nova Scotia and recorded his experiences in a journal (1790). A* Narrative of the Lord's Wonderful Dealings
with John Marrant *was published in 1785.*

[101] Envy and pride are the leading lines to all the misery that mankind
           has suffered from the beginning of the world to this present day.
                       Sermon, African Lodge, Boston, Massachusetts
                       [June 24, 1789]

[102] Unhappily, too many Christians, so called, take their religion not
           from the declarations of Christ, but from the writings of those
           they esteem learned.
                       Sermon, African Lodge, Boston, Massachusetts
                       [June 24, 1789]

RICHARD ALLEN

(1760 - 1831)   Philadelphia, Pennsylvania

Richard Allen was founder and first bishop of the African Methodist Episcopal Church, the oldest Afro-American religious denomination in America. Allen's memoirs, The Life Experience and Gospel Labors of the Right Reverend Richard Allen, *were published in 1887.*

[103] We left our master's house, and I may truly say it was like leaving our father's house, for he was a kind, affectionate and tenderhearted master.

> *The Life Experience and Gospel Labors of*
> *the Right Reverend Richard Allen* [1887]

[104] . . . A Black man, although reduced to the most abject state human nature is capable of, short of madness, can think, reflect and feel injuries, although it may not be with the same degree of keen resentment and revenge that you, who have been our great oppressors would manifest, if reduced to the pitiable condition of a slave.

> *The Life Experience and Gospel Labors of*
> *the Right Reverend Richard Allen* [1887]

[105] . . . the vile habits often acquired in a state of servitude are not easily thrown off. . . .

> *The Life Experience and Gospel Labors of*
> *the Right Reverend Richard Allen* [1887]

[106] We who know how bitter the cup is of which the slave hath to drink, O, how ought we to feel for those who yet remain in bondage.

> *The Life Experience and Gospel Labors of*
> *the Right Reverend Richard Allen* [1887]

JOSÉ MANUEL VALDÉS
(c. 1760 - 1843)   Lima, Peru

José Valdés rose from poverty to become one of Peru's most distinguished physicians and the winner of many honors for his medical research. Also a poet, Valdés published a collection of mystical verse, Poésias espirituales escritas a beneficio y para el uso de las personas sensibles y piadosas *(Spiritual poems written for the benefit and use of reasonable and devout persons) in 1818. The following poems have been translated from the Spanish.*

[107]   So it practices the profession
        Of friendship; it becomes beautiful in contemplation
        Of infinite goodness:
        And when it is pleading for pardon
        For the evil which it knows to be within,
        And for the evil which it does not know,
        It is like unto a dove that weeps while singing.
                        The Perfect Soul [c. 1824]

[108]   Look for me in the heavens
        That sing of my glory:
        Look for me in the stars,
        Of wondrous revolutions:
        Look for me in the birds,
        That claw the air:
        Look for me in the flowers
        And fruits ever pleasing:
        Look for me in the high seas
        Of frothy waters,
        That the weak sand
        Retains on the beaches.
        Look for me in the brutes
        And look for me in so many
        Other marvels
        That attract man's attention;
        For the universe
        That I made from nothingness
        With sonorous voices
        Extols my power.
                Conversation Between Jesus and the Soul [c. 1830]

JAMES FORTEN

(1766 - 1842)   Philadelphia, Pennsylvania

Born of free parents, James Forten was a prosperous businessman and one of Philadelphia's most prominent citizens. An active abolitionist, Forten was a colleague of Robert Allen and Absalom Jones, and in 1833 also provided the needed funds for William L. Garrison to found The Liberator.

[109]   Punish the guilty man of colour to the utmost limit of the laws, but sell him not in slavery! If he is in danger of becoming a publick [sic] charge prevent him! If he is too indolent to labour for his own subsistence, compel him to do so; but sell him not in slavery. By selling him you do not make him better but commit a wrong without benefitting the object of it or society at large.

> *Letters from a Man of Colour on a Late Senate Bill before the Senate of Pennsylvania*, Letter I [April 1813]

[110]   It seems almost incredible that the advocates of liberty should conceive the idea of selling a fellow creature to slavery.

> *Letters from a Man of Colour on a Late Senate Bill before the Senate of Pennsylvania*, Letter II [1813]

[111]   If men, though they know that the law protects all, will dare, in in defiance of law, to execute their hatred upon the defenseless black, will they not by the passage of this bill believe him still more a mark for their venom and spleen. Will they not believe him completely deserted by authority, and subject to every outrage brutality can inflict—too surely they will, and the poor wretch will turn his eyes around to look in vain for protection. Pause, ye rulers of a free people before you give us over to despair and violation—we implore you for the sake of humanity, to snatch us from the pinnacle of ruin—from that gulph [sic], which will swallow our rights as fellow creatures; our privileges as citizens; and our liberties as men.

> *Letters from a Man of Colour on a Late Senate Bill before the Senate of Pennsylvania*, Letter IV [1813]

HENRI CHRISTOPHE

(1767 - 1820)   Grenada, West Indies

Henri Christophe succeeded Jean Jacques Dessalines as emperor of Haiti and created an absolute autocracy that eventually led to his downfall. The Dessalines era is illuminated in Black Triumvirate: a Study of L'Ouverture, Dessalines, Christophe *by Charles Moran (1957). The following quotations have been translated from the French.*

[112]   We will sooner bury ourselves beneath the ruins of our native
        country than suffer an infraction of our political rights.
                    Manifesto of the King [September 18, 1814]

[113]   We should understand that we are still surrounded by
        quicksands. . . .
                    Proclamation [January 1, 1816]

[114]   Descendants of Africans, my brethren, the friends of humanity
        have asserted that we are susceptible of improvement like the
        whites; our traducers affirm the contrary; it is for us to decide the
        question. It is by the wisdom of our conduct, our success in the
        arts and sciences, that we shall secure the triumph of our
        respected and illustrious patrons, and confound, forever, the
        malice and unfounded assertions of our implacable enemies.
                    Proclamation [January 1, 1816]

DAVID WALKER

(1785 - 1830)   Wilmington, North Carolina

Born free, David Walker was a fervent abolitionist and Boston agent for Freedom's Journal. *His* Appeal in Four Articles, *an impassioned condemnation of slavery published in 1829, stirred great controversy. Walker died under mysterious circumstances shortly after its publication.*

[115]   The Americans say that we are ungrateful—but ask them, for
        heaven's sake, what we should be grateful to them for . . .
        murdering our fathers and mothers? Or do they wish us to return

thanks to them for chaining and handcuffing us, branding us, cramming fire down our throats, or for keeping us in slavery, and beating us nearly or quite to death to make us work in ignorance and miseries to support them and their families. They certainly think that we are a gang of fools.

Appeal in Four Articles, IV [1829]

[116]   Treat us like men and we will be your friends.

Appeal in Four Articles, IV [1829]

[117]   . . . remember Americans, that as miserable, wretched, degraded and abject as you have made us in the preceding, and in this generation, to support you and your families, some of you . . . will yet curse the day you were born.

Appeal in Four Articles, IV [1829]

ABRAHAM
(born c. 1787)   Florida

Abraham was a full-blooded African who joined the Seminoles as a young fugitive slave. He became one of their most influential leaders and played a key role as interpreter-diplomat during the Seminole wars.

[118]   We do not live for ourselves only, but for our wives and children, who are as dear to us as those of any other men.

Letter to General T. S. Jesup [April 25, 1838]

GEORGE MOSES HORTON
(1797 - c. 1883)   Northampton County, North Carolina

George Moses Horton, who remained a slave until emancipation, learned to read by memorizing hymns. Among his surviving works are Poems By a Slave *(1837) and* Naked Genius *(1865).*

[119]   Such is the quiet bless [bliss] of soul,
             When in some calm retreat
         Where pensive thoughts like streamlets roll,
             And render silence sweet.
                        On The Poetic Muse (s. 5) [c. 1828]

[120]   Must I dwell in slavery's night
         And all pleasure take its flight
         Far beyond my feeble sight,
                             Forever?
                        The Slave's Complaint (s. 2) [1829]

[121]   Coo sweetly, oh thou harmless Dove,
         And bid thy mate no longer rove
             In cold, hybernal vales;
         Let music rise from every tongue,
         Whilst winter flies before the song,
             Which floats on gentle gales.
                        On Spring (s. 2) [1829]

[122]   My genius from a boy,
             Has fluttered like a bird within my heart;
         But could not thus confined her powers employ,
             Impatient to depart.
                        George Moses Horton, Myself (s. 4) [1864]

SOJOURNER TRUTH

(c. 1797 - 1883)   Ulster County, New York

Sojourner Truth, who could neither read nor write, won a national reputa-
tion with powerful lectures against slavery and, after emancipation, for
women's rights. Her autobiography, Narrative of Sojourner Truth, *was pub-*
lished in 1875 and was reprinted in 1970.

[123]   Look at me! Look at my arm! I have plowed and planted, and
             gathered into barns, and no man could head me—and ain't I a
             woman? I could work as much and eat as much as a man (when
             I could get it), and bear de lash as well—and ain't I a woman?
             I have borne 13 chillern and seen 'em mos' all sold off into
             slavery, and when I cried out with a mother's grief, none but
             Jesus heard—and ain't I a woman?
                        Address, Women's Rights Convention, Akron, Ohio [1851]

[124]   If de fust woman God ever made was strong enough to turn the
          world upside down all 'lone, dese togedder ought to be able to
          turn it back and get it right side up again, and now dey asking to
          do it, de men better let 'em.
                          Address, Women's Rights Convention Akron, Ohio [1851]

[125]   . . . I know a little mite 'bout woman's rights, too. I come forth to
          speak about woman's rights and want to throw in my little mite
          to keep the scales a-movin'.
                          Address, Mob Convention, New York, New York
                          [September 8, 1853]

[126]   Ef women want any rights more'n dey's got, why don't dey jes'
          take 'em, and not be talkin' about it.
                          Comment [c. 1863]

[127]   There is a great stir about colored men getting their rights, but not
          a word about colored women; and if colored men get their rights,
          and not colored women theirs, you see, the colored men will be
          masters over the women and it will be as bad as before. So I am
          for keeping the thing going while things are stirring, because if we
          wait till it is still, it will take a great while to get it going again.
                          Address, Annual Meeting of Equal Rights Convention,
                          New York, New York [May 9, 1867]

[128]   I go fur adgitatin'. But I believe dere is works belongs wid
          adgitatin', too.
                          Address Commemorating the Eighth Anniversary of Negro
                          Freedom in the United States, Tremont Temple, Boston,
                          Massachusetts [January 1, 1871]

[129]   I . . . can't read a book but I can read de people.
                          Address Commemorating the Eighth Anniversary of Negro
                          Freedom in the United States, Tremont Temple, Boston,
                          Massachusetts [January 1, 1871]

[130]   The majority rules. If dey want anything, dey git it. If dey want
          anything not right, dey git it, too.
                          Address, Rochester, New York [1871]

[131]   It is the mind that makes the body.
                          Interview, Battle Creek, Michigan [c. 1877]

[132]   This colored people going to be a people.
                          Interview, Battle Creek, Michigan [c. 1877]

[133]   Religion without humanity is a poor human stuff.
                            Interview, Battle Creek, Michigan [c. 1877]

[134]   [To a chastiser who commented that she couldn't get to heaven with
        smoke on her breath]:

        Yes, chile, but when I goes to heaven I 'spects to leave my breff
        behind.
                            Comment [c. 1879]

[135]   [On Horace Greeley]:

        You call him a self-made man; well, I'm a self-made woman.
                            Comment [c. 1880]

[136]   Truth burns up error.
                            Comment [c. 1882]

JUAN FRANCISCO MANZANO
(1797 - 1854)   Havana, Cuba

*The vivid poetry of Juan Manzano, written primarily during his slavery years,
was published as* Poems by a Slave in the Island of Cuba *(1840). The
following selections have been translated from the Spanish.*

[137]   Whoever spent the night on an estate
        In time of crop, and had endured of late
        Fatigue and toil, that amply might dispose
        A weary trav'ller to enjoy repose.
        And roused at midnight, heard the frightful bell,
        The dismal conch's loud blast at change of spell,
        The crack of whips, the hurried tramp of men,
        The creaking mill, the driver's threats, and then
        The sudden scream, the savage bloodhounds growl,
        The shout prolonged, the "stokers" ceaseless howl;
        All the dread noise that's requisite to keep
        The jaded cattle and the slaves from sleep;
        To rouse the weak, to drown the women's cries,
        And cause one deaf'ning uproar to uprise.

Whoever found this tumult at its height,
This Cuban Babel's strife at dead of night;
Whoever listened to these horrid sounds,
And might not deemed, hell had enlarged her bounds,
Made this plantation part of her domain,
And giv'n its owners, slaves, and lust of gain.
            The Sugar Estate, Canto II (s. 1) [c. 1822]

[138] Such is the merchant in his trade of blood;
      The Indian savage in his fiercest mood
      Is not more cruel, merciless in strife,
      Ruthless in war, and reckless of man's life!
      To human suffering, sympathy and shame,
      His heart is closed, and wealth is all his aim.
      Behold him now in social circles shine,
      Polite and courteous, bland—almost benign,
      Calm as the grave, yet affable to all,
      His well-taught smile has nothing to appeal;
      It plays like sunbeams on a marble tomb,
      Or coldly glancing o'er the death like a gloom,
      Creeps o'er his features, as the crisping air,
      On Lake Asphaltes steals and stagnates there.
      Serene as summer how the Euxine looks
      Before the gale its slumb'ring rage provokes.
      Who would imagine, while the calm is there,
      Or think, beneath such gently swelling waves,
      Thousands of human beings find their graves.
      But who can ponder here and reconcile
      The scowl of murder, with its merchant's smile.
            from *The Slave Trade Merchant* [c. 1825]

[139] 'Tis not alone the wretched negro's fate
      That calls for pity, sad as it may be;
      There's more to weep for in that hapless state
      Of men who proudly boast that they are free,
      Whose moral sense is warped to that degree,
      That self-debasement seems to them unknown,
      And life's sole object, is for means to play,
      To roll a carriage, or to seek renown
      In all the futile follies of the town.
            To Cuba (s. 4) [c. 1829]

[140]   To think unmoved of millions of our race,
        Swept from thy soil by cruelties prolonged,
        Another clime then ravaged to replace
        The wretched Indians; Africa then wronged
        To fill the void where myriads lately thronged,
        And add new guilt to that long list of crimes,
        That cries aloud, in accents trumpet-tongued,
        And shakes the cloud that gathers o'er these climes,
        Portending evil and disastrous times.
                    To Cuba (s. 6) [c. 1829]

[141]   Thou knowest, dear Florence, my sufferings of old,
        The struggles maintained with oppression for years,
        We shared them together, and each was consoled
        With the whispers of love that were mingled with tears.
                    The Dream (s. 1) [c. 1830]

JAMES P. BECKWOURTH

(1798 - 1867)   Fredericksburg, Virginia

*Patriot, Indian fighter and Crow Indian Chief, James P. Beckwourth lived
the adventurous life of the frontiersman. He discovered a pass through the
Sierra Nevadas that today still bears his name. Beckwourth's autobiography,
recorded between 1854 and 1855, was published in 1892.*

[142]   [On his discovery of Beckwourth Pass]

        It was the latter end of April when we entered upon an extensive
            valley at the northwest extremity of the Sierra range. . . . Swarms
            of wild geese and ducks were swimming on the surface of the cool
            crystal stream, which was the central fork of the Rio de las
            Plumas, or sailed the air in clouds over our heads. Deer and
            antelope filled the plains, and their boldness was conclusive
            that the hunter's rifle was to them unknown. Nowhere visible
            were any traces of the white man's approach, and it is probable
            that our steps were the first that ever marked the spot.
                    Autobiography of James P. Beckwourth [1892]

ALEXANDER SERGEYEVICH PUSHKIN

(1799 - 1837)   Moscow, Russia

*Alexander Pushkin, grandson of the Afro-Russian general Ibrahim Han-
nibal, was one of Russia's great writers. Among his best known works are*
Eugene Onegin *(1823),* Boris Godounov *(1831), and* Queen of Spades *(1834).
The following quotations have been translated from the Russian.*

[143]   Blessed is the man who to himself has kept
  The high creations of his soul;
  Who from his friends as from the grave,
  Expected nothing of esteem!
  Who sang his songs alone, obscure,
  And did not wear the crown of fame
  That rots so soon, its laurel torn
  And trampled by the senseless mob
  That quickly flouts a former choice.
  For what is fame, that it deceives
  More than the glittering dreams of hope:
  A lover's whisper? The abuse of boors?
  Or the lean, worthless rapture of the fool?
     Fame [1823]

[144]   Marriage castrates the soul.
    Letter to Peter Andreevich Vyazemsky [May, 1826]

[145]   Beneath the deep blue sky of her own native land,
  She weary grew, and, drooping, pined away.
  She died and passed, and over me I oft-times feel
  Her youthful shadow fondly hovering;
  And all the while a gaping chasm divides us both.
  In vain I would my aching grief awake:
  From tongue indifferent I heard the fatal news,
  With ear indifferent I learned her death.
  And yet 'tis true, I loved her once with ardent soul,
  My heart of hearts enwrapt in her alone;
  With all the tenderness of languor torturing,
  With all the racking pains of fond despair!
  Where now my love, my pains? Alas, my barren soul
  For her, so light and easy of belief,
  For memory of days that nothing can recall,
  To song or tears is dead and voiceless now.
    Elegy [June 29, 1826]

[146] And now, my chubby critic, fat burly cynic,
       Forever mocking and deriding my sad muse,
       Draw near, and take a seat, I pray, close beside me,
       And let us come to terms with this accursed spleen.
       But why that frown? Is it so hard to leave our woes,
       A moment to forget ourselves in joyous song?
       And now, admire the view! That sorry row of huts;
       Behind a level long descent of blackish earth,
       Above, one layer thick of gray, unbroken clouds.
       But where the river? In the court there, by the fence,
       Sprout two lean and withered trees to glad the eye;
       Just two, no more, and one of them, you will observe
       By autumn rains has long been bared of its last leaf;
       The scanty leaves upon the other only wait
       The first loud breeze, to fall and foul the pond below.
       No other sign of life, no dog to watch the yard.
       But stay, Ivan I see, and two old women near;
       With head unbared, the coffin of his child he bears,
       And from afar too drowsy sexton loudly shouts,
       And bids him call the priest, and church door to unlock;
       "Look sharp! The brat we should have buried long ago!"
                     A Study [1830]

JOHN BROWNE RUSSWURM

(1799 - 1851)   Port Antonio, Jamaica

*John B. Russwurm, along with Samuel Cornish, established America's first
Afro-American newspaper,* Freedom's Journal *(1827). Russwurm emigrated
to Liberia in 1828 as representative for the Maryland Colonization Society,
and remained there until his death.*

[147] It is the irresistible course of events that all men who have been
       deprived of their liberty shall recover this precious portion of
       their indefeasible inheritance. It is vain to stem the current;
       degraded man will rise in his native majesty and claim his rights.
       They may be withheld from him now, but the day will arrive
       when they must be surrendered.
                     Commencement Address, Bowdoin College,
                     Brunswick, Maine [September 6, 1826]

[148]   We wish to plead our own cause. Too long have others spoken for
us.

> Editorial, *Freedom's Journal* [March 16, 1827]

[149]   . . . the greatest stimulus ever presented to the man of color in the
United States has been the promotion of men of his race to
offices of great trust and responsibility. . . .

> Despatch to John B. Latrobe, President, Maryland
> Colonization Society [Cape Palmas, Liberia,
> [December 30, 1845]

SIMON CHRISTIAN OLIVER

(c. 1800 - 1848)   Grenada

*Simon Oliver was born in Grenada but spent most of his adult life in British
Guiana (Guyana), where he taught at a secondary school in Buxton. Although
he wrote many poems, few of them have survived.*

[150]   Oh! ye first of August freed men who now liberty enjoy;
Salute the day and shout hurrah to Queen Victoria;
Oh this glad day the galling chains of Slavery were broke
From off the necks of Afric's sons, who bled beneath
its yoke.
With hearts and voice you should rejoice, to God the
glory give;
Now freedom is your happy lot, as freedmen you should live;
Your minds you ought to cultivate as well as till the ground,
And virtuous actions imitate wherein true bliss abound.
To your masters then you'll fill a glass and drink with
grateful glee,
And to all those of the same class who nobly set you free.
Then you should sing, *God save the Queen*, oh, may she
live forever;
Great Britain your true friend has been—forsake you,
may she never.

> Untitled [August 1, 1838]

ALEXANDER DUMAS (père)

(1802 - 1870)   Villers-Cotterets, France

Alexander Dumas (père) *was one of France's most distinguished novelists. The Three Musketeers (1844) and* The Count of Monte Cristo *(1854) number among his most popular fiction adventures. The following quotations from his memoirs have been translated from the French.*

[151]   Youth never despairs, for it is still in harmony with the Divine.
        My Memoirs [1802-21]

[152]   Oh, how great and glorious art is! It shows more devotion than a
        friend, is more faithful than a mistress, more consoling than a
        confessor.
        My Memoirs [1822-25]

[153]   Men's minds are raised to the level of the women with whom they
        associate. . . .
        My Memoirs [1826-30]

[154]   . . . the man of genius . . . does not steal, he conquers. . . .
        My Memoirs [1831-32]

WILLIAM WHIPPER

(c. 1802 - 1895)   Columbia, Pennsylvania

William Whipper managed a prosperous lumber business he inherited from his master. He edited an early black newspaper, The National Reformer, *and helped establish the American Moral Reform Society to promote better education among Afro-Americans.*

[155]   The spirit of war can never be destroyed by all the butcheries and
        persecutions the human mind can invent.
        Non-Resistance to Offensive Aggression [1837]

[156]   If men's superiority over the brute creation consists only in his
        reasoning powers and rationality of mind, his various methods of
        practicing violence towards his fellow creatures has in many cases

placed him on a level with, and sometimes below, many species
of the quadruped race.

Non-Resistance to Offensive Aggression [1837]

[157]   There is scarcely a single fact more worthy of indelible record than
the utter inefficiency of human punishments to cure human evils.

Non-Resistance to Offensive Aggression [1837]

[158]   Human passion is the hallucination of a distempered mind.

Non-Resistance to Offensive Aggression [1837]

JOSÉ MARÍA HEREDIA

(1803 - 1839)   Santiago, Cuba

*Cuban poet and patriot, José María Heredia was the first romantic poet of
Spanish America. A translation of his sonnets,* The Trophies, *was published
in 1900. Heredia's work also appears in the anthology,* Spanish American
Literature in Translation, *Vol. 1 (1963).*

[159]   The noonday burns: beneath the terrible light
The languid stream rolls on her leaden waves;
From blinding zenith falls the day aplomb;
All Egypt feels the unrelenting Phra.
Those sphinxes vast which never close their eyes,
Stretching their flanks beneath the yellow sands,
Follow with look mysterious and long
The towering lines of distant obelisks.
Alone to break upon the blank, still sky,
There wheels far off the vultures' endless flight;
The heat hath lulled to sleep both man and beast.
The burning soil is sparkling and unmoved;
And silent in the midst of such hot joy
The brass Anubis barks toward the sun.

The Vision of Khem, I [c. 1822]

[160]   In deepest hollow of the moving dune,
In night that has no morning, stars, nor moon,
Let the seafarer find at last her rest!
O Earth! O Sea! pity her anxious shade!

And where her bones sank deep on Hellas shore
O earth rest light on her and Sea be still!
                    The Shipwreck (ll. 12-17) [c. 1823]

[161]   No sound of insect or of plundering bee:
        All sleeps beneath the great sun-burdened trees,
        Where through the foliage sifts down a light
        Like sombre velvet soft as emerald moss.
        Piercing the shady dome the splendid noon
        Hovers aloft, and o'er my half-closed eyes
        The furtive flashes form a rosy net
        Stretching itself across the heated shade.
        Against the woven gauze of fiery rays
        Flutters a swarm of brilliant butterflies
        Inebriate with light and rich perfumes.
        While I with trembling fingers seize each thread
        And in the golden meshes of that net,
        A willing hunter, bind my captive dreams.
                            The Siesta [c. 1828]

[162]   Blue glaciers, peaks of marble and of slate,
        Moraines whose winds from Néthou unto Bègle,
        Tear, twirl and twist the fields of wheat and rye,
        Steep hills, lakes, forests full of shade and rest!
        Deep caves, dark valleys which in ancient times
        The outlaws, rather than obey the rule,
        Did make with bear and wolf and eagle their haunt,
        Cliffs, torrents, deep abysses, be ye blest!
        Fleeing the workhouse and the rigid town,
        One Geminus the slave has vowed this stone
        To the Hills, the Sacred Guardians of Freedom:
        And on these summits clear where silence hangs
        In air inviolable, immense and pure,
        I think I hear again the freeman's cry!
                        To the Divine Mountains [c. 1830]

MARIA W. STEWART

(1803 - 1879)   Hartford, Connecticut

Maria W. Stewart was one of the earliest Afro-American women to speak in public. A selection of her speeches, Productions of Maria W. Stewart, *was published in 1835.*

[163]   . . . it was asserted that we are "a ragged set crying for liberty." I reply to it, the whites have so long and so loudly proclaimed the theme of equal rights and privileges that our souls have caught the flame, ragged as we are.

> Address, Franklin Hall, Boston, Massachusetts
> [September 21, 1832]

[164]   Talk without effort is nothing.

> Address, African Masonic Hall, Boston, Massachusetts
> [February 27, 1833]

[165]   The unfriendly whites first drove the native American from his much-loved home. Then they stole our fathers from their peaceful and quiet dwellings and brought them hither, and made bondmen and bondwomen of them and their little ones. They have obliged our brethren in labor, kept them in utter ignorance, nourished them in vice and raised them in degradation; and now that we have enriched their soil and filled their coffers, they say that we are not capable of becoming like white men, and that we can never rise to respectability in this country. They would drive us to a strange land. But before I go, the bayonet shall pierce me through. African rights and liberty is a subject that ought to fire the breast of every free man of color in these United States. . . .

> Address, African Masonic Hall, Boston, Massachusetts
> [February 27, 1833]

JAMES W. C. PENNINGTON

(born 1807)   Washington County, Maryland

Fugitive slave James W. C. Pennington received a Doctor of Divinity degree from the University of Heidelberg, Germany. He lectured frequently against slavery both in the United States and abroad. His autobiography, Fugitive Blacksmith, *was published in 1850.*

[166]   I called you master when I was with you from the mere force of
         circumstances, but I never regarded you as master. The nature
         which God gave me did not allow me to believe that you had any
         more right to me than I had to you, and that was just none at all.
                         Letter to His Former Master [1844]

[167]   There is one sin that slavery committed against me which I can
         never forgive. It robbed me of my education. The injury is
         irreparable.
                         Fugitive Blacksmith [1850]

[168]   There is not one feature of slavery to which the mind recurs with
         more gloomy impressions than to its disastrous influence upon
         the families of the masters, physically, pecuniarily, and mentally.
                         Fugitive Blacksmith [1850]

SOLOMON NORTHRUP

(born c. 1808)   Minerva, New York

Solomon Northrup was born free but was kidnapped and sold into bondage in Louisiana, where he remained in slavery twelve years before regaining his freedom. His experiences are recorded in his autobiography, Twelve Years a Slave *(1853).*

[169]   It is not the fault of the slaveholder that he is cruel, so much as it is
         the system under which he lives.
                         Twelve Years a Slave [1853]

[170]   Men may write fictions portraying lowly life as it is, or as it is not,
         may expatiate with owlish gravity upon the bliss of ignorance,
         discourse flippantly from armchairs of the pleasures of slave life;
         but let them toil with him in the field, sleep with him in the
         cabin, feed with him on the husks; let them behold him scourged,

> hunted, trampled on, and they will come back with another story
> in their mouths.
>> *Twelve Years a Slave* [1853]

[171]   Oh, ye pleasure-seeking sons and daughters of idleness, who move
with measured step, listless and snail-like through the slow-
winding cotillion; if ye wish to look upon the celerity, if not the
"poetry of motion," upon genuine happiness rampant and
unrestrained, go down to Louisiana and see the slaves dancing in
the starlight of a Christmas night.
>> *Twelve Years a Slave* [1853]

GABRIEL DE LA CONCEPCIÓN VALDÉS

(1809 - 1844)   Havana, Cuba

*Gabriel Valdés, who published his first volume of poetry in 1838, was active
in the Cuban fight for independence. He was arrested for his alleged participation in a revolutionary uprising and executed for treason. The following
poem has been translated from the Spanish.*

[172]   Almighty God! whose goodness knows no bound,
    To Thee I flee in my severe distress;
O let thy potent arm my wrong redress,
    And rend the odious veil by slander wound
About my brow. The base world's arm confound,
    Who on my front would not the seal of shame impress.
God of my sires, to whom all kings must yield,
    Be Thou alone my shield, protect me now.
All power is His, to whom the sea doth owe
    His countless stores; who clothed with light heaven's
        field,
And made the Sun, and air, and polar seas congeal'd;
    All plants with life endow'd, and made the rivers flow.

All power is thine, 't was thy creative might
    This godly frame of things from chaos brought,
Which unsustain'd by Thee would still be naught;
    As erst it lay deep in the womb of night,
Ere thy dread word first called it into light;
    Obedient to Thy call it lived, and moved and thought.

Thou know'st my heart, O God, supremely wise,

Thine eye, all-seeing, cannot be deceived;
By Thee my inmost soul is clear perceived,
  As objects gross are through transparent skies
By mortal ken. Thy mercy exercise,
  'Lest slander foul exult o'er innocence aggrieved.

But if 't fixed by the decree divine,
  That I must bear the pain of guilt and shame,
And that my foes this cold and senseless frame
  Shall rudely treat with scorn and shouts malign;
Give thou the word, and I my breath resign
  Obedient to Thy will; blest be thy holy name.

Prayer to God [1844]

IRA FREDERICK ALDRIDGE

(c. 1810 - 1867)   Belaire, Maryland

Although Ira Aldridge began his theatrical career in New York City, he gained fame in Europe as a leading Shakespearean actor, toured the continent for three decades, and received many honors. Aldridge's life is chronicled in Ira Aldridge, the Negro Tragedian *by Herbert Marshall (1958) and* Actor in Exile *by Mary Malone (1969).*

[173] Son of the land whose swarthy race, late known
       For nought but bloodshed and the murderous groan;
       Mark'd by the God of Havoc and of strife
       To raise the war-whoop, wield the murderous knife,
       To roam unfettered, void of reason's light—
       Lone tribe of mankind in chaotic night.
       Borne on the bellows of the trackless sea,
       From genial climes came learning's purity.
       Bright as the snowflake bursting from the deep—
       Severing the bonds of nature wrapt in sleep—
       Shone the mild beam to illuminate the mind
       Of him, the savage—still of human kind;
       To mould the soul of Nature's hallowed sway—
       To drive the clouds of darkness far away—
       To array in robes of friendship, pure and bright,
       The fellow brotherhood of Day and Night.
       Link'd with the sister arts, the Drama's pile,
       Its beauteous structure towered within our isle;
       And though exotic was each lovely flower
       Yet still they bloom'd in night and noontide hour.

'Twas wandering in those bowers of classic bloom,
The Drama's radiance did my heart illume;
Enraptured, from the hallowed bower I seized
A blossom that my youthful fancy pleased,
And, wonderful to tell, I straight became
A wandering son, fired with ambitious flame,
Though nature to my aspect has denied,
The rose and lily, which in you're allied,
'Child of the Sun,' with brow of ebon hue,
I stand before you but with soul as true;
For in this favored land, where'er we roam,
To me has ever ope'd the stranger's home;
From you I've caught that warm and kindly ray
That cheered me onwards in this world's lone way.
If to my native shores I do return,
Within my heart's fane ever shall your kindness burn.
O'er my lone grave, perhaps in desert spot,
Shall wave the lotus but 'forget you not.'
More I could say, but what would it avail—
To you I've told my turn, my heartfelt tale.
The moment's come, and severed is the spell—
Scotia's kind children, Hail and Fare you well.

Farewell Appearance Address, Glasgow, Scotland
[November 1860]

ROBERT PURVIS

(1810 - 1898)   Charleston, South Carolina

Robert Purvis, a brilliant orator, was among the youngest of Philadelphia's black abolitionists. He was founder of the Vigilante Committee of Philadelphia, the forerunner of the Underground Railroad.

[174]   This is the red man's country by natural right, and the black man's by virtue of his suffering and toil.

Letter to Senator S. C. Pomroy on the Colonization
Question [August 28, 1862]

[175]   I elect to stay on the soil of which I was born and on the plot of ground which I have fairly bought and honestly paid for. Don't advise me to leave, and don't add insult to injury by telling me it is for my own good; of that I am to be the judge.

Letter to Senator S. C. Pomroy on the Colonization
Question [August 28, 1862]

CHARLES LENOX REDMOND

(1810 - 1873)   Salem, Massachusetts

Charles Lenox Redmond was a leading black abolitionist and orator prior to the rise of Frederick Douglass. He was an original member of Philadelphia's antislavery society and vice-president of its New England chapter.

[176]   We need more radicalism among us before we can speak as becomes
        a suffering, oppressed and persecuted people.
                      Letter to a Friend [March 7, 1841]

[177]   . . . what a burning shame it is that many of the pieces on the
        subject of slavery and the slave trade, contained in different
        school books, have been lost sight of, or been subject to the
        pruning knife of the slaveholding expurgatorial system! To make
        me believe that those men who have regulated the educational
        institutions of our country have humanity in their hearts, is to
        make me believe a lie. . . .
                      Letter to William Lloyd Garrison [March 5, 1842]

[178]   . . . let American religion and wrong, American religion and
        cruelty, American religion and prostitution, American religion
        and piracy, American religion and murder, cold-blooded, and
        calculated by America's largest measure, shake hands.
                      Letter to the West Newberry Antislavery Society
                      [September 16, 1842]

DAVID RUGGLES

(1810 - 1849)   Norwich, Connecticut

Born free, David Ruggles gave up a grocery business to devote full time to the antislavery movement. He was editor and publisher of the first black periodical, Mirror of Liberty *(1838), and was a key agent with the Underground Railroad in New York City.*

[179]   Let the iron that enters into the soul of the slave; let the bloody
        whip of the cruel taskmaster; let the cries, tears, groans and
        blood of three millions of American bondmen tell how large is
        the stream of pity that flows in America to wash the wounds of
        bleeding humanity!
                      The "Extinguisher" or the Extinguished [1834]

[180]   Prejudice is not so much dependent upon natural antipathy as upon education.

The "Extinguisher" or the Extinguished [1834]

[181]   A man is sometimes lost in the dust of his own raising.

The "Extinguisher" or the Extinguished [1834]

[182]   To me nothing is more disgusting than to see my race bleached to a pallid, sickly hue by the lust of those cruel and fastidious white men whose prejudices are so strong that they can't come in sight of a colored skin. Ah, no! His natural "prejudices" forbid it! Oh delicacy, thou hast run mad and chased thy sister chastity out of bounds of southern states . . . God knows the truth is appalling enough to make a devil start, disgraceful enough to crimson the face of the whole heavens and make the angels blush.

The "Extinguisher" or the Extinguished [1834]

[183]   I have had the pleasure of helping 600 persons in their flight from bondage. In this I have tried to do my duty, and mean to persevere until the last fetter shall be broken, and the last sigh heard from the lips of a slave.

Address, Boston, Massachusetts [August 1, 1841]

[184]   When we, a proscribed, outraged, disfranchised and downtrodden people shall *know* our condition and live in obedience to the laws of our being, ignorance, slavery and all other evils afflicting us will be no more, and we shall be free indeed.

Letter to the Editor of the *Albany Northern Star* [1844]

DANIEL ALEXANDER PAYNE

(1811 - 1893)   Charleston, South Carolina

Daniel Alexander Payne, a pioneer in Afro-American education, was an influential bishop in the African Methodist Episopal Church and achieved distinction as an early president of Wilberforce University in Ohio. Payne's autobiography, Recollections of Seventy Years, *was published in 1888.*

[185]   Fly, glittering orbs! on rapid pinions fly.
        With angel swiftness through the blazing sky!
        O usher in that morn of light and love,

When God, descending from the climes above,
With word omnific shall to all proclaim
The doom of slavery, sin, and every blame:
Bid Peace shed all her radiance o'er the globe,
With love divine all human hearts enrobe:
Say to all nations, "Hear my voice with glee—
Be free! be free! ye ransomed lands, be free!"

Poem composed for the soiree of the Vigilant Committee
of Philadelphia (s. 8) [May 7, 1841]

MARTIN ROBISON DELANEY

(1812 - 1885)   Charles Town, West Virginia

Martin R. Delaney was a physician, author, explorer, and pioneer black nationalist. For two years he co-edited The North Star *with Frederick Douglass, and he was the first black field officer to serve in the Civil War. Among biographies of Delaney is* Life and Public Services of Martin R. Delaney *by Frank A. Rollin (1969).*

[186] The policy of all those who proscribe any people induces them to select, as the objects of proscription, those who differed from themselves.

The Condition, Elevation, Emigration and Destiny of the Colored People in the U.S. Politically Considered [1852]

[187] The colored people of today are not the colored people of a quarter century ago, and require very different means and measures to satisfy their wants and demands, and to effect their advancement.

The Condition, Elevation, Emigration and Destiny of the Colored People in the U.S. Politically Considered [1852]

JOHN JASPER

(1812 - 1901)   Fluvanna County, Virginia

John Jasper, a slave for fifty years before he was freed, entered the ministry and gained popularity throughout the South for his spirited sermons. Jasper's biography, John Jasper, the Unmatched Negro Philosopher *(1908) was written by William E. Hatcher.*

[188]   Yer know dat God ordains kings an' ruler, an' wat kinder bodders
        some of us, He don't always make it a p'int ter put up good men.
                        The Stone Cut Out of the Mountain, Sermon [July 20, 1884]

[189]   God done settled it dat one woman is enough fer a man, an' two is a
        war on yer hands.
                        Dem Seben Women [c. 1889]

[190]   In our day mens is awful pleniful wid us, tho' I kin not say dat de
        quality is fust-class in ve'y many.
                        Dem Seben Women [c. 1889]

[191]   We rarely goes down by ourse'fs.
                        Where Sin Come From [c. 1892]

JERMAIN WESLEY LOGUEN

(c. 1813 - 1872)   Davidson County, Tennessee

*A chronic runaway, Jermain Loguen finally made it to Canada and free-
dom. He eventually returned to the United States where he became a
bishop in the AME Zion Church. Loguen's autobiography,* The Reverend
Jermain W. Loguen as a slave and as a freeman, *was published in 1859.*

[192]   . . . I value my freedom, to say nothing of mother, brothers and
        sisters, more than your whole body; more indeed than my own
        life; more than all the lives of all the slaveholders and tyrants
        under heaven.
                        Letter to his former mistress [March 28, 1860]

[193]   . . . you say that I am a thief because I took the old mare along with
        me. Have you got to learn that I had a better right to the old
        mare, as you call her, than Mannaseth Loguen had me? Is it a
        greater sin for me to steal his horse, than it was for him to rob my
        mother's cradle and steal me? Have you got to learn that human
        rights are mutual and reciprocal, and if you take my liberty and
        life, you forfeit your own liberty and life?
                        Letter to his former mistress [March 28, 1860]

JAMES McCUNE SMITH

(1813 - 1865)   New York, New York

James McCune Smith, physician, scientist, writer, and abolitionist, earned his medical degree from the University of Glasgow, Scotland, and established the first black pharmacy in New York City.

[194]   Freedom and Liberty are synonyms. Freedom is an essence;
        Liberty an accident. Freedom is born with a man; Liberty may be
        conferred on him. Freedom is progressive; Liberty is
        circumscribed. Liberty may be taken away from a man; but, on
        whatsoever soul Freedom may light, the course of that soul is
        thenceforth onward and upward. Society, customs, laws, armies,
        are but as scythes in its giant grasp if they oppose, instruments
        to work its will if they assent. Humankind welcome the birth of a
        free soul with reverence and shoutings, rejoicing in the advent of
        a fresh offshoot of the Divine Whole, of which this is but a part.
                     Freedom—Liberty, Autographs for Freedom [1854]

HENRY BIBB

(born 1815)   Shelby County, Kentucky

Henry Bibb, a fugitive slave, settled in Canada, founded a weekly, The Voice of Fugitives, *and established a one thousand, three hundred-acre haven for escaped slaves.* Narrative of the Life and Adventures of Henry Bibb *was published in 1849.*

[195]   You may perhaps think hard of us for running away from slavery,
        but as to myself, I have but one apology to make for it . . . that I
        did not start at an earlier period. I might have been free long
        before I was.
                         Letter to W. H. Gatewood (his former master)
                         [March 28, 1844]

[196]   Let us come together by the thousands from all parts of this slave-
        holding nation and . . . kindle up the sacred fires of liberty upon
        the altars of our hearts, which shall never be extinguished until
        the last slave of America is free.
                         Letter to Frederick Douglass announcing the National
                         Convention of Colored Freedmen, Detroit, Michigan
                         [August 23, 1848]

[197]   Among other good trades I learned the art of running away to
        perfection. I made a regular business of it, and never gave it up
        until I broke the bands of slavery.
                    Narrative of the Life and Adventures of Henry Bibb [1849]

[198]   . . . I never had religion enough to keep me from running away
        from slavery in my life.
                    Narrative of the Life and Adventures of Henry Bibb [1849]

[199]   . . . I was regarded as property, and so was the ass; and I thought if
        one piece of property took off another, there could be no law
        violated in the act; no more sin committed in this than if one
        jackass had rode off another.
                    Narrative of the Life and Adventures of Henry Bibb [1849]

WILLIAM WELLS BROWN

(1815 - 1884)   Lexington, Kentucky

Ex-slave William Wells Brown was an abolitionist and self-taught writer.
His works include Narrative of William Wells Brown *(1847) and* Clotel
(1853), the first novel written by an Afro-American.

[200]   This is called "the land of the free and the home of the brave"; it is
        called the "asylum of the oppressed"; and some have been
        foolish enough to call it the "Cradle of Liberty." If it is the
        "Cradle of Liberty," they have rocked the child to death.
                    Address, Female Antislavery Society, Salem, Massachusetts
                    [November 14, 1847]

[201]   My mother's name was Elizabeth. She had seven children. . . . No
        two of us were children of the same father.
                    Narrative of William Wells Brown [1847]

[202]   . . . the acts committed daily upon slave women of America should
        not only cause the blood to chill, but to stop its circulation.
                    Letter to Captain Enoch Price (his former master)
                    [November 23, 1849]

[203]   This was a southern auction, at which the bones, muscles, sinews,
        blood and nerves of a young lady of sixteen were sold for five-
        hundred dollars; her moral character for two-hundred; her

improved intellect for one-hundred; her Christianity for
four-hundred; and her chastity and virtue for three-hundred
dollars more. And this, too, in a city thronged with churches,
whose tall spires look like so many signals pointing to heaven and
whose ministers preach that slavery is a God-ordained institution.
Clotel [1853]

[204]   Black men, don't be ashamed to show your colors, and to own them.
My Southern Home [1880]

HENRY HIGHLAND GARNET

(1815 - 1882)   Kent County, Maryland

*Teacher, minister and editor, Henry Highland Garnet was an uncompro-
mising advocate of black equality, and his orations drew large audiences.
Garnet was the first Afro-American to speak in the nation's capitol, and he
served as United States Minister to Liberia (1881-82).*

[205]   Let your motto be resistance, resistance, RESISTANCE! No
          oppressed people have ever secured their liberty without
          resistance.
Address to the Slaves of the U.S. [1843]

[206]   . . . rather die free men than live to be slaves.
Address to the Slaves of the U.S. [1843]

FREDERICK DOUGLASS

(1817 - 1895)   Tuckahoe, Maryland

*Frederick Douglass, abolitionist, journalist, orator, and diplomat, was an
outstanding figure in American history. He founded* The North Star *and
held various government posts, including that of consul general to Haiti
(1889-91).* The Life and Writings of Frederick Douglass *(5 vols.) was
published in 1950.*

[207]   If a slave has a bad master, his ambition is to get better; when he

gets better, he aspires to have the best; and when he gets the best, he aspires to be his own master.

> *An Appeal to the British People* Reception speech,
> Finsburg Chapel, Moorfields, England [May 12, 1846]

[208]   I glory in conflict, that I may hereafter exult in victory.

> *Farewell Speech to the British People*, London, England
> [March 30, 1847]

[209]   Give a hungry man a stone and tell him what beautiful houses are made of it; give ice to a freezing man and tell him of its good properties in hot weather; throw a drowning man a dollar, as a mark of your good will; but do not mock the bondman in his misery by giving him a Bible when he cannot read it.

> *Bibles for the Slaves* [June, 1847]

[210]   I am your fellow-man but not your slave.

> Letter to Thomas Auld (his former master), Rochester,
> N.Y. [September 8, 1848]

[211]   It's a poor rule that won't work both ways.

> Address, Boston, Massachusetts [June 8, 1849]

[212]   America cannot always sit as a queen in peace and repose. Prouder and stronger governments than hers have been shattered by the bolts of a just God.

> *Government and Its Subjects*, *The North Star*
> [November 9, 1849]

[213]   To imagine that we shall ever be eradicated is absurd and ridiculous. We can be remodified, changed, and assimilated, but never extinguished.

> *The Destiny of Colored Americans*, *The North Star*
> [November 16, 1849]

[214]   The white man's happiness cannot be purchased by the black man's misery.

> *The Destiny of Colored Americans*, *The North Star*
> [November 16, 1849]

[215]   The very accompaniments of the slave system stamp it as an offspring of hell itself. To insure good behavior, the slaveholder relies on *the whip*; to induce proper humility, he relies on *the*

whip. . . ; to bind down the spirit of the slave, to imbrute and
destroy his manhood, he relies on *the whip*, the chain, the gag, the
thumb-screw, the pillory, the Bowie knife, the pistol, and the
bloodhound.

> Address, Rochester, New York [December 1, 1850]

[216] If there were no other fact descriptive of slavery than that the slave
is dumb, this alone would be sufficient to mark the slave system
as a grand aggregation of human horrors.

> Address, Rochester, New York [December 1, 1850]

[217] Oppression makes a wise man mad.

> *The Meaning of July Fourth for the Negro*, Address
> Rochester, New York [July 5, 1852]

[218] O, had I the ability and could I reach the nation's ear, I would
today pour out a fiery streak of biting ridicule, blasting reproach,
withering sarcasm, and stern rebuke. For it is not light that is
needed but fire; it is not the gentle shower but thunder. We need
the storm, the whirlwind, and the earthquake. The feeling of the
nation must be quickened; the conscience of the nation must be
aroused; the propriety of the nation must be started; the
hypocrisy of the nation must be exposed, and its crimes against
God and man denounced.

> *The Meaning of July Fourth for the Negro*, Address
> Rochester, New York [July 5, 1852]

[219] To make a contented slave you must make a thoughtless one.

> *My Bondage and My Freedom* [1855]

[220] They who study mankind with a whip in their hands will always go
wrong.

> Address, Geneva, New York [August 1, 1860]

[221] The midnight sky and the silent stars have been the witnesses of
your devotion to freedom and of your own heroism.

> Letter to Harriet Tubman [August 29, 1868]

[222] The simplest trues often meet the sternest resistance and are slowest
in getting general acceptance.

> *The Woman's Sufferage Movement*, Essay published in *The
> New National Era* [October 6, 1870]

[223]   Human law may know no distinction among men in respect of
        rights, but human practice may.

>   Address, Louisville, Kentucky [September 1883]

[224]   Woman knows and feels her wrongs as a man cannot know and feel
        them, and she also knows as well as he can know, what measures
        are needed to redress them.

>   *The Woman's Sufferage Movement*, Address published in
>   *Woman's Journal* [April 14, 1888]

[225]   A government that can give liberty in its constitution ought to have
        the power to protect liberty in its administration.

>   Address, Republican National Convention
>   Chicago, Illinois [June, 1888]

[226]   It is better to be part of a great whole than to be the whole of a
        small part.

>   Interview, Anacostia, Washington, D.C. [January, 1889]

[227]   The only excuse for pride in individuals or races is the fact of their
        own achievements.

>   Address, Bethel Literary and Historical Association,
>   Washington, D.C. [April, 1889]

[228]   A nation within a nation is an anomaly.

>   Address, Bethel Literary and Historical Association,
>   Washington, D.C. [April, 1889]

[229]   No man can point to any law in the U.S. by which slavery was
        originally established. Men first make slaves and then make laws.

>   Address, Bethel Literary and Historical Association,
>   Washington, D.C. [April, 1889]

[230]   The price of liberty is eternal vigilance.

>   Address, Bethel Literary and Historical Association,
>   Washington, D.C. [April, 1889]

[231]   A little learning, indeed, may be a dangerous thing, but the want of
        learning is a calamity to any people. . . .

>   Address, Colored High School Commencement
>   Baltimore, Maryland [June 22, 1894]

[232]   . . . the upstart of today is the elite of tomorrow.
                          Address, Colored High School Commencement
                          Baltimore, Maryland [June 22, 1894]

SAMUEL RINGGOLD WARD

(1817 - 1866)   Eastern Shore, Maryland

Samuel Ringgold Ward rose to prominence between 1830 and 1860 as a dynamic antislavery orator and opponent of the 1850 Fugitive Slave Law. His life experiences are recorded in Autobiography of a Fugitive Negro *(1855).*

[233]   God helping me wherever I shall be, at home, abroad, on land or
        sea, in public or private walks, as a man, a Christian, especially
        as a black man, my labours will be antislavery labours, because
        mine must be an antislavery life.
                          Autobiography of a Fugitive Negro [1855]

[234]   It is not a question about what the Negro is capable of; it is an
        undeniable truth in demonstration of what he has done and is
        doing.
                          Autobiography of a Fugitive Negro [1855]

[235]   What an ever-present demon the spirit of Negro hate is! How it
        haunts, tempts, wounds the black man wherever his arch-enemy,
        the American goes!
                          Autobiography of a Fugitive Negro [1855]

CHARLES LEWIS REASON

(1818 - 1898)   New York, New York

Refused admittance to the Episcopal Theological Seminary because he was an Afro-American, Charles Lewis Reason instead became a teacher, specializing in languages and math. He taught in New York City schools and was also a professor of literature at New York Central College.

[236]   Come! rouse ye brothers, rouse! nor let the voice
        That shouting, calls you onward to rejoice,

Be heard in vain! but with ennobled souls,
Let all whom now an unjust law controls,
Press on in strength of mind, in purpose bent,
To live by right; to swell the free tones sent
On Southern airs, from this, your native State,
A glorious promise for the captive's fate
Then up! and vow no more to sleep, till freed
From partial bondage to a life indeed.

> from *The Spirit Voice of Liberty Call to the Disfranchised of the State of New York* [July 20, 1841]

[237] The church to her great charge untrue,
    Keeps Christian guard, o'er slavery's den!
Her coward laymen, wrong pursue,
    Her recreant priesthood, say—amen.

> from *Freedom* [1847]

ALEXANDER CRUMMELL

(1819-1898)   Eastern Shore, Maryland

Alexander Crummell was an outstanding Episcopal clergyman and black nationalist. He spent two decades as a missionary in Liberia and in 1897 founded the American Negro Academy, the first organization of Afro-American intellectuals. Crummell's speeches, Africa and America, *first published in 1891, were reprinted in 1979.*

[238] Everywhere on earth men like to hold onto power; like to use their inferiors as tools and instruments; plume and pride themselves as superior beings; look with contempt upon the labouring classes and strive by every possible means to use them to their own advantage.

> *The Dignity of Labor, Its Value to a New People*, Address, Working Men's Club, Philadelphia, Pennsylvania [1881]

[239] The evil of gross and monstrous abominations, the evil of great organic institutions crop out long after the departure of the institutions themselves.

> Address, Freedman's Aid Society, Ocean Grove, New Jersey [August 15, 1883]

[240]   Any movement that passes by the female sex is an ephemeral thing.
        Without them, no true nationality, patriotism, religion,
        cultivation, family life, or true social status is a possibility.
>   Address, Freedmen's Aid Society, Ocean Grove, New
>   Jersey [August 15, 1883]

[241]   Error moves with quick feet . . . and truth must never be lagging
        behind.
>   Address, high school graduating class, Washington, D.C.
>   [June 6, 1884]

[242]   Strive to make something of yourselves; then strive to make the
        most of yourselves.
>   Address, high school graduating class, Washington, D.C.
>   [June 6, 1884]

[243]   We read the future by the past.
>   *The Race Problem in America*, Address, Protestant
>   Episcopal Church Congress, Buffalo, New York
>   [November 20, 1888]

[244]   The race problem is a moral one. . . . Its solution will come
        especially from the domain of principles. Like all the other great
        battles of humanity, it is to be fought out with the weapons of
        truth.
>   *The Race Problem in America*, Address, Protestant
>   Episcopal Church Congress, Buffalo, New York
>   [November 20, 1888]

[245]   This country should be agitated and even convulsed till the battle
        of liberty is won and every man in the land is guaranteed fully
        every civil and political right. . . .
>   *The Race Problem in America*, Address, Protestant
>   Episcopal Church Congress, Buffalo, New York
>   [November 20, 1888]

[246]   If this nation is not truly democratic, then she must die.
>   *The Race Problem in America*, Address, Protestant
>   Episcopal Church Congress, Buffalo, New York
>   [November 20, 1888]

[247]   It is a sad reflection . . . that a sense of the responsibility which
        comes with power is the rarest of things.
                    Sermon [c. 1894]

[248]   Cheapness characterizes almost all the donations of the American
        people to the Negro. . . .
                    *The Attitude of the American Mind toward the Negro
                    Intellect*, Address, first annual meeting of the American
                    Negro Academy [December 28, 1897]

[249]   It is only by closing the ears of the soul, or by listening too intently
        to the clamors of sense, that we become oblivious of their
        utterances. . . .
                    Rightmindedness, Address, Garnet Lyceum, Lincoln
                    University, Oxford, Pennsylvania [c. 1897]

HARRIET ROSS TUBMAN

(1820 - 1913)   Dorchester County, Maryland

*As principal conductor for the Underground Railroad, Harriet Tubman led
hundreds of slaves to freedom. Tubman also supported women's rights,
and during the Civil War she served as a nurse, spy, and scout for the
Union Army.* Harriet Tubman, *a biography written by Earl C. Conrad,
was published in 1969.*

[250]   . . . I was conductor of the Underground Railroad for eight years
        and I can say what most conductors can't say—I never ran my
        train off the track or lost a passenger.
                    Inscription, Harriet Tubman Memorial
                    Auburn, New York

[251]   [On her escape from slavery]:

        . . . there was one of two things I had a right to, liberty or death. If I
        could not have one, I would have the other, for no man should
        take me alive. I should fight for my liberty as long as my strength
        lasted, and when the time came for me to go, the Lord would let
        them take me.
                    Harriet, the Moses of Her People [1869]

JAMES MONROE WHITFIELD

(1822 - 1871)   Boston, Massachusetts

The few facts known about James Whitfield place him in an active role during the decade before the Civil War. A black separatist, Whitfield supported the back to Africa philosophy, or resettlement outside the United States. A collection of his verse, America and Other Poems, *was published in 1853.*

[252]   How long, oh gracious God! how long
     Shall power lord it over right?
The feeble, trampled by the strong,
     Remain in slavery's gloomy night?
In every region of the earth,
     Oppression rules with iron power,
And every man a sterling worth,
     Whose soul disdains to cringe, or cower
Beneath a haughty tyrant's rod,
     And, supplicating, kiss the rod,
That wielded by oppression's might,
     Smites to the earth his dearest right,
The right to speak, and think, and feel,
     And spread his uttered thoughts abroad,
To labor for the common weal,
     Responsible to none but God—
          How Long (ll. 1-16) [c. 1850]

[253]   Now, when the hopes and joys are dead
     That gladdened once the heart of youth,
All romantic visions fled
     That told of friendship, love and truth,
Turn we unto that steadfast friend
     Who guards our steps where'er they rove,
Whose power support us to the end,
     Whose word is trust, whose name is love.
          Delusive Hope [1853]

MIFFLIN WISTAR GIBBS

(born 1823)   Philadelphia, Pennsylvania

Mifflin Gibbs was publisher of Mirror of the Times, *California's First Afro-American newspaper, and in 1873 was elected the first Afro-American municipal judge in the nation. Gibbs also served as United States consul at Tamatave, Madagascar (1897-1901), and published an autobiography,* Shadow and Light *(1902).*

[254]   Locality, nationality, race, sex, religion or social manner may
        differ, but the accord of desire for civil liberty . . . is ever the
        same.
                            Shadow and Light [1902]

[255]   Peace is the exhaustion of strife, and is only secure in her triumphs
        in being in instant readiness for war. . . .
                            Shadow and Light [1902]

[256]   The adaptability of the Negro to conditions that are at the
        time inevitable has been the paladium that has sustained and
        multiplied him amid the determined prejudice that has ever
        assailed him.
                            Shadow and Light [1902]

ALEXANDER DUMAS (fils)

(1824 - 1895)   Paris, France

The son of novelist Alexander Dumas reigned as a leading nineteenth-century French satirist, whose dramas focused on social and moral attitudes of the time. One of this best known works, La Dame aux Camélias *(1852), served as a model for Giuseppe Verdi's* La Traviata. *The following quotations have been translated from the French.*

[257]   Alas! The journey of life is beset with thorns to those who have to
        pursue it alone.
                            Le Demi-Monde, act III, scene i [1855]

[258]   You should not attempt to outwit a woman.
                            Le Demi-Monde, act III, scene i [1855]

[259]   She is a proverb of propriety.
                    Le Demi-Monde, act IV, scene i [1855]

[260]   The human heart is a strange mystery.
                    Le Demi-Monde, act V, scene i [1855]

[261]   . . . love without esteem cannot go far or reach high. It is an angel
        with only one wing.
                    Advice to a Son, Man-Woman [1872]

WILLIAM G. ALLEN

(born c. 1825)   Urbanna County, Virginia

*William G. Allen graduated from Oneida Institute in Whitsboro, New
York, and was later professor of Greek and German at New York Central
College. Allen published two narratives,* The American Prejudice against
Color *(1853) and* A Short Personal Narrative *(1860).*

[262]   O, the length and breadth, the height and depth, the cruelty and the
        irony of prejudice which can so belittle human nature.
                    The American Prejudice against Color [1853]

[263]   Exacerbated, forever, be this wretched slavery—this disturbing
        force. It kills the white man, kills the black man, kills the master,
        kills the slave, kills everybody and everything. Liberty is . . . the
        first condition of human progress and the special handmaiden of
        all that in human life is beautiful and true.
                    The American Prejudice against Color [1853]

FRANCES ELLEN WATKINS HARPER

(1825 - 1911)   Baltimore, Maryland

*Frances Ellen Watkins Harper was in great demand as an antislavery orator;
she also fought for women's rights and supported the Temperance movement. Her best known work is* Iola Leroy, or the Shadows Uplifted *(1892).*

[264]   Oh, could slavery exist long if it did not sit on a commercial throne?
                    Letter, Temple, Maine [October 20, 1854]

[265]   A hundred thousand new-born babes are annually added to the
        victims of slavery; twenty thousand lives are annually sacrificed
        on the plantations of the South. Such a sight should send horror
        through the nerves of civilization and impel the heart of
        humanity to lofty deeds. So it might if men had not found out a
        fearful alchemy by which his blood can be transformed into gold.
        Instead of listening to the cry of agony, they listen to the ring of
        dollars and stoop down to pick up the coin.
                        Address, Antislavery Society Convention, New York City
                        [May 13, 1857]

[266]   The respect that is only bought by gold is not worth much. It is no
        honor to shake hands politically with men who whip women and
        steal babies.
                        Our Greatest Want, The Anglo-African Magazine
                        [June 1859]

[267]   The true aim of female education should be not a development of one
        or two, but all the faculties of the human soul, because no perfect
        womanhood is developed by imperfect culture.
                        The Two Offers, The Anglo-African Magazine
                        [September, 1859]

[268]   I would prefer to see slavery go down peaceably by men breaking
        off their sins by righteousness and their iniquities by showing
        justice and mercy to the poor, but we cannot tell what the future
        may bring forth. God writes national judgments upon national
        sins. . . .
                        Letter to John Brown [November 25, 1859]

JOHN S. ROCK

(born 1825)   Salem, New Jersey

An abolitionist and brilliant pre-Civil War orator, John S. Rock was also a
successful Boston dentist and lawyer. He was the first Afro-American attorney
to plead before the U.S. Supreme Court.

[269]   The black man is not a coward.
                        Address, Boston Antislavery Society [March 5, 1858]

[270]   . . . no man shall cause me to turn my back upon my race. With it I
        will sink or swim.
                    Address, Boston Antislavery Society [March 5, 1858]

[271]   When I contrast the fine, tough muscular system, the beautiful, rich
        color, the full broad features and the gracefully frizzled hair of
        the Negro, with the delicate physical organization, wan color,
        sharp features and lank hair of the Caucasian, I am inclined to
        believe that when the white man was created, nature was pretty
        well exhausted—but determined to keep up appearances, she
        pinched up his features, and did the best she could under the
        circumstances.
                    Address, Boston Antislavery Society [March 5, 1858]

[272]   When the avenues of wealth are opened to us we will become
        educated and wealthy, and then the roughest-looking colored
        man that you ever saw . . . will be pleasanter than the harmonies
        of Orpheus, and black will be a very pretty color. It will make our
        jargon, wit—our words, oracles; flattery will then take the place
        of slander, and you will find no prejudice in the Yankee
        whatsoever.
                    Address, Boston Antislavery Society [March 5, 1858]

[273]   The free people of color have succeeded in spite of everything, and
        we are today a living refutation of that shameless assertion that
        we cannot take care of ourselves.
                    Address, Massachusetts Antislavery Society
                    [January 23, 1862]

[274]   Today, our heads are in the lion's mouth, and we must get them out
        the best way we can. To contend against the Government is as
        difficult as it is to sit in Rome and fight with the Pope.
                    Address, Massachusetts Antislavery Society
                    [January 23, 1862]

[275]   There is no prejudice against color among the slaveholders. Their
        social system and one million mulattoes are facts which no
        arguments can demolish.
                    Address, Massachusetts Antislavery Society
                    [January 23, 1862]

JOHN MERCER LANGSTON
(1829 - 1897)   Louisa County, Virginia

John Mercer Langston worked with the Freedmen's Bureau, served as dean and vice-president of Howard University, was minister to Haiti (1877-85), and was elected congressional representative from Virginia (1888). Langston's personal papers are housed at Fisk University.

[276]   . . . white Americans cannot stand as idle spectators to the struggle, but must unite with us in battling against this fell enemy if they themselves would save their own freedom.
> *The World's Antislavery Movement: Its Heroes and Its Triumphs*. Address, Xenia, Ohio [August 2, 1858]

[277]   While one man leans against another, or in soul fears him, he is subservient; and in his subserviency loses his freedom as he does the real dignity of his manhood.
> *The Exodus*. Address, Washington, D.C. [October 7, 1879]

[278]   Want makes us all work.
> *The Future of the Colored American* [c. 1882]

[279]   Abuse us as you will . . . we will increase and multiply until, instead of finding every day five-hundred black babies turning up their bright eyes to greet the rays of the sun, the number shall be five-thousand and go on increasing. There is no way to get rid of us.
> Address, 51st Congress, 2nd Session [January 16, 1891]

OSBORNE PERRY ANDERSON
(1830 - 1872)   West Fallowfield, Pennsylvania

Osborne Perry Anderson was one of five Afro-Americans who accompanied John Brown on his raid at Harper's Ferry, Virginia. Anderson wrote his account of the incident in A Voice From Harper's Ferry *(1861).*

[280]   [On his black comrades]:
> . . . are they not part of the dark deeds of this era, which will assign their perpetrators to infamy, and cause after generations to blush at the remembrance?
> *A Voice from Harper's Ferry* [1861]

EDWARD WILMOT BLYDEN

(1832 - 1912)   Saint Thomas, U.S. Virgin Islands, West Indies

A dedicated Islamic scholar and diplomat, Edward Blyden spent a short time in America before emigrating to Liberia, where he served as Secretary of State. Christianity, Islam, and the Negro Race *(1877), one of Blyden's best known works, was reprinted in 1967.*

[281] All peoples need to pass through a period of discipline and pupilage before they can really enjoy and manage liberty and independence.
> *Our Origin, Dangers, and Duties*, Independence Day
> Address, Monrovia, Liberia [July 26, 1865]

[282] No man can determine his own force of mind.
> *Our Origin, Dangers, and Duties* Independence Day
> Address, Monrovia, Liberia [July 26, 1865]

[283] Where there is no future before a people, there is no hope.
> *Our Origin, Dangers, and Duties,* Independence Day
> Address, Monrovia, Liberia [July 26, 1865]

[284] The captive Jews could not sing by the waters of Babylon, but the Negroes in the dark dungeon of American slavery made themselves harps and swept them to some of the most thrilling melodies.
> *Christianity, Islam, and the Negro Race* [1877]

[285] The inspiration of the race is the race.
> *The African Problem and the Methods of Its Solution*
> [1890]

HENRY McNEAL TURNER

(1833 - 1915)   Newberry, South Carolina

Editor, author, and bishop in the AME Church, Henry McNeal Turner favored emigration to Africa for Afro-Americans, and he played a key role in the expansion of AME Church activities on the African continent. Respect Black, the Writings and Speeches of Henry McNeal Turner *was published in 1971.*

[286]   The Fourth of July—memorable in the history of our nation as the great day of independence to its countrymen—had no claims upon our sympathies. They made a flag and threw it to the heavens, and bid it float forever; but every star in it was against us. . . .

> Address, Emancipation Day Anniversary Celebration, Augusta, Georgia [January 1, 1866]

[287]   The Negro is the junior race of the world. We have a grand future.

> Interview, *The Baltimore Afro-American* [May 16, 1884]

[288]   In some places in America black is supposed to symbolize the devil and white symbolize God. But this is partially wrong, for the devil is white and never was black.

> Interview, *The Baltimore Afro-American* [May 16, 1884]

[289]   We have as much right biblically and otherwise to believe that God is a Negro as . . . white people have to believe that God is a fine looking, symmetrical and ornamented white man. Every race of people since time began who have attempted to describe their God by words or by paintings, or by carvings . . . have conveyed the idea that the God who made them and shaped their destinies was symbolized in themselves; and why should not the Negro believe that he resembles God as much as other people?

> *God Is a Negro*. Editorial, *The Voice of Missions* [February, 1898]

JOHN ANTHONY COPELAND

(1833 - 1859)   Raleigh, North Carolina

Born of free parents, John Copeland attended college in Oberlin, Ohio. He was hanged for participation in John Brown's raid at Harper's Ferry, West Virginia.

[290]   I am well in both body and mind.
> Letter to his family on the day of his execution
> [December 16, 1859]

[291]   . . . it is not the mere fact of having to meet death which I should regret (if I should express regret I mean), but that such an unjust institution should exist as the one which demands my life, and not my life only, but the lives of those to whom my life bears but the relative value of zero to the infinite.
> Letter to his family on the day of his execution
> [December 16, 1859]

CHARLOTTE L. FORTEN

(1837 - 1914)   Philadelphia, Pennsylvania

Charlotte L. Forten, granddaughter of James Forten, attended school in Massachusetts, became a teacher, and taught newly freed slaves on Saint Helena Island, South Carolina. An edition of The Journal of Charlotte L. Forten *was published in 1961.*

[292]   I love to walk on the Sabbath, for all is so peaceful; the noise and labor of everyday life has ceased; and in perfect silence we can commune with nature and with Nature's God. . . .
> *The Journal of Charlotte L. Forten* [May 28, 1854]

[293]   Tomorrow school commences and although the pleasure I shall feel in again seeing my beloved teacher, and in resuming my studies will be much saddened by recent events, yet they shall be fresh incentive to more earnest study, to aid me in fitting myself for laboring in a holy cause, for enabling me to do much towards changing the condition of my oppressed and suffering people.
> *The Journal of Charlotte L. Forten* [June 4, 1854]

[294]   . . . hatred of oppression seems to me so blended with hatred of the oppressor I cannot separate them. I feel that no other injury could be hard to bear, so very hard to forgive, as that inflicted by cruel oppression and prejudice. How can I be a Christian when so many in common with myself, for no crime suffer so cruelly, so unjustly? It seems vain to try.

The Journal of Charlotte L. Forten [August 11, 1854]

[295]   Oh, it is hard to go through life meeting contempt with contempt, hatred with hatred, fearing, with too good reason, to love and trust hardly anyone whose skin is white—however loveable and congenial in seeming.

The Journal of Charlotte L. Forten [September 12, 1855]

[296]   Dear children, born in slavery but free at last! May God preserve to you all the blessings of freedom and may you be in every possible way fitted to enjoy them. My heart goes out to you. I shall be glad to do all I can to help you.

The Journal of Charlotte L. Forten [October 29, 1862]

AMANDA BERRY SMITH

(1837 - 1915)   Long Green, Maryland

Amanda Smith, a popular evangelist in her time, traveled extensively both in the United States and abroad. She spent eight years as a Methodist missionary in Liberia and recorded her experiences in An Autobiography *(1893).*

[297]   [On her father]:

. . . he used to make brooms and husk mats and take them to market with the produce. This work he would do nights after his day's work. . . . Then in harvest time, after working for his mistress all day, he would walk three and four miles and work in the harvest field till one and two o'clock in the morning, then go home and lie down and sleep for an hour or two, then up and at it again. He had an important and definite object before him, and was willing to sacrifice sleep and rest in order to accomplish it. It was not his own liberty alone, but the freedom of his wife and five children.

An Autobiography [1893]

JOAQUIM MARIA MACHADO DE ASSIS

(1839 - 1908)   Rio de Janeiro, Brazil

Joaquim Maria Machado de Assis is considered one of Brazil's great writers. His prodigious output covers poetry, short stories, and several major novels, including Dom Casmurro *(1900),* Esau and Jacob *(1904), and* The Psychiatrist and other Stories *(c. 1905), all available in English translation from the Portuguese.*

[298] Let no one trust the happiness of the moment; there is in it a drop
       of gall.
       Epitaph for a Small Winner [1881]

[299] . . . there is nothing in the world so monstrously vast as our
       indifference.
       Epitaph for a Small Winner [1881]

[300] One endures with patience the pain in the other fellow's stomach.
       Epitaph for a Small Winner [1881]

[301] We kill time; time buries us.
       Epitaph for a Small Winner [1881]

[302] Do not feel badly if your kindness is rewarded with ingratitude;
       it is better to fall from your dream clouds than from a third-story
       window.
       Epitaph for a Small Winner [1881]

[303] Absolute truth is incompatible with an advanced state of
       society. . . .
       Epitaph for a Small Winner [1881]

[304] . . . there is only one genuine misfortune: not to be born.
       Epitaph for a Small Winner [1881]

[305] . . . one cannot honestly attribute to a man's basic character
       something that is obviously the result of a social pattern.
       Epitaph for a Small Winner [1881]

[306] A life without fighting is a dead sea in the universal organism.
       Epitaph for a Small Winner [1881]

[307] Insanity is a matter of degree.
       Epitaph for a Small Winner [1881]

[308]   Life is won, the battle is still lost.
Dom Casmurro [1900]

[309]   . . . habitual use of the superlative makes the mouth prolix.
Dom Casmurro [1900]

[310]   . . . nothing is more unseemly than to give very long legs to very
brief ideas.
Dom Casmurro [1900]

[311]   Destiny is not only a dramatist, it is also its own stage manager.
Dom Casmurro [1900]

[312]   Vanity is the beginning of corruption.
Dom Casmurro [1900]

[313]   Purgatory is a pawnshop which lends on all virtues, for high
interest and short terms.
Dom Casmurro [1900]

[314]   Eternal truths demand eternal hours.
Esau and Jacob [1904]

[315]   . . . time is an invisible web on which everything may be
embroidered.
Esau and Jacob [1904]

[316]   Abolition is the dawn of liberty, we await the sun: the black
emancipated, it remains to emancipate the white.
Esau and Jacob [1904]

[317]   Death is a phenomenon like life; perhaps the dead live.
Esau and Jacob [1904]

[318]   It's the occasion that makes the revolution.
Esau and Jacob [1904]

[319]   If two refuse, no one fights.
Esau and Jacob [1904]

[320]   Oh, that we cannot see the dreams of one another!
A Woman's Arms [date unknown]

[321]   Out of the sighs of one generation are kneaded the hopes of the
next.
Education of a Stuffed Shirt [date unknown]

WILLIAM HARVEY CARNEY

(born 1840)   Norfolk, Virginia

At the age of twenty-three, William Carney joined the Union Army and was assigned to the Fifty-fourth Massachusetts Colored Infantry Volunteers. He was the first Afro-American soldier awarded the Congressional Medal of Honor for heroism during the battle of Fort Wagner.

[322]   The old flag never touched the ground, boys.
                    Comment to his comrades after the battle of Fort Wagner
                    [July, 1863]

OSWALD DURAND

(1840 - 1906)   Cap Haitien, Haiti

Oswald Durand, sometimes referred to as the "mistral of Haiti," was a poet, dramatist and editor who wrote many of his works in Creole. The following poem has been translated from the French.

[323]   As Lise, however, my mother was white,
                Her eyes were blue where sleeping tears gleamed,
        Whenever she blushed or in fear or delight,
                Pomegranates burst into bloom it seemed.

        Her hair was golden, too! In wind and the light
                It covered her forehead where pale griefs dreamed.
        My father was blacker than I. Yet deemed
                Sacred their union the Church and right.

        Behold, strange contrast on her white breast
                A child as golden and brown as the maize,
        Ardent, too, as the sun in our land always.
                I, orphan, loved Lise at youth's intensest,
        But her face grew pale at such words from me,
                The Black Man's son held a terror you see.
                            The Black Man's Son [Date unknown]

BLANCHE KELSO BRUCE

(1841 - 1898)   Farmville, Virginia

Blanche K. Bruce, the only Afro-American of his time to serve a full term in the United States Senate, was a member of committees on pensions, education, and labor. After completing his term, Bruce continued in government service until his death.

[324]   It will not accord with the laws of nature or history to brand the
        colored people as a race of cowards.
                Address, U.S. Senate [March 31, 1876]

[325]   I have confidence not only in my country and her institutions but
        in the endurance, capacity and destiny of my people.
                Address, U.S. Senate [March 31, 1876]

WILLIAM H. CROGMAN

(1841 - 1931)   Saint Martin, West Indies

William Crogman traveled all over the world as a merchant seaman before graduating from Pierce Academy in Massachusetts. He specialized in Greek and Latin at Atlanta University and taught at Clark College.

[326]   Freedom is the open gate into a life of vast . . . responsibilities.
                Address, Henry Ward Beecher's Church
                Brooklyn, New York [October 14, 1883]

[327]   It is a grand and awful thing to be a free man.
                Address, Henry Ward Beecher's Church
                Brooklyn, New York [October 14, 1883]

[328]   . . . to make a slave skillful is to make him dangerous.
                Address, Atlanta, Georgia State Capitol, Twenty-sixth
                Anniversary of the Emancipation Proclamation
                [January 1, 1889]

[329]   Old civilizations die hard, and old prejudices die harder.
                Address, Atlanta, Georgia State Capitol, Twenty-sixth
                Anniversary of the Emancipation Proclamation
                [January 1, 1889]

JOHN HENRY SMYTH

(1844 - 1908)   Richmond, Virginia

John Henry Smyth taught for several years after his graduation from Howard University Law School. He entered the United States Diplomatic Service in 1878 and served over seventeen years, including two interims as minister to Liberia.

[330]   I have no prejudice . . . against man or woman on account of race, color or creed. But I have a preference for my race and color that I have for no other. . . .
>   Preface, *Speeches* [1891]

[331]   First a race, then part of a nation.
>   Address, Vermont Avenue Baptist Church, Washington, D.C. [April 16, 1891]

[332]   Cultivate race love.
>   Address, Vermont Avenue Baptist Church, Washington, D.C. [April 16, 1891]

[333]   In the twilight of time, aye, mid the night of the ages when time was young, the African had birth. Throughout historic times uninterruptedly this race has existed. When time shall have become hoary with age, when the end shall be, we shall as a race be the last to look upon the earth. . . .
>   Address, Vermont Avenue Baptist Church, Washington, D.C. [April 16, 1891]

JOSEPH BURRITT SEVELLI CAPPONI

(born c. 1846)   Florida

Little is known about Joseph Sevelli Capponi, who was a graduate of Biddle University (today Johnson C. Smith University). He was principal of Warren Academy in Saint Augustine, Florida, and he practiced law in Texas.

[334]   . . . the black man for 245 years has plowed, hoed, chopped, cooked, washed, walked, run, fought, bled and died for the white man not because he enjoyed it or gained by it, but simply because the stronger man was on top and had him down; and for the time being he had to grin and bear it or strike and die in a pile.
Ham and Dixie, "What Manner of Man is He?" [1895]

[335]   . . . if the Negro succeeds at all, he must succeed as a Negro and not as a mere imitator or pliant tool in the hands of other races.
Ham and Dixie, "What Manner of Man is He?" [1895]

[336]   . . . I love the Negro's melody, the Negro's humor, the Negro's pathos, the Negro's wit and the Negro's blackness, because these are original and God-given, and they can never be destroyed.
Ham and Dixie, "What Manner of Man is He?" [1895]

[337]   Wisdom is greater than knowledge, for wisdom includes knowledge and the due use of it.
Ham and Dixie, "The Five Pillars" [1895]

[338]   Solve your own problem by curing your own defects.
Ham and Dixie, "Work Out Your Own Salvation" [1895]

ARCHIBALD HENRY GRIMKÉ

(1849 - 1930)   Charleston, South Carolina

Harvard-educated Archibald Grimké was half-brother of the famous abolitionist sisters, Angelina and Sarah Grimké. He edited HUB, *a small Boston newspaper, served as United States consul to Santo Domingo (1884), and was president of the American Negro Academy for over a decade. Many of Grimké's writings were published in the American Negro Academy's* Occasional Papers.

[339]   [On Denmark Vesey]:

> In judging the black man, oh, ye critics and philosophers, judge
> him not hastily before you have tried to put yourselves in his
> place. You may not even then succeed in doing him justice, for
> while he had his faults, and was sorely tempted he was,
> nevertheless, in every inch of him, from the soles of his feet to
> the crown of his head, a man.
>
> *Right on the Scaffold, or Martyrs of 1882* [1901]

[340]   . . . slavery is a breeding bed, a sort of composte heap where the
best qualities of both races decay and become food for the worst.

> Address, Annual Meeting of the American Negro Academy
> [December 28, 1915]

[341]   You may ransack the libraries of the world, and turn over all the
documents of recorded time, to match the Preamble of the
Constitution as a piece of consummate political dissimulation
and mental reservation as an example of how men juggle
deliberately and successfully with their moral sense, how they
raise above themselves huge fabrics of falsehood and go willingly
to live and die in a make-believe world of lies. The muse of
history, dipping her iron pen in the generous blood of the Negro,
has written large across the page of that Preamble and the face of
the Declaration of Independence the words, "sham,"
"hypocrisy."

> *The Shame of America or the Negro's Case Against the
> Republic* [1924]

THOMAS EZEKIEL MILLER

(1849 - 1938)   Ferebeeville, South Carolina

*Thomas E. Miller, a graduate of Lincoln University, studied law, passed the
bar in 1875, and set up private practice in Beaufort, South Carolina. He was
elected state senator in 1880, participated in the South Carolina Con-
stitutional Convention (1895), and was president of the State Colored
College in Orangeburg, South Carolina.*

[342]   It is not the fear of negro supremacy in the South that causes the
southern election of officers to suppress the negro vote, but it is
the fear of the rule of the majority regardless of race. The master
class does not want to surrender to the rule of the people, and

they use the frightful bugbear of negro rule to scare the white man and drive him under the yoke that has been bearing heavily upon him for more than a century.

> Address, House of Representatives [February 14, 1891]

[343] I shall not be muffled here. Muffled drums are instruments of the dead. I am in part the representative of the living; of those whose rights are denied; of those who are slandered by the press, on the lecture platform, in the halls of legislation, and oftentimes by men in the livery of heaven, and I deem it my supreme duty to raise my voice, though feebly, in their defense.

> Address, House of Representatives [February 14, 1891]

[344] We are no more aliens to this country or to its institutions than our brothers in white. We have instituted it; our forefathers paid dearly for it. The broken hearts of those who first landed here is the first price that was paid for the blessings for which we now contend. By the God of right, by the God of justice, by the God of love, we will stay here and enjoy it, share and share alike with those who call us aliens, and invite us to go. Together we planted the tree of liberty and watered its roots with our tears and blood, and under its branches we will stay and be sheltered.

> Address, South Carolina State Convention
> [October 26, 1895]

GEORGE WASHINGTON WILLIAMS

(1849 - 1891)   Bedford Springs, Pennsylvania

George Washington Williams was a soldier in the Union Army. He attended Howard University, Newton Theological Seminary, and was the first Afro-American elected to the Ohio Legislature. Williams also wrote History of the Negro Race in America, 1619-1880 *(1883).*

[345] I have tracked my bleeding countrymen through widely scattered documents on American history; I have listened to their groans, their clanking chains and melting prayers until woes of a race and the agonies of centuries seem to crowd upon my soul as a bitter reality. Many pages of this history have been blistered with my tears; and although having lived but a little more than a generation, my mind feels as if it were cycles old.

> Preface, *History of the Negro Race in America, 1619-1880,*
> Vol. II [1883]

FRANCIS JAMES GRIMKÉ

(1850 - 1937)   Charleston, South Carolina

Francis Grimké, brother of Archibald H. Grimké, served over fifty years as
a minister of the Fifteenth Street Presbyterian Church in Washington,
D.C., and was a member of the Howard University Board of Trustees. The
Works of Francis J. Grimké *(a collection of his papers) was published in*
1942.

[346]   The Negro is bound to get his rights, or else there will be trouble.
> *Signs of a Brighter Future*, Sermon [December 4, 1900]

[347]   Slavery is gone . . . but the spirit of it still remains.
> *God and the Race Problem*, Sermon [May 3, 1901]

[348]   The Negro is no longer running like he used to do.
> Sermon, Union Thanksgiving Service, Plymouth
> Congregational Church, Washington, D.C.
> [November 27, 1919]

[349]   It is only what is written upon the soul of man that will survive the
wreck of time.
> *Stray Thoughts and Meditations* [1914 - 1934]

[350]   A pretty good test of a man's religion is how it affects his
pocketbook.
> *Stray Thoughts and Meditations* [1914 - 1934]

[351]   Race prejudice can't be talked down, it must be lived down.
> *Stray Thoughts and Meditations* [1914 - 1934]

[352]   It is not the grade of work that determines the respectability, but
the grade of man who does the work.
> *Stray Thoughts and Meditations* [1914 - 1934]

[353]   It is the impact of life that tells.
> *Stray Thoughts and Meditations* [1914 - 1934]

ALBERY ALLISON WHITMAN

(1851 - 1902)   Hart County, Kentucky

Albery A. Whitman was a Methodist minister and, in later years, a financial agent. Whitman's works were published in various magazines and in two collections of his poems: Not a Man and Yet a Man *(1877) and* Twasinta's Seminoles or, Rape of Florida *(1890).*

[354]   The cabin dance, the banjo and the song,
Are courted yet by Afric's humble throng.
They drown their sorrows in a sea of mirth,
They crush young griefs as soon as they find birth
Neath dance's heel; and on the banjo string
A theme of hope, that forces woe to sing.

> *Not a Man and Yet a Man* [1877], "In the House of the Aylors" (s. 11)

[355]   Ah! ye whose eyes with pity doth run o'er,
When mournful tales come from a heathen shore,
Of babes by mothers thrown to crocodile;
The scaly terror of the languid Nile;
Of Brahma's scar and Islam's wanton rites,
And bloody raids on Zion's sacred heights!
Ye who hear these and pray for God to come,
Behold yon mother fleeing from her home!
A master's child upon her frantic breast,
And by a master's savage bloodhounds prest;
And this, too, where in every steepled town,
The crucifix on human wrong looks down!
Think then no more of heathen lands to rove,
While in America there breathes a slave!

> *Not a Man and Yet a Man* [1877], "The Flight of Leeona" (s. 17)

WILLIAM SAUNDERS SCARBOROUGH

(1852 - 1926)   Bibb County, Georgia

William S. Scarborough was a distinguished educator and linguist whose textbook, First Lessons in Greek, *was used extensively in Northern schools. Scarborough traveled internationally and headed the Classical Language Department at Wilberforce University in 1877.*

[356]   We have too many dudes whose ideal does not rise above the
        possession of a new suit, a cane, a silk hat, patent leather shoes, a
        cigarette, and a good time. . . .
                The Educated Negro and His Mission [1903]

[357]   The masses must move, but it must be the classes that move
        them. . . .
                The Educated Negro and His Mission [1903]

[358]   The quiet shaft of ridicule oftimes does more than argument. . . .
                The Educated Negro and His Mission [1903]

[359]   The race must make a common cause to meet a common enemy and
        win common friends.
                The Educated Negro and His Mission [1903]

[360]   So mixed are we that we know not who we are or what we are, and
        cannot even agree upon a suitable name for ourselves—so mixed
        that if all were counted to us who bear our blood we would have
        at least 25 [million] rather than 10 million charged up to our
        census account.
                Race Integrity, The Voice of the Negro [May 1907]

GEORGE HENRY WHITE

(1852 - 1918)										Rosindale, North Carolina

George H. White was an outstanding lawyer and served as United States representative from North Carolina during the Reconstruction. After leaving politics, he established a bank and entered the real estate business.

[361]   You tie us and then taunt us for a lack of bravery, but one day we will break the bonds. You may use our labor for two and a half centuries and then taunt us for our poverty, but let me remind you we will not always remain poor. You may withhold even the knowledge of how to read God's word and learn the way from earth to glory and then taunt us for our ignorance, but we would remind you that there is plenty of room at the top, and we are climbing.

> *Defense of the Negro Race, Charges Answered*
> Farewell address to the U.S. Congress [January 29, 1901]

[362]   This . . . is perhaps the Negro's temporary farewell to the American Congress, but . . . Phoenix-like he will rise up some day and come again.

> *Defense of the Negro Race, Charges Answered*
> Farewell address to the U.S. Congress [January 29, 1901]

JOSEPHINE SILONE YATES

(1852 - 1912)										New York, New York

Educator and writer Josephine Silone Yates taught for many years at Lincoln Institute in Missouri. As president of the National Association of Colored Women she worked for more effective participation of Afro-American women in American society.

[363]   A democracy cannot long endure with the head of a God and the tail of a demon.

> Editorial, *The Voice of the Negro* [July, 1904]

JOSÉ JULIEN MARTÍ
(1853 - 1895)   Havana, Cuba

Poet and newspaper journalist José Martí was an activist in the Cuban fight for independence. In May 1895 he was killed in the battle of Dos Ríos. Martí's poems appear in various English anthologies, and his Complete Works *(in Spanish) was published in 1925. The following selections have been translated from the Spanish.*

[364]   A poem is something sacred. Let no one
        Take it for anything except itself.
        Let one force it to his will, as slaves
        Are forced with tear-filled eyes by mistress cruel,
        And then, pale and unloving it will come,
        Like that unhappy slave who, while she may
        Obey behests with weak, unwilling hands
        Will comb her mistress' tresses; and some tower
        That rises like a cake against the sky,
        She'll press the hair in form, or with false curls
        Destroy the flowing line of noble brow
        That shows the soul's essential honesty.
        But while the slave obeys her mistress' whims,
        Her melancholy heart, like a red bird
        With wounded wings, dreams she is soaring far
        From there to where her absent sweetheart is.
        God's curse on masters and on tyrants, too,
        Who force the luckless bodies to abide
        In places where their hearts unwilling dwell!
                    Poetry is Sacred [c. 1878]

[365]   . . . the injustice of this world is great, as is the ignorance of its
        sages, and there are many who still honestly believe that the
        Negro is incapable of the intelligence and spirit of the white man.
                    My Race [April, 1893]

[366]   The beautiful night makes sleep impossible.
        The cricket chirps, the lizard shrills, and
        its chorus responds. Even through the darkness
        one can see the wood is of *cupey* and *pagua*, low,
        thorny palm; the fireflies circle slowly about;
        above the twittering nests, I hear the music
        of the forest, blended and soft, like delicate
        violins; the music rises and falls, comes
        together and breaks off, spreads wing and settles,

hovers and soars, always subtle and minimum --
a myriad of fluid sound. What wings brush the
leaves? What tiny violin, and sections of
violins draws notes and soul from the leaves:
What dance of souls of leaves?

> *From Cabo Haitiano to Dos Ríos,* Excerpt from his diary
> [1895]

JAMES ALLEN BLAND

(1854 - 1911)   Flushing, New York

James Allen Bland composed over six hundred songs and was a nationally acclaimed minstrel performer as star of Haverly's European Minstrels. "Carry Me Back to Old Virginny," one of his hit songs, is the official state song of Virginia.

[367]   Carry me back to old Virginny,
        There's where the cotton and the corn and 'tatoes grow,
        There's where the birds warble sweet in the springtime,
        There's where this old darky's heart am long'd to go.
> *Carry Me Back to Old Virginny* (s. 1) [c. 1847]

[368]   Oh, dem golden slippers!
        Oh, dem golden slippers!
        Golden slippers I'se gwine to wear
        Because dey look so neat:
        Oh, dem golden slippers!
        Oh, dem golden slippers!
        Golden slippers I'se gwine to wear,
        To walk de golden street.
> *Oh, Dem Golden Slippers!* (Chorus) [c. 1879]

[369]   In the evening by the moonlight
        You could hear us darkies singing,
        In the evening by the moonlight
        You could hear the banjo ringing,
        How the old folks would enjoy it,
        They would sit all night and listen,
        As we sang in the evening by the moonlight.
> *In the Evening by the Moonlight* [c. 1886]

NAT LOVE
(1854 - 1921)   Davidson County, Tennessee

Nat Love numbered among the better known Afro-American cowboys who rode the Western plains. He was once adopted by an Indian tribe, and Jesse James and Bat Masterson were among his acquaintances. Love recalled his experiences in The Life and Adventures of Nat Love *(1907).*

[370]   Some of the slaves, like us, had kind and indulgent masters. These were lucky indeed, as their lot was somewhat improved over their less fortunate brothers, but even their lot was the same as that of the horse or cow of the present day. They were never allowed to get anything in the nature of education, as smart negroes were not in much demand at that time, and the reason was too apparent. Education meant the death of the institution of slavery in this country, and the slave owners took good care that their slaves got none of it.

The Life and Adventures of Nat Love [1907]

[371]   The name of Deadwood Dick was given to me by the people of Deadwood, South Dakota, July 4, 1876 after I had proven myself worthy to carry it, and after I had defeated all comers in riding, roping, and shooting, and I have always carried the name with honor since that time.

The Life and Adventures of Nat Love [1907]

JOHN WESLEY EDWARD BOWEN
(1855 - 1933)   New Orleans, Louisiana

Educator, theologian, and writer, John W. E. Bowen received a doctorate from Boston University, and was minister of Asbury Methodist Episcopal Church in Washington, D.C. Bowen taught Hebrew at Howard University and edited the early periodical, The Voice of the Negro.

[372]   While I do not believe that whatever is is right, I do believe that whatever is ought to be known.

Sermon, Asbury Methodist Episcopal Church
Washington, D.C. [January 31, 1892]

[373]   We must learn that the purity of woman is the purity of the family,
        and the purity of the family is the purity of the race, and
        whosoever dares to touch the character of a single girl or is a foe
        to the purity of the family is an enemy of the race and in league
        with hell.
                            Sermon, Asbury Methodist Episcopal Church
                            Washington, D.C. [January 31, 1892]

[374]   It remains to be seen what God will do in ebony. . . .
                            Sermon, Asbury Methodist Episcopal Church
                            Washington, D.C. [January 31, 1892]

[375]   It is impossible to raise and educate a race in the mass. All
        revolutions and improvements must start with individuals.
                            Sermon, Asbury Methodist Episcopal Church
                            Washington, D.C. [February 14, 1892]

[376]   We are not old enough to read the deep lessons of these times.
                            Sermon, Asbury Methodist Episcopal Church
                            Washington, D.C. [February 14, 1892]

[377]   . . . when we shall be removed from the struggles of recent times in
        the social and political world to the centuries beyond, in which
        the prejudices engendered in the participants of the strife shall be
        known only through the cold type of history, then under the
        unblurred eye and the cold sympathetic logic of the patient
        historian the period of servitude of the Negro will shine forth
        with a luster unapproachable in American history.
                            An Appeal to the King, Address, Atlanta Exposition,
                            Atlanta, Georgia [October 21, 1895]

TIMOTHY THOMAS FORTUNE

(1856 - 1928)   Marianna, Florida

Timothy Thomas Fortune was a leading black journalist of the late 1800s and editor of The New York Age. *After leaving this post Fortune joined the staff of Booker T. Washington, while continuing to publish articles until his death. Fortune also published a collection of essays,* Black and White: Laud, Labor and Politics in the South *(1884), and a book of poetry,* Dreams of Life *(1905).*

[378]   Let the history of the past be spread before the eyes of a candid and
          thoughtful people; let the bulky roll of misgovernment,
          incompetence, and blind folly be enrolled on the one hand, and
          then turn to the terrors of the midnight assassin and the lawless
          deeds which desecrate the sunlight of noontide, walking abroad
          as a phantom armed with the desperation of the damned.
                    Political Independence of the Negro, Address, Colored
                    Press Association, Washington, D.C. [June 27, 1882]

[379]   There is no strength in a Union that enfeebles.
                    Political Independence of the Negro, Address, Colored
                    Press Association, Washington, D.C. [June 27, 1882]

[380]   Mob law is the most forcible expression of an abnormal public
          opinion; it shows that society is rotten to the core.
                    Political Independence of the Negro Address, Colored
                    Press Association, Washington, D.C. [June 27, 1882]

[381]   Progress goes forward ever, backward never.
                    Black and White: Land, Labor and Politics in the South
                    [1884]

[382]   Human, it may be, to err, and to forgive divine, but for man to
          extend forgiveness too far is positively fatal.
                    Black and White: Land, Labor and Politics in the South
                    [1884]

[383]   . . . . the truth should be told, though it kill.
                    Black and White: Land, Labor and Politics in the South
                    [1884]

[384]   From hill to hill let Freedom ring!
          Let tyrants bend the knee!

Why should the people have a king,
When every man a king should be!
Every Man a King (s. 1) [c. 1904]

[385]   Such power has love—a potion dread
That kills or cures the heart and head!
Filling the soul with glorious light
Of darkness of the fearsome night!
It lifts to heaven's fruition fair,
Or dashes down to hell's despair!
It leads through valleys where the blooms
Are ripening for the mills and looms,
By streams that oaks and cedars shade,
While wildly rushing through the glade!
It toils o'er rugged mountains steep,
Where snows in wakeless slumber sleep!
The Bird of Ellerslee, Canto III (s. 20) [1905]

BOOKER TALIAFERRO WASHINGTON

(1856 - 1915)   Hale's Ford, Virginia

Educator, lecturer, and controversial statesman, Booker T. Washington was internationally acclaimed during his lifetime. He was an organizer of the National Negro Business League and founder of Tuskegee Institute, one of America's oldest black colleges. Volume 8 of a projected fifteen-volume edition of the Booker T. Washington Papers *was recently published.*

[386]   One problem thoroughly understood is of more value than a score poorly mastered.
Address, The Alabama State Teacher's Association,
Montgomery, Alabama [April 11, 1888]

[387]   The world cares very little about what a man or woman knows; it is what the man or woman is able to do. . . .
Address, The Alabama State Teacher's Association,
Selma, Alabama [June 5, 1895]

[388]   We can feel more in five minutes than the white man can in a day.
Address, The Alabama State Teacher's Association,
Selma, Alabama [June 5, 1895]

[389] Nobody cares anything for a man that hasn't something that
       somebody wants.
                         Address, The Alabama State Teacher's Association,
                         Selma, Alabama [June 5, 1895]

[390] No race can prosper till it learns that there is as much dignity in
       tilling a field as in writing a poem.
                         Cotton States Exposition Address, Atlanta, Georgia
                         [September 19, 1895]

[391] It is in all things pure and social we can be as separate as the fingers,
       yet one as the hand in all things essential to mutual progress.
                         Cotton States Exposition Address, Atlanta, Georgia
                         [September 19, 1895]

[392] No race can wrong another race simply because it has the power to
       do so without being permanently injured in morals.
                         Democracy in Education, Address, Institute of Arts and
                         Sciences, Brooklyn, New York [September 30, 1896]

[393] A sure way for one to lift himself up is by helping to lift someone
       else.
                         Daily Resolves [1896]

[394] . . . do a common thing in an uncommon way.
                         Daily Resolves [1896]

[395] A great deal of prejudice against the Negro exists in this country,
       but it stops when it comes to buying.
                         Solving the Negro Problem, Address, Central Presbyterian
                         Church, Denver, Colorado [January 26, 1900]

[396] . . . you can't make a good Christian out of a hungry man.
                         Solving the Negro Problem, Address, Central Presbyterian
                         Church, Denver, Colorado [January 26, 1900]

[397] Every individual and every race that has succeeded has had to pay
       the price which nature demands from all.
                         National Negro Business League Address, Boston,
                         Massachusetts [August 24, 1900]

[398] A race is not measured by its ability to condemn, but to create.
                         The Rights and Duties of the Negro, Address, National
                         Afro-American Council, Louisville, Kentucky
                         [June 2, 1903]

[399] Let us hold up our heads and with firm and steady tread go manfully forward. No one likes to feel that he is continually following a funeral procession.

> *The Rights and Duties of the Negro* Address, National Afro-American Council, Louisville, Kentucky [June 2, 1903]

[400] No race can accomplish anything till its mind is awakened. . . .

> *The Negro's Part in the South's Upbuilding* [1904]

[401] If I have learned much from things, I have learned more from men.

> *My Larger Education* [1911]

[402] I used to be a hater of the white race, but I soon learned that hating the white man did not do him any harm. . . .

> Address, Fourth American Peace Conference, St. Louis, Missouri [May 1, 1913]

[403] We must not become discouraged.

> *What Cooperation Can Accomplish*, Address, Negro Organization Society, Norfolk, Virginia [November 12, 1914]

[404] At the bottom of education, at the bottom of politics, even at the bottom of religion itself, there must be for our race . . . economic foundation, economic prosperity, economic independence.

> *National Negro Business League Address*, Boston, Massachusetts [August 19, 1915]

CHARLES WADDELL CHESTNUTT

(1858 - 1932)   Cleveland, Ohio

Charles W. Chestnutt never finished grade school, yet he prepared himself to teach, established a legal and stenography business, studied law, passed the bar exam, and wrote over fifty short stories, numerous essays, and three novels: The House behind the Cedars *(1900),* The Marrow of Tradition *(1901), and* The Colonel's Dream *(1905).*

[405] Time touches all things with destroying hand.

> *The House behind the Cedars* [1900]

[406] W'ite folks has deir troubles jes' ez well ez black folks, an' sometimes feel 'em mo', 'cause dey ain't ez use' ter 'em.

> *The House behind the Cedars* [1900]

[407]   We shall come up . . . slowly and painfully perhaps, but we shall
         win our way.
                    The Marrow of Tradition [1901]

[408]   The ability to thrive and live under adverse circumstances is the
         surest guaranty of the future.
                    The Marrow of Tradition [1901]

[409]   The Negro was here before the Anglo-Saxon was evolved, and his
         thick lips and heavy-lidded eyes looked out from the inscrutable
         face of the sphinx across the sands of Egypt, while yet the
         ancestors of those who now oppress him were living in caves
         practicing human sacrifice, and painting themselves with
         woad—and the Negro is here yet.
                    The Marrow of Tradition [1901]

[410]   I ain' no w'ite folks nigger. . . . I don' call no man "Marster." I
         don' wan' nothin' but w'at I wo'k fer, but I wants all er dat. I
         never moles's no w'ite man, 'less'n he moles's me fus'.
                    The Marrow of Tradition [1901]

[411]   Race prejudice is the devil unchained.
                    The Marrow of Tradition [1901]

[412]   Those who set in motion the forces of evil cannot always control
         them afterwards.
                    The Marrow of Tradition [1901]

[413]   We are all puppets in the hands of Fate and seldom see the strings
         that move us.
                    The Marrow of Tradition [1901]

[414]   . . . our boasted civilization is but a veneer which cracks and scales
         off at the first impact of primal passions.
                    The Marrow of Tradition [1901]

[415]   In matters of taste, the majority is always wrong.
                    The Colonel's Dream [1905]

[416]   Environment controls the making of men.
                    The Colonel's Dream [1905]

CHARLES THOMAS WALKER

(1858 - 1921)   Hephzibah, Georgia

Charles Thomas Walker attended Atlanta Baptist Seminary, was ordained at the age of nineteen, and because of his oratorical eloquence became known as the "Black Spurgeon."

[417]   . . . God made us men long before men made us citizens.
> *An Appeal to Caesar*, Sermon, Carnegie Hall, New York, New York [May 27, 1900]

[418]   Until the rights of man are recognized, guaranteed, and maintained in this nation, social disorder will continue to gnaw the heart, and the gangrene of corruption will continue.
> *An Appeal to Caesar*, Sermon, Carnegie Hall, New York, New York [May 27, 1900]

[419]   Dollars not only count but they rule.
> *An Appeal to Caesar*, Sermon, Carnegie Hall, New York, New York [May 27, 1900]

EGBERT MARTIN

(1859 - 1887)   Demarara, British Guiana [Guyana]

Egbert Martin (pseudonym "Leo") was a popular South American writer whose Poetical Works *was published in 1883.*

[420]   Men's hearts are like harps that quiver
        In one peculiar key.
> *Erring Ones* (s. 4, l. 1) [1875]

[421]   O sovereign Night! to thee is kindly given
        The gentler power that draws us nearer heaven;
        Thine is the subtler spell and nobler art
        To touch the finer chords within the heart;
        Thine is the hand which lays contention by,
        And softly wipes the tear from sorrow's eye,
        And lulls the erring senses into calm,
        And spreads o'er every wound some cooling balm;
        Thine is the hour that calls from mem'ry's voice
        And strain which makes the very soul rejoice—
> *The Joys of Night* (s. 8) [c. 1879]

[422]   Judge not thy brother!
            There are secrets in his heart that you might weep to see.
                    Judge Not Thy Brother (ll. 1-2) [c. 1881]

[423]   While with just thought to know she lives,
                The aged grandam heeds nor old, nor young;
            But ever and again some proverb gives
                That in her youthful days was said or sang,
                Repeating o'er and o'er the rune,
                Until it grows a weary tune
                Like bells in monotones cadence rung.
                    The Negro Village (s. 9) [c. 1882]

ESTEBAN MONTEJO

(1860 - c. 1965)   Plantation, Northern Cuba

*Esteban Montejo spent his youth on a sugar plantation and as a runaway
lived ten years alone in the forest. After slavery was abolished, Montejo
came out of hiding, worked again in the fields, and fought in the Cuban
struggle for independence. His story is told in* The Autobiography of a
Runaway Slave, *published in 1968.*

[424]   I was a runaway from birth.
                    The Autobiography of a Runaway Slave [1968]

[425]   The deputy overseer slept inside the barracoon [slave shack] and
            kept watch. . . . Everything was based on watchfulness and the
            whip.
                    The Autobiography of a Runaway Slave [1968]

[426]   Life was hard and bodies wore out.
                    The Autobiography of a Runaway Slave [1968]

[427]   The spirit is the reflection of the soul.
                    The Autobiography of a Runaway Slave [1968]

[428]   Even if I had to die tomorrow, I would not give up my pride.
                    The Autobiography of a Runaway Slave [1968]

BABIKR BEDRI

(1861 - 1954)   Atabara, Sudan

Babikr Bedri was a pioneer in Sudanese education and one of his country's leading intellectuals. Volume I of Bedri's Memoirs, *translated from the Arabic, was published in 1969.*

[429] Let love between us so divided be
       That thou mayst feel the fire that burns in me.
       And let my days be e'en as God hath willed,
       If only in thy arms they be fulfilled.
                    Untitled [c. 1900]

[430] When God wills that an event will occur, He sets the causes that will
       lead to it.
                    Memoirs [1969]

JOSEPH SEAMON COTTER, SR.

(1861-1959)   Bardstown, Kentucky

Joseph Seamon Cotter was a teacher and school principal who lived and taught most of his life in Louisville, Kentucky. Among his works are a play in verse, Caleb, the Degenerate *(1903); short stories; and* Links of Friendship *(1898), a collection of poetry.*

[431] How oft inflated hope carries us on,
       In search of ancient truth's deferred dawn,
       And then, with eyes grown dim and lips grown mute,
       We hurry back in failure's parachute.
                    Hope [1898]

[432] Faith is essential to prosperity,
       Although no moral knoweth what it be;
       For, without it, the wise man, like the fool,
       Would swap the ocean for a stagnant pool.
                    Faith [1898]

[433] God makes a man. Conditions make his creed.
                    Caleb, the Degenerate [1903]

REVERDY CASSIUS RANSOM

(1861 - 1959)   Flushing, Ohio

Reverdy Ransom was a prominent bishop in the African Methodist Episcopal Church. He preached a social gospel advocating church leadership in community welfare and equal rights for Afro-Americans. A collection of his speeches, The Spirit of Freedom and Justice, *was published in 1926.*

[434]   [On slavery]:

> It is no longer a question of property in human flesh or of the boundary lines of slavery. Today it is subtle, complex, involved. Then it struck men, now it strikes manhood; then it chained the intellect, now it removes the fetters from the mind but sets bounds as to the sphere of its exercise.
>
> > *The Martyrdom of John Brown*, Sermon delivered in celebration of the 50th anniversary of the hanging of John Brown. Faneuil Hall, Boston, Massachusetts [December 2, 1909]

[435]   . . . we ask not that others bear our burden, but do not obstruct our pathway, and we will throw off our burdens as we run.

> *Wendell Phillips*, Sermon, Plymouth Congregational Church, Brooklyn, New York [November 29, 1911]

[436]   There is a strong effort to make a case against the Negro as "the sick man of America." His case has been diagnosed by doctors of every school of thought who have treated him for all the deadly diseases in the mental, moral, social, industrial and political catalogue, yet he continues to grow strong on the same meat and exercise that are the daily bread of all normal, healthy Americans. The trouble is not with the Negro, but with the physicians who are paranoics on the Negro question.

> *Wendell Phillips*, Sermon, Plymouth Congregational Church, Brooklyn, New York [November 29, 1911]

[437]   The white man held onto us in the days of slavery; we are holding onto him in the day of freedom, and we will not let him go until we are seated securely by his side in the full enjoyment of every right he holds as his most sacred heritage.

> *Wendell Phillips*, Sermon, Plymouth Congregational Church, Brooklyn, New York [November 29, 1911]

[438]   I see, now near at hand, the opening day
            of the darker races of mankind in which
        Americans of African descent stand forth
        Among the first Americans.
                            from *Prophesy* [c. 1915]

[439]   Race prejudice and race antagonism are by no means confined to
            the United States, but this country is pre-eminent in the ignoble
            distinction it has achieved in the matter of treating a fellow
            human being on the basis of the color of his skin.
                            Crossing the Color Line [c. 1916]

IDA B. WELLS BARNETT

(1862 - 1931)   Holly Springs, Mississippi

Newspaper journalist and editor Ida Wells Barnett was best known for her crusade against lynching at the turn of the century. In later years she devoted her time to the black women's club movement and civil rights. Crusade for Justice: The Autobiography of Ida B. Wells *was published in 1970.*

[440]   The appeal to the white man's pocket has ever been more effectual
            than all the appeals ever made to his conscience.
                            United States Atrocities [1892]

[441]   True chivalry respects all womanhood, and no one who reads the
            record, as it is written in the faces of the million mulattoes in the
            South will, for a minute, conceive that the southern white man
            had a very chivalrous regard for the honor due the woman of his
            own race or respect for the womanhood which circumstances
            placed in his power.
                            A Red Record [1895]

KELLY MILLER

(1863 - 1939)   Winnsborough, South Carolina

Kelly Miller, a noted Afro-American intellectual of his time, was dean of the Howard University College of Liberal Arts for over a decade. Miller wrote for various periodicals and two collections of essays: Out of the House of Bondage *(1914), and* The Everlasting Stain *(1924).*

[442]   White man's civilization is as much a misnomer as the white man's multiplication table. It is the equal inheritance of anyone who can appropriate and apply it.
As to the Leopard's Spots, Race Adjustment [1908]

[443]   If initiative is the ability to do the right thing, then efficiency is the ability to do the thing right.
Out of the House of Bondage [1914]

[444]   If God or Nature intended any indelible difference between the races, He could easily have accomplished the purpose by making them immiscible. It requires great audacity to reenact laws of the Almighty, to say nothing of enacting laws for the Almighty.
Is Race Difference Fundamental, Eternal and Inescapable?
An Open Letter to Warren G. Harding [1917]

[445]   Every caste system in the world is based on vocation. Social stratification rests on employment.
Is Race Difference Fundamental, Eternal and Inescapable?
An Open Letter to Warren G. Harding [1917]

[446]   The white man boasts of his God-given right to rule, but he should prove his right to rule by ruling right.
An Appeal to Conscience [1918]

[447]   Revolution accelerates evolution.
Radicalism and the Negro [1918]

[448]   Tradition is the dead hand of human progress.
Radicalism and the Negro [1918]

[449]   The leaders of any suppressed people should speak boldly, even though they may be ambassadors in bonds.
Radicals and Conservatives [c. 1918]

[450]   When reform becomes impossible, revolution becomes imperative.
The Negro in the New World Order [c. 1919]

[451]   Revolutions never go backward.
                    Power and Principle [c. 1920]

[452]   . . . conscienceless efficiency is no match for efficiency quickened
        by conscience.
                    Power and Principle [c. 1920]

[453]   The only reconstruction worthwhile is a reconstruction of thought.
                    Reconstruction of Thought [c. 1922]

[454]   No race can speak for another or give utterance to its striving goal.
                    Race Leadership [c. 1923]

[455]   It is human instinct to heed the cry of the oppressed. But if the
        oppressed fail to give the outcry, there will be no indication for
        the oppressor to heed.
                    Unrest among the Weaker Races [c. 1923]

MARY CHURCH TERRELL

(1863 - 1954)   Memphis, Tennessee

Mary Church Terrell, civic leader, writer, and lecturer, was the first president
of the National Association of Colored Women, a charter member of the
NAACP, and actively involved in the fight for equal rights. Her auto-
biography, Confessions of a Colored Woman in a White World, *was*
published in 1940.

[456]   A white woman has one handicap to overcome: that of sex. I have
        two—both sex and race.
                    Confessions of a Colored Woman in a White World [1940]

[457]   . . . never once in my life have I even been tempted to "cross the
        color line" and deny my racial identity. I could not have
        maintained my self-respect if I had continuously masqueraded as
        being something I am not.
                    Confessions of a Colored Woman in a White World [1940]

[458]   I will always protest against the double standard of morals.
                    Confessions of a Colored Woman in a White World [1940]

LENA MASON
(1864 - 1924)   Sedalia, Missouri

Lena Mason was an evangelist and poet who lectured and preached through-out the East and Midwest for more than twenty-five years.

[459]   When the Negro gained his freedom
            Of body and of soul,
        He caught the wheels of progress,
            Gave them another roll.
        He was held near three long centuries
            In slavery's dismal cave,
        But now he is educated
            And unfitted for a slave.
                          The Negro and Education (s. 6) [c. 1894]

[460]   White man, stop lynching and burning
        This black race trying to thin it;
        for if you go to heaven or hell,
        You will find some Negroes in it.
                          A Negro in It [c. 1902]

CHARLES VICTOR ROMAN
(1864 - 1934)   Williamsport, Pennsylvania

Charles V. Roman, an ophthalmologist, did his internship in London, England. He later taught at Meharry Medical College and was editor of the National Medical Association Journal. *Roman also published a collection of essays,* American Civilization and the Negro *(1916).*

[461]   Racial solidarity and not amalgamation is the desired . . . goal of
        the American Negro. Phyletic triumph through racial solidarity,
        rather than phyletic oblivion in the Lethan waters of
        miscegenation will be the teaching of that scholarship.
                   A Knowledge of History Conducive to Racial Solidarity
                   Address, Wilberforce University [February 24, 1911]

[462]   As black contains by absorption all the colors of the rainbow,
        though it does not reflect them, so the Negro has in him all the
        elements of civilization and may yet reflect them as brilliantly as
        any sons of men.
                   A Knowledge of History Conducive to Racial Solidarity
                   Address, Wilberforce University [February 24, 1911]

[463]   Losses always attend moving.
A Knowledge of History Conducive to Racial Solidarity
Address, Wilberforce University [February 24, 1911]

[464]   No civilization can become world-wide and enduring if a white skin
is the indispensable passport to justice and distinction. This
would exclude . . . the majority of mankind.
Science and Christian Ethics [c. 1912]

[465]   The ignorant are always prejudiced and the prejudiced are always
ignorant.
Science and Christian Ethics [c. 1912]

[466]   If the majority rules, then the earth belongs to colored people.
American Civilization and the Negro, "Dominating Forces"
[1916]

[467]   Violence of language leads to violence of action. Angry men seldom
fight if their tongues do not lead the fray.
American Civilization and the Negro, "Dark Pages in the
White Man's Civilization" [1916]

[468]   A . . . universal human stupidity is the belief that our neighbor's
success is the cause of our failure.
American Civilization and the Negro, "What the Negro
May Reasonably Expect of the White Man" [1916]

[469]   The Negro has been grateful to his friends, forgiving to his enemies
and has frequently disappointed the prophets.
American Civilization and the Negro, "What Has the
American Negro Done? What Ought He to Do? What Will
He Do?" [1916]

[470]   'Tis a long way from slavery to freedom. Sometimes the freedman
is absolutely incapable of becoming a freeman.
American Civilization and the Negro, "What Has the
American Negro Done? What Ought He to Do? What Will
He Do?" [1916]

[471]   No human folly can surpass the conceit of ignorance.
American Civilization and the Negro, "Racial Differences"
[1916]

[472]   The man who believes his neighbor is foreordained to hell, is prone
to raise hell for him.
American Civilization and the Negro, "The Solution" [1916]

[473]   All men have reason, but all men do not reason equally well.
                        American Civilization and the American Negro, "Some
                        Basic Problems" [1916]

[474]   Those who believe in ghosts always see them.
                        The Horoscope of Prince Ham [c. 1918]

[475]   No race ever rises above its average man.
                        The Horoscope of Prince Ham [c. 1918]

MATTHEW HENSON

(1866 - 1955)   Charles County, Maryland

*A skilled navigator with a fluent command of the Eskimo language, Matthew
Henson accompanied Admiral Robert E. Peary on all of his polar expedi-
tions. Henson was the first man to reach the North Pole in 1909, and he
recounted his exploits in* A Negro Explorer at the North Pole *(1912).*

[476]   We were crossing a lane of moving ice. Commander Peary was in
         the lead setting the pace, and a half hour later the four boys and
         myself followed single file. They had all gone before, and I was
         standing and pushing at the upstanders of my sledge, when the
         block of ice I was using as a support slipped from underneath my
         feet, and before I knew it the sledge was out of my grasp, and I
         was floundering in the water of the lead. I did the best I could. I
         tore my hood from off my head and struggled frantically. My
         hands were gloved and I could not take hold of the ice, but before
         I could give the "Grand Hailing Sigh of Distress," . . . Ootah
         had grabbed me by the nape of the neck, the same as he would
         have grabbed a dog, and with one hand he pulled me out of the
         water, and with the other hurried the team across.
                        A Negro Explorer at the North Pole [1912]

[477]   Since my return to civilization seven years ago, my mind often
         reverts to life in the Arctic, and there steals over me a great desire
         to return to those "Frozen Ice Fields" once more.
                        Autograph to Arthur A. Schomburg [1916]

RANDALL ALBERT CARTER
(born 1867)   Fort Valley, Georgia

Randall Albert Carter was an influential figure in the Colored Methodist Episcopal Church. Appointed bishop in 1914, Carter was an early advocate of international religious ecumenicalism, and he traveled extensively to promote this cause.

[478]   [On race prejudice]:

Do not deceive yourselves into believing in this country you will escape this curse of the age. Often it will be veiled and stealthy. Frequently, it will walk openly and unafraid, but it will be the same illogical and unreasoning thing. Learn to expect it, and face it, and conquer it.

Whence and Whether, Commencement address, Paine College, Augusta, Georgia [May 30, 1923]

RUBÉN DARÍO
(1867 - 1916)   Metapa, Nicaragua

Poet Rubén Darío was of Spanish, Indian, and African ancestry, and he is considered an outstanding figure in Latin American literature. Poet-errant: A Biography of Rubén Darío, *by Charles Watland, was published in 1965. The following poems have been translated from the Spanish.*

[479]   The treacheries of ambition never cease.
            To Columbus (s. 6, l. 1) [1892]

[480]   The sun, a disc of translucent glass,
            creeps to the zenith like an invalid;
            the sea wind rests in the shade, its head
            pillowed on its black bugle.
                        Symphony in Gray Major (s. 2) [1896]

[481]   I know there are those who ask: Why does he not
            sing with the same wild harmonies as before?
            But they have not seen the labors of an hour,
            the work of a minute, the prodigies of a year.

I am an agèd tree that, when I was growing,
uttered a vague, sweet sound when the breeze caressed me.
The time for youthful smiles has now passed by;
now, let the hurricane swirl my heart to song!
                    In Autumn [c. 1898]

[482]   That childless lady despises
        her own exquisite figure
        when the cook comes by in the street with her six
        children and a seventh on the way.
                    Thistles [c. 1900]

WILLIAM EDWARD BURGHARDT DU BOIS

(1868 - 1963)   Great Barrington, Massachusetts

Historian, scholar, educator, and sociologist, W. E. B. Du Bois was the first Afro-American to receive a Ph.D. from Harvard University, and he was a founding member of the NAACP. Among his numerous works are: The Souls of Black Folk *(1903),* The Gift of Black Folk *(1924), and* Du Bois: Speeches and Addresses *(2 vols., 1970).*

[483]   Black mother of the iron hills that
            guard the blazing sea.
        Wild spirit of a storm-swept soul
            a-struggling to be free,
        Where 'neath the bloody finger marks,
            thy riven bosom quakes,
        Thicken the thunders of God's voice,
            and lo! a world awakes.
                    from *The Burden of Black Women* [1896] (Later published
                    as "Riddle of the Sphinx")

[484]   I believe in Pride of race and lineage and self: in pride of self so
        deep as to scorn injustice to other selves; in pride of lineage so
        great as to despise no man's father; in pride of race so chivalrous
        as neither to offer bastardy to the weak nor beg wedlock of the
        strong, knowing that men may be brothers in Christ, even though
        they be no brothers-in-law.
                    Credo [1900]

[485]   It is a hard thing to live haunted by the ghost of an untrue dream. . . .
                    The Souls of Black Folk [1903]

[486]   One ever feels his twoness—an American, a Negro; two souls, two
         thoughts, two unreconciled strivings; two warring ideals in one
         dark body, whose dogged strength alone keeps it from being torn
         asunder.
                              The Souls of Black Folk [1903]

[487]   To be a poor man is hard, but to be a poor race in a land of dollars
         is the very bottom of hardships.
                              The Souls of Black Folk [1903]

[488]   The problem of the twentieth century is the problem of the color
         line.
                              The Souls of Black Folk [1903]

[489]   There is in this world no such force as the force of a man determined
         to rise. The human soul cannot be permanently chained.
                              Race Prejudice, Speech, Republican Club of New York
                              [March 5, 1910]

[490]   Business pays. Philanthropy begs.
                              Business and Philanthropy, *Crisis* [June, 1911]

[491]   Oppression costs the oppressor too much if the oppressed stand up
         and protest. The protest need not be merely physical—the
         throwing of stones and bullets—if it is mental, spiritual; if it
         expresses itself in silent, persistent dissatisfaction, the cost to the
         oppressor is terrific.
                              Our Own Consent, Editorial, *Crisis* [January, 1913]

[492]   If there is anybody in this land who thoroughly believes that the
         meek shall inherit the earth, they have not often let their presence
         be known.
                              The Gift of Black Folk [1924]

[493]   Listen to the Winds, O God the Reader, that wail
         across the whipchords stretched taut on broken
         human hearts; listen to the Bones, the bare bleached
         bones of slaves that line the lanes of Seven Seas
         and beat eternal tom-toms in the forests of the
         laboring deep; listen to the Blood, the cold thick
         blood that spills its filth across the fields and
         flowers of the Free; listen to the Souls that
         wing and thrill and weep and scream and sob and
         sing above it all. What shall these things mean,
         O God the Reader? You know. You know.
                              The Gift of Black Folk [1924]

[494] We shall never secure emancipation from the tyranny of the white
       oppressor until we have achieved it in our own souls.
                    Patient Asses, Editorial, *Crisis* [March, 1930]

[495] If the unemployed could eat plans and promises they would be able
       to spend the winter on the Riviera.
                    As the Crow Flies, Crisis [January, 1931]

[496] The fall of capitalism began when it made razor blades that would
       get dull in a month instead of those that would easily last 10 years
       at the same cost.
                    As the Crow Flies, Crisis [January, 1933]

[497] What joy it is to "investigate" the Negro. We don't dare study
       wealth or politics or the morals of Peachtree Street; but
       "niggers"—Lord! Any fool can make a doctor's thesis on them
       full of lies that universities love to publish.
                    As the Crow Flies, Crisis [January, 1933]

[498] . . . it is the spirit that knows Beauty, that has music in its soul and
       the color of sunsets in its headkerchiefs; that can dance on a
       flaming world and make the world dance, too. Such is the soul of
       the Negro.
                    Dusk of Dawn [1940]

[499] The white world has its jibes and cruel caricatures; it has its loud
       guffaws; but to the black world alone belongs the delicious
       chuckle.
                    Dusk of Dawn [1940]

[500] The greatest and most immediate danger of white culture, . . . is its
       fear of the Truth, its childish belief in the efficacy of lies as a
       method of human uplift.
                    Dusk of Dawn [1940]

[501] The social sciences from the beginning were deliberately used as
       instruments to prove the inferiority of the people of the world,
       who were being used as slaves for the comfort and culture of the
       masters.
                    *Prospect of a World Without Racial Conflict, American
                    Journal of Sociology* [March 1944]

[502] Freedom always entails danger.
                    Freedom to Learn, Midwest Journal [Winter, 1949]

[503] We are peddling freedom to the world and daring them to oppose it
and bribing them kindly to accept it and dropping death on those
whose refuse it. . . .

What is Wrong with the United States?, Speech, Madison
Square Garden, New York City [May 13, 1952]

[504] As you live, believe in life. Always human beings will live and
profess to greater, broader and fuller life. The only possible
death is to lose belief in this truth simply because the great end
comes slowly, because time is long.

Last Message [written June 26, 1957]

JAMES DAVID CORROTHERS

(1869 - 1917)   Calvin, Michigan

*During his lifetime, James Corrothers was, among other things, a lumber-
jack, boxer, and bootblack. He attended Northwestern University, was an
ordained minister, and wrote for various newspapers and periodicals. In
addition, he wrote a novel,* The Black Cat Club *(1902).*

[505] We want to live as free men; not as half slaves
        'mong the free,
    With free men's rights and homes in this fair
        Land of Liberty!
    'Tis not to enter white men's homes, but to enjoy our own,
    In the land for which our fathers died—
        the only we have known!

The Gift of the Greatest God (s. 10) [1901]

[506] Do de other feller, befo' he do you.

The Black Cat Club [1902]

[507] A good run's bettah 'n' a bad stan'.

The Black Cat Club [1902]

[508] Many a man have died f'om havin' too much bravery; but common
sense nevah killed nobody.

The Black Cat Club [1902]

[509] Him dat fights an' run away,
    'll lib to fight anothah day.

The Black Cat Club [1902]

[510]   To be a Negro in a day like this
            Demands strange loyalty. We serve a flag
        Which is to us white freedom's emphasis.
            Ah! one must love when Truth and Justice lag,
        To be a Negro in a day like this.
                        At the Closed Gates of Justice (s. 3) [1913]

[511]   Dey was hard times jes 'fo' Christmas
            round our neighborhood one year;
        So we held a secret meetin', whah de
            white folks could n't hear,
        To 'scuss de situation, an' to see whut
            could be done
        Towa'd a fust-class Christmas Dinneh an'
            a little Christmas fun.

        Rufus Green, who called de meetin', ris'
            an' said: "In dis here town,
        An' throughout de land, de white folks
            is a-tryin' to keep us down,"
        S' 'e: "Dey's bought us, sold us, beat us;
            now dey 'buse us 'ca'se we's free;
        But when dey tetch my *stomach*, dey 's
            done gone to fur foh *me*!

        "Is I right?" "You sho is, Rufus!" roared
            a dozen hungry throats.
        "Ef you 'd keep a mule a-wo'kin', don't
            you tamper wid his oats.
        Dat 's sense," continued Rufus. "But
            dese white folks nowadays
        Has done got so close an' stingy you can't
            live on whut dey pays.

        "Here 't is Christmas-time, an', folkses,
        I's indignan 'nought to choke.
        Whah 's our Christmas dinneh comin'
            when we 's mos' completely broke?
        I can't hahdly 'fo'd a toothpick an' a
            glass o' water. Mad?
        Say, " 'nt desp'ut! Dey jes better treat
            me nice, dese white folks had!"

        Well, dey 'bused de white folks scan'lous,
            till old Pappy Simmons ris',

Leanin' on his cane to spote him, on
    account his rheumatis',
An' s' 'e: "Chilun, whut's dat wintry
    wind a-sighin' th'ough de street
'Bout yo' wasted summeh wages; But,
    no matteh, we mus' *eat*.
"Now, I seed a a beau'ful tuhkey on a
    certain gemmun's fahm
He's a-growin' fat an' sassy, an'
    a-struttin' to a chahm.
Chickens, sheeps, hogs, sweet pertaters—
    all de craps is fine dis year;
All we needs is a *committee* foh to tote
    de goodies here."

Well, we lit right in an' voted dat it was
    a gran' idee,
An' de dinneh we had Christmas was
    worth trabblin' miles to see;
An' we eat a full an' plenty, big an'
    little, great an' small,
Not beca'se we was dishonest, but
    indignant, sah. Dat 's all.

                  An Indignation Dinner [1915]

JAMES WELDON JOHNSON

(1871 - 1938)   Jacksonville, Florida

*James Weldon Johnson, a respected poet among Afro-Americans, was also
a critic, teacher and diplomat. He served as United States consul to Venezuela
and Nicaragua, and was an executive director of the NAACP. In addition
to poetry, Johnson wrote a novel,* Autobiography of an Ex-Colored Man
(1912) and an autobiography, Along This Way *(1933).*

[512] Lift every voice and sing
      Till earth and heaven ring,
      Ring with the harmonies of Liberty;
      Let our rejoicing rise
      High as the listening skies,
      Let it resound loud as the rolling sea.

Sing a song full of the faith that the dark past has
    taught us,
Sing a song full of the faith that the present has
    brought us,
Facing the rising sun of our new day begun,
Let us march on till victory is won.
                        Lift Every Voice and Sing (s. 1) [1900]

[513] So often has thou to thy bosom pressed
       The golden head, the face and brow of snow;
       So often has it 'gainst thy broad, dark breast
       Lain, set off like a quickened cameo.
       Thou simple soul, as cuddling down that babe
       With thy sweet croon, so plaintive and so wild,
       Came ne'er the thought to thee, swift like a stab,
       That it some day might crush thy own black child?
                        Black Mammy (s. 2) [1917]

[514] Sinner, oh, sinner,
       Where will you stand
       In that great day when God's a-going to rain down fire?
       Oh, you gambling man—where will you stand?
       You whore-mongering man—where will you stand?
       Liars and backsliders—where will you stand,
       In that great day when God's a-going to rain down fire?
                        The Judgment Day (s. 7) [1927]

WILLIAM TECUMSEH VERNON

(1871 - 1944)   Lebanon, Missouri

*Lincoln University graduate, minister, and educator, William T. Vernon
devoted most of his life to the education of young Afro-Americans. He was
a president of Western University, a church-supported school in Quindaro,
Kansas; he also spent several years in Africa as an African Methodist
Episcopal bishop. Vernon published a collection of his speeches,* The
Upbuilding of a Race, *in 1904.*

[515] Temples fall, statues decay, mausoleums perish, eloquent phrases
       declaimed are forgotten, but good books are immortal.
                        Sermon, Western University, Quindaro, Kansas [1900]

[516] Be yourself.
>   Sermon, Western University, Quindaro, Kansas [1900]

[517] Keep your counsel; the world knowing your plans will seek to
>   destroy them.
>   Sermon, Western University, Quindaro, Kansas [1900]

[518] Do not despise or hate your neighbor because he has been a success;
>   take care of your own case.
>   Sermon, Western University, Quindaro, Kansas [1900]

[519] Men get out of life what they put into it, but at an increased rate of
>   interest.
>   Sermon, African Methodist Episcopal Church Conference,
>   Cape Girardeau, Missouri [October, 1900]

[520] We, the free, must set about our unfinished tasks of freeing others.
>   Sermon, African Methodist Episcopal Church Conference,
>   Cape Girardeau, Missouri [October 1900]

[521] We want not only brainy leaders but brainy followers.
>   Sermon, African Methodist Episcopal Church Conference,
>   Cape Girardeau, Missouri [October 1900]

[522] . . . all our liberty ends where moral wrong begins.
>   *The Mission of the Teacher*, Address, Missouri State
>   Teachers Association [December 26, 1901]

[523] The man of vast wealth must learn that by amassing wealth at the
>   expense of the soul and body of the man who earns bread by the
>   sweating face in poverty, he only builds to his own ruin.
>   *The Mission of the Teacher*, Address, Missouri State
>   Teacher's Association [December 26, 1901]

[524] Today's listeners many times surpass yesterday's preachers.
>   *The Mission of the Teacher*, Address, Missouri State
>   Teacher's Association [December 26, 1901]

[525] Omniscience alone may dare to visit the mistakes of buried sires on
>   breathing sons or adjust accounts between the living and the
>   dead.
>   *A Plea for a Suspension of Judgment*, Address, Kansas City
>   Day Club, Kansas City, Missouri [1905]

[526] With education symmetrical and true we will take the dead mass
       buried by slavery's hand and touch them to life. This beauteous
       angel, which has always done its work for those on earth, will
       roll away the stone from the tomb where is buried a race, and my
       people will come forth to their glory and the amazement of the
       world.
                     A Plea for a Suspension of Judgment, Address, Kansas City
                     Day Club, Kansas City, Missouri [1905]

[527] For nearly 300 years we've sung the sorry songs. We shall yet sing
       the songs of rejoicing and triumph.
                     A Plea for a Suspension of Judgment, Address, Kansas City
                     Day Club, Kansas City, Missouri [1905]

[528] Wound us and we bleed; fatally so and we die;
           crush our spirits and our hearts ache, and with anguished
           souls we suffer on.
                     A Plea for a Suspension of Judgment, Address, Kansas City
                     Day Club, Kansas City, Missouri [1905]

[529] Humanity, returning to first principles where man will be just to
       fellow man, at the altar of truth will bow, the sable son of earth
       will be called brother, and the story of how he rose to higher
       estate will be the theme of dreamers and of those who write the
       truths that undo fiction by their strangeness.
                     A Plea for a Suspension of Judgment, Address, Kansas City
                     Day Club, Kansas City, Missouri [1905]

PAUL LAURENCE DUNBAR
(1872 - 1906)   Dayton, Ohio

*During his short lifetime, Paul Laurence Dunbar carved a solid niche in
Afro-American literature as a poet, novelist, and short story writer. His*
Complete Poems *(1913) remains a popular collection today.*

[530] We wear the mask that grins and lies,
           It hides our cheeks and shades our eyes,—
           This debt we pay to human guile;
           With torn and bleeding hearts we smile,

And mouth with myriad subtleties.
And should the world be overwise,
In counting all our tears and sighs?
Nay, let them only see us, while
    We wear the mask!

We smile, but, O Great Christ, our cries
To thee from tortured souls arise.
We sing, but oh the clay is vile
Beneath our feet, and long the mile;
But let the world dream otherwise
    We wear the mask!
                    We Wear the Mask [1895]

[531]   An angel, robed in spotless white,
        Bent down and kissed the sleeping Night.
        Night woke to blush; the sprite was gone.
        Men saw the blush and called it Dawn.
                    Dawn [1895]

[532]   Fiddlin' man jes' stop his fiddlin',
            Lay his fiddle on de she'f;
        Mockin'-bird quit tryin' to whistle,
            'Cause he jes' so shamed hisse'f.
        Folks a-playin' on de banjo
            Draps dey fingahs on de strings—
        Bless yo' soul—fu'gits to move 'em.
            When Malindy sings.
                    When Malindy Sings (s. 5) [1895]

[533]   The man who simply sets and waits
            Fur good to come along,
        Ain't worth the breath that one would take
            To tell him he is wrong.
        Fur good ain't flowin' round this world
            Fur every fool to sup;
        You've got to put yor see-ers on,
            An' go an' hunt it up.
                    My Sort o' Man (s. 7) [c. 1896]

[534]   Money is a great dignifier.
                    The Ordeal at Mt. Hope [1898]

[535] ... human bein's is cur'ous articles.
The Intervention of Peter [1898]

[536] I said de right kin' o' price allus pays. But de wrong kin'—oomph,
well, you'd bettah look out!
Mammy Peggy's Pride [1898]

[537] I know why the caged bird sings!
Sympathy (s. 3, 1. 7) [1899]

[538] The rain streams down like harp-strings from the sky;
The wind that world-old harpist sitteth by;
And ever as he sings his low refrain
He plays the harp-strings of the rain.
Rain Songs [1901]

[539] Only the rich are lonesome.
The Sport of Gods [1901]

[540] ... the underdog does not stop to philosophize about his position.
The Fanatics [1902]

[541] Blue bird sass de robin,
Robin sass him back,
Den de blue bird scol' him
'Twell his face is black.
Wouldn' min' de quoilin'
All de mo'nin' long,
'Cept it wakes me early,
Case hit's done in song.
Spring Fever (s. 2) [1903]

SUTTON ELBERT GRIGGS
(1872 - 1930)   Denison, Texas

Sutton E. Griggs, a Baptist minister, was in great demand as a speaker on racial issues. He established Orion Publishing Company in Nashville to print his works. Among Griggs' five novels are Imperium in Imperio *(1899) and* Unfettered *(1902).*

[542]   De greatest t'ing in de wul is edification. Ef our race ken git dat we ken git eberyt'ing else.
Imperium in Imperio [1899]

[543]   The courts of the land are the facile instruments of the Anglo-Saxon race. They register its will as faithfully as the thermometer does the slightest caprice of the weather.
Imperium in Imperio [1899]

[544]   . . . in judging a people we must judge them according to the age in which they lived and the influence that surrounded them.
Imperium in Imperio [1899]

[545]   I hed ter sell dis ole body ter de doctah ter git money ter lib on while heah.
Unfettered [1902]

[546]   . . . it often requires more courage to read some books than it does to fight a battle.
Unfettered [1902]

[547]   . . . a race that does not read must ever be a laggard race.
Unfettered [1902]

ETZER VILAIRE

(born 1872)   Jérémie, Haiti

*Etzer Vilaire, a poet of the Parnassian school, was honored by the French
Academy, and his works were published in various anthologies. In addition,
Vilaire practiced law, was a higher court judge, and a well known figure in
the Haitian civil service. The poems that follow have been translated from
the French.*

[548]   All things are silent even homes everywhere.
        It rains. Along roads nowhere can you see
        A soul that lives. It rains. I can hear sadly
        Its song which descends slow and dull up there.
        Night falls.
                    A night so chill, so filled with shadows
        'Tis but shadows expiring among greater shadows.
                    Soir Triste [Date Unknown]

[549]   Water—pale light-flash across dark green,
            Where the winds play. Far—night's horizon seen
        Topping mountains which are sublime and serene.
        In dusky velvet of fields that dream,
        Through leafage, I see little huts which seem
        Big nests. Clouds that drift over all
        Till confused they tremble, vague images fall.

                    The moon dreams and floats high,
        Caressing the waves which caress the shore
        A ray starts to dance on the sleeping sea.
        With a pencil of light dawn streaks the sky.
                    Landscape [Date Unknown]

WILLIAM CHRISTOPHER HANDY
(1873 - 1958)   Florence, Alabama

*William Christopher Handy was a bandleader and cornetist during the early
days of jazz, and he gained fame as the top blues composer of all time.
Handy's autobiography,* Father of the Blues *(1941), is a chronicle of the
early jazz era.*

[550]   Saint Louis woman wid her diamon' rings
        Pulls dat man roun' by her apron strings.
        'Twant for powder an' for store-bought hair
        De man I love would not gone nowhere.
                    St. Louis Blues (s. 1, ll. 8-11) [1914]

[551]   You'll never miss the water
        Till your well runs dry.
                    Joe Turner's Blues (s. 1, ll. 1-2) [1915]

[552]   I woke up this morning with the Blues all 'round my bed
        Thinking about what you, my baby, said.
        Do say the word and give my poor heart ease,
        The Blues ain't nothing but a fatal heart disease.
                    Shoeboot's Serenade (s. 2, ll. 1-4) [1915]

[553]   I put ashes in my sweet papa's bed
        So that he can't slip out.
        Hoodoo in his bread
        Goofer dust all about—
        I'll fix him!
        Conjuration is in his socks and shoes
        Tomorrow he'll have those mean
        Sundown Blues.
                    from *Sundown Blues* [1926]

[554]   Want to go down where the father of the waters
        And all of his daughters like the human stream
        Flow leisurely 'long.
        They wear the world there like a loose garment
        And without adornment,
        All day a dream, all night a song.
        Lawd sent boll-wee-vil,
        All kinds of upheaval; like Egypt land
        He had his plan, He had his plan—
        Made the work borrow gladness from sorrow
        'Way down South where the blues began.
                    Way Down South Where the Blues Began (chorus 2) [1932]

ARTHUR ALFONSO SCHOMBURG

(1874 - 1938)   San Juan, Puerto Rico

Arthur Schomburg was a founder of the Negro Society for Social Research and owned one of the finest private libraries on people of African descent. It formed the nucleus for what is today the Schomburg Center for Research in Black Culture in New York City.

[555]   The American Negro must remake his past in order to make his
          future. . . .
                    The Negro Digs up His Past [1925]

[556]   . . . pride of race is the antidote to prejudice.
                    The Negro Digs up His Past [1925]

[557]   History must restore what slavery took away, for it is the social
          damage of slavery that the present generation must repair and
          offset.
                    The Negro Digs up His Past [1925]

BERT WILLIAMS

(1875 - 1922)   New Providence, Nassau, West Indies

Bert Williams was a famous black-face vaudeville comedian, a composer, and a Ziegfeld Follies star. His long partnership with George Walker produced a string of successes, including introduction of the cakewalk. Nobody: The Story of Bert Williams, *by Ann Charters, was published in 1970.*

[558]   . . . I have never been able to discover that there was anything
          disgraceful in being a colored man. But I have often found it
          inconvenient—in America.
                    Comment [c. 1911]

[559]   The man with the real sense of humor is the man who can put
          himself in the spectator's place and laugh at his own misfortunes.
                    Comment [c. 1915]

[560]   Troubles are funny only when you can pin them to one particular
          individual; the fellow who is the goat must be the man who is
          singing the song or telling the story.
                    Comment [c. 1917]

[561]   I was thinking about all the honors that are showered on me in the theater, how everyone wishes to shake my hand or get an autograph, a real hero you'd naturally think. However, when I reach a hotel, I am refused permission to ride on the passenger elevator, I cannot enter the dining room for my meals, and am Jim Crowed generally. But I am not complaining, particularly since I know this to be an unbelievable custom. I am just wondering. I would like to know when (my prediction) the ultimate changes come, if the new human beings will believe such persons as I am writing about actually lived?

Letter to a friend [1922]

MARY McLEOD BETHUNE

(1875 - 1955)   Mayesville, South Carolina

Mary McCleod Bethune won national recognition for her political, educational, and humanitarian achievements. She founded the National Council of Negro Women and in 1904 established Bethune-Cookman College in Florida. The Mary McLeod Bethune Papers are housed at Dilliard University in New Orleans, Louisiana.

[562]   Invest in the human soul. Who knows, it might be a diamond in the rough.

Address, delivered at a gathering in her honor, Los Angeles, California [September 21, 1926]

[563]   . . . I am my mother's daughter, and the drums of Africa beat in my heart. They will not let me rest while there is a single Negro boy or girl without a chance to prove his worth.

Faith That Moved a Dump Heap [c. 1943]

[564]   I leave you love.

My Last Will and Testament [1955]

[565]   Love builds. . . .

My Last Will and Testament [1955]

[566]   Knowledge is the prime need of the hour.

My Last Will and Testament [1955]

GEORGE REGINALD MARGETSON
(born 1877)   Saint Kitts, West Indies

George Margetson graduated with honors from the Moravian School in Saint Kitts and came to the United States in 1897. Among his several published volumes of verse are England and the West Indies *(1906) and* Songs of Life *(1910).*

[567]   For we should know precisely what we are,
        To judge of such another's rights doth mar;
        And we should know likewise what not are we,
        If we would realize what we hope to be.
                        England and the West Indies (s. 9) [1906]

[568]   Here in a cumbrous corner of the earth,
        Where lie stupendous stores of tragic worth,
        Amidst the howling of a murderous throng,
        Ethiopia bravely drags her train along.
                        Ethiopia's Flight (s. 1) [1907]

[569]   Life is half insanity
            As we choose to make it.
                        Life (s. 2, ll. 3-4) [1910]

[570]   This is the native rampart
        Of Nature's chosen sons,
        While 'tis the haunted prison
        Of her despised ones.
        This is the fruitful Eden
        Where fortune bids us dwell
        This is the white man's Heaven,
        But 'tis the Negro's hell.
                        The Fledgling Bard and the Poetry Society Part II, II [1916]

WILLIAM STANLEY BEAUMONT BRAITHWAITE

(1878 - 1962)   Boston, Massachusetts

William Stanley Beaumont Braithwaite, poet and literary critic, wrote book reviews for the Boston Transcript *and published several collections of poetry, including* Lyrics of Life and Love *(1904) and* The House of Falling Leaves *(1908).*

[571]   I am glad daylong for the gift of song,
          For time and change and sorrow;
          For the sunset wings and the world-end things
          Which hang on the edge of tomorrow.
          I am glad for my heart whose gates apart
          Are the entrance-place of wonders,
          Where dreams come in from the rush and din
          Like sheep from the rains and thunders.
                              Rhapsody [1904]

[572]   Over the seas tonight, love,
              Over the darksome deeps,
          Over the seas tonight, love,
              Slowly my vessel creeps.
          Over the seas tonight, love,
              Waking the sleeping foam—
          Sailing away from thee, love,
              Sailing from thee and home.
          Over the seas tonight, love,
              Dreaming beneath the spars—
          Till in my dreams you shine, love,
              Bright as the listening stars.
                              Sea Lyric [1904]

[573]   Between the sunlight and the sea
          Time hoists her sails, pulls anchor free;
          The ship of Life moves on its keel—
          Humanity commands the wheel
          And steers for one more Hope to be
          Between the sunlight and the sea.
                          Off the New England Coast (s. 3) [1908]

[574]   When Time shall close the door unto the house
        And opens that of Winter's soon to be,
        And dreams go moving through the ruined boughs—
        He who went in comes out a Memory.
        From his deep sleep no sound may e'er arouse,—
        The moaning rain, nor wind-embattled sea.
                        The House of Falling Leaves (Part IV, s. 2) [1908]

JACK JOHNSON
(1878 - 1946)   Galveston, Texas

Jack Johnson was the first black heavyweight champion of the world. His autobiography, Jack Johnson in the Ring and Out *(1927), was reprinted in 1969 as* Jack Johnson is a Dandy.

[575]   I know the bitterness of being accused and harrassed by
        prosecutors. I know the horror of being hunted and haunted. I
        have dashed across continents and oceans as a fugitive, and have
        matched my wits with the police and secret agents seeking to
        deprive me of one of the greatest blessings man can have—
        liberty.
                        Jack Johnson in the Ring and Out [1927]

[576]   The possession of muscular strength and the courage to use it in
        contests with other men for physical supremacy does not
        necessarily imply a lack of appreciation for the finer and better
        things of life. . . . A man's vocation is no measure for the inner
        feelings nor a guarantee of his earnest desire to live right and
        attain the highest standards.
                        Jack Johnson in the Ring and Out [1927]

ANGELINA WELD GRIMKÉ

(1880 - 1958)   Boston, Massachusetts

Angelina Weld Grimké, daughter of the eminent Archibald H. Grimké, was a schoolteacher, writer, and women's rights activist. She wrote numerous short stories and Rachel, *a three-act play published in 1920.*

[577]   Grey trees, grey skies, and not a star
            Grey mist, grey hush;
        And then frail, exquisite, afar
            A hermit thrush.
                    Dawn [1927]

[578]   There is a tree, by day,
            That, at night,
            Has a shadow,
        A hand huge and black,
        With fingers long and black
            All through the dark,
        Against the white man's house,
            In the little wind,
        The black hand plucks and plucks
            At the bricks.
        The bricks are the color of blood and very small.
            Is it a shadow?
                    Tenebris [1927]

[579]   —I weep—
        Not as the young do noisily
        Not as the aged rustily,
            But quietly.
        Drop by drop the great tears
        Splash upon my hands,
        And save you saw them shine,
        You would not know
            I wept.
                    I Weep [1927]

[580]   They knew, those gone, bent backs, the lash's cut
         On crimsoning and shudd'ring flesh, and thirst
         And hunger and all weariness yet durst
         Nor pause nor rest; but toil and toil till shut
         Of day set them to fall in noisome hut
         Herded e'en in sleep. Tortured, accursed,—
         These knew this life as death, and death at worst
         As Peace, when earth above their bones was put.
         But we their children, bone of them and blood
         Bound, by new fetters tortured, still have seen
         A light we know that soul and mind are free;
         That sorrow, tears and evil, all are good;
         We know it matters not what we have been
         But this and always this: what we shall be.
                        Then and Now [c. 1929]

JOEL AUGUSTUS ROGERS

(1880 - 1966)   Negril, Jamaica

Noted black historian and newspaper journalist Joel Rogers wrote several definitive works on people of African descent and was the first Afro-American international war correspondent. Among Rogers' popular works is The World's Greatest Men of Color *(1946).*

[581]   Strip American democracy and religion of its verbiage and you find
         the Neanderthal.
                        Critical Excursions and Reflections, The Messenger
                        [May, 1924]

[582]   He who has a message and no propaganda will not get very far.
                        Critical Excursions and Reflections, The Messenger
                        [June, 1924]

[583]   The Negro has a field all to himself in musical expression. His
         enemies will listen to his music where they will hear nothing else.
                        The Temple of Music, New York Amsterdam News
                        [September 4, 1929]

WILLIAM PICKENS
(1881 - 1954)   Anderson County, South Carolina

William Pickens, educator and orator, was an honor graduate of both Talladega College and Yale University. He taught at Talladega and was a dean at Morgan State College. Pickens published his autobiography, Heir of Slaves, *in 1911 and a collection of essays,* The New Negro, His Political, Civil and Mental Status, *in 1916.*

[584]   . . . the man who succeeds is never conceded the right to fail.
        Heir of Slaves [1911]

[585]   The runaway Negro was the vanguard, the first hero in the struggle
        to free his race.
        Fifty Years after Emancipation [written c. 1912]

[586]   The best time to do a thing is when it can be done.
        Fifty Years after Emancipation [written c. 1912]

[587]   The race is as the man.
        Education [written c. 1914]

[588]   If prejudice could reason, it would dispel itself.
        The New Negro [written c. 1914]

[589]   The primary motive of the black man is not a desire for a mixed
        family but for the protection of his own colored family. He
        believes that a law to compel fathers to marry the mothers would
        break up more miscegenation in a week than a law prohibiting
        the marriage will break up in 25 years.
        The Ultimate Effects of Segregation [written c. 1914]

[590]   One of the greatest handicaps to our mutual adjustments is the
        American white man's general ignorance of the Negro race.
        The Ultimate Effects of Segregation [written c. 1914]

[591]   Till this day the Negro is seldom frank to the white man in
        America. He says what he does not mean; he means what he does
        not say.
        The Negro, a Test for Our Civilization [written c. 1915]

[592] The struggle of the Negro is not a struggle of days, but of decades.
The Negro, a Test for Our Civilization [written c. 1915]

[593] Modern science has not done away with races, but it has certainly dispensed with racial geography.
Letter to Marcus Garvey [July 24, 1922]

[594] There is no prospect that man will ever be without religion, but there is every prospect that he will soon be beyond our present religious beliefs.
Preachers Defend Hell [written February, 1923]

[595] . . . the very idea of hell is a helluvanidea.
Things Nobody Believes, The Messenger [February, 1923]

[596] . . . every age thinks it is perfect, especially in religion.
Intelligent Christianity, The Messenger [April, 1923]

[597] Race is but a date in history. . . .
Address, National Council of Social Work, Toronto, Canada [June 26, 1924]

[598] For two generations the lynchers of America tried to justify lynching by the cry of rape. This appeal to sex fooled about everybody except the fellows who got lynched—and they could not tell.
Sex and the American Race Problem
[written February 14, 1927]

[599] In the struggle for human rights for Negroes in America, a few hundred dollars from the Negroes themselves will go much further than thousands of dollars from the best of our philanthropists.
The Menace of Philanthropy [1931]

[600] Living together is an art. . . .
Address, Meeting of the Congregationalists
Oak Park, Illinois [November 2, 1932]

[601]   . . . colored Americans, in their fight for equality, must disabuse white people's minds of the opinion that the only equality the Negro desires is the association of white people.
It Pays to Kick, Atlanta World [January 7, 1935]

[602]   Negro quartets and choruses have sung more money for their education out of white people's pockets than forty Booker Washingtons could ever have argued out of them.
Address, National Folk Festival, Washington, D.C. [April 26, 1940]

JESSIE REDMON FAUSET

(1882 - 1961)   Fredericksville, New Jersey

Jessie Fauset emerged as a writer during the 1920s Harlem Renaissance. A Cornell University graduate, she taught French and Latin at Dunbar High School in Washington, D.C., and wrote four novels: There is Confusion *(1924),* Plum Bun *(1928),* The Chinaberry Tree *(1931), and* Comedy American Style *(1933).*

[603]   . . . I'm sick of planning life with regard to being colored. I'm not in the least ashamed of my race. I don't mind in the least that once we were slaves. Every race in the world has at some time occupied a servile position. But I do mind having to take it into consideration every time I want to eat outside my home, every time I enter a theatre, every time I think of a profession.
Plum Bun [1928]

[604]   Biology transcends society.
The Chinaberry Tree [1931]

[605]   . . . colored people are at a point where they will bear watching. They are on their way upward, their eyes on the stars.
Address, R. H. Macy Co., New York City [May 23, 1931]

[606]   I'm perfectly satisfied to be an American Negro, tough as it all is.
Comedy American Style [1933]

ANNE SPENCER

(1882 - 1975)   Henry County, Virginia

Anne Spencer, who could not read and write until the age of eleven, graduated in 1899 as valedictorian of her normal school class and became a librarian. Her poems appear in several anthologies including Countee Cullen's Caroling at Dusk *(1927).*

[607] I proudly love being a Negro woman. It's so involved and
            interesting. We are the problem—the great national game of
            taboo.

                              Comment [1927]

[608] We trekked into a far country
            My friend and I.
        Our deeper content was never spoken,
        But each knew all the other said.
        He told me how calm his soul was laid
        By the lack of anvil and strife.
        "The wooing kistrel," I said, "Mutes his mating-note
        To please the harmony of this sweet silence."
        And when at the day's end
        We laid tired bodies 'gainst
        The loose warm sands,
        And the air fleeced its particles for a coverlet;
        When star after star came out
        To guard their lovers in oblivion—
        My soul so leapt that my evening prayer
        Stole my morning song!

                              Translation [1927]

[609] Oh, you are cruel;
            You ask too much;
            Offered a hand, a finger tip
            You must have a soul to clutch.

                              Neighbors [1927]

WALTER EVERETTE HAWKINS

(born 1883)   Warrenton, North Carolina

Little is known about Walter E. Hawkins, who was a brilliant student and graduate of Kittrell College. Hawkins worked for many years as a United States postal clerk and published a small volume of verse, Chords and Dischords *(1909).*

[610]   And it was in a Christian land,
        With freedom's towers on every hand,
        Where shafts to civic pride arise
        To lift America to the skies.
        And it was on a Sabbath day,
        While men and women went to pray,
        Well-groomed in fashion's bright design,
        Right proudly wending to their shrine.
        The bell up in the steeple spoke,
        Its ringing notes the silence broke,
        And on the pulsing Sabbath air
        Poured out its chimes, a call to prayer.
        He passed the crowd in humble mode
        While going to his meek abode.
        From out the crowd arose a cry,
        And epithets began to fly;
        And so this Christian mob did turn
        From prayer to rob, to lynch and burn.
        A victim helplessly he fell
        To tortures truly kin to hell;
        They bound him fast and strung him high,
        Then cut him down lest he should die
        Before their energy was spent
        In torturing to their heart's content.
        They tore his flesh and broke his bones,
        And laughed in triumph at his groans;
        They chopped his fingers, clipped his ears
        And passed them round as souvenirs.
        They bored hot irons in his side
        And reveled in their zeal and pride;
        They cut his quivering flesh away
        And danced and sang as Christians may;
        Then from his side they tore his heart
        And watched its quivering fibres dart.

And then upon his mangled frame
They piled the wood, the oil and flame.
Lest there be left one of his creed,
One to perpetuate his breed;
Lest there be one to bear his name
Or build the stock from which he came,
They dragged his bride up to the pyre
And plunged her headlong in the fire,
Full-freighted with an unborn child,
Hot embers on her form they piled.
And then they raised a Sabbath song,
The echo sounded wild and strong,
A benediction to the skies
That crowned the human sacrifice.
A little boy stepped out the crowd,
His face was pale, his accents loud:
"My ma could not get to the fun,
And so I came, her youngest son,
To get the news of what went on."
He stirred the ashes, found a bone,—
(A bit of flesh was hanging on.)
He bore it off a cherished prize,
A remnant of the sacrifice.

And this where men are civilized,
Where culture is so highly prized;
Where liberty with blood was bought,
And all the "Christian virtues" taught,
Where nations boast their God has sent
The angel of Enlightenment.
But while you sing your country's pride
Where men for liberty have died,
Compare the strain with double stress
To her reward for harmlessness,
When burning flesh makes sporty time,
And innocence is greatest crime.
Alas! no doubt, the heathen reads
Of Christian lands and Christian deeds;
But blest is he who never sees
Grim sacrifices such as these,
Which culture wrings from the despised
To pay for being civilized.
Blest are those souls unhurt by sounds

Of strife where love of God abounds,
Who have not learned the curse of faith
Accompanied by the curse of death;
Blest are those who know not the shame
Which Christians do in Jesus' name.
O heathen souls on heathen strand,
What think you of a Christian land,
Where Christians on a Sabbath day
Upon their helpless brothers prey,
And oft their drowsy minds refresh
Thru sport of burning human flesh?
But none dare tell who led the band,
And this was in a Christian Land.

The Mob Victim [1909]

SHELTON BROOKS

(born 1886)   Amesburg, Ontario, Canada

A child prodigy, Shelton Brooks entered show business as a Detroit café
performer and later topped his career as a vaudeville headliner. Also a
successful songwriter, Brooks produced several hits, including "Some of
These Days," theme song of Sophie Tucker.

[611] I'll be down to get you in a taxi honey
       You better be ready about half past eight,
       Now dearie, don't be late,
       I want to be there when the band starts playing.
       Remember when we get there Honey,
        The two steps I'm goin' to have 'em all,
       Goin' to dance out both my shoes,
       When they play the "Jelly Roll Blues"
       Tomorrow night, at the Darktown Strutters' Ball

The Darktown Strutters' Ball (chorus) [1917]

GEORGIA DOUGLAS JOHNSON

(1886 - 1967)   Atlanta, Georgia

Georgia Douglas Johnson, a graduate of Oberlin, was a gifted musician and composer. She also wrote poetry, plays, and a newspaper column. Her best known collection of poetry, Bronze, *was published in 1922.*

[612]   I've learned of life this bitter truth
Hope not between the crumbling walls
Of mankind's gratitude to find repose,
But rather,
Build within thy own soul
Fortresses!
Lesson [1924]

[613]   I wonder—
        as I see them pass unheeded down the way
(The women who were once beloved, imperious and gay)
Holding with pale hands, pale hands the cup
Of Life's discarded wine
If memories
Are bliss enough
To make the dregs divine
I Wonder [1927]

MARCUS MOZIAH GARVEY

(1887 - 1940)   Saint Ann's Bay, Jamaica, West Indies

Marcus Garvey became an influential leader during the 1920s and organized the first mass movement among Afro-Americans, the Universal Negro Improvement Association (UNIA). Garvey's Philosophy and Opinions, *in two volumes, was published in 1923 and 1925.*

[614]   A man's bread and butter is only insured when he works for it.
Philosophy and Opinions, I [1923]

[615]   The whole world is run on bluff.
Philosophy and Opinions, I [1923]

[616] The Negro who lives on the patronage of philanthropists is the most dangerous member of society, because he is willing to turn back the clock of progress to do so.
Philosophy and Opinions, I [1923]

[617] Men who are in earnest are not afraid of the consequences.
Philosophy and Opinions, I [1923]

[618] We have to liberate ourselves.
Philosophy and Opinions, I [1923]

[619] If you have no confidence in self you are twice defeated in the race of life. With confidence, you have won even before you have started.
Philosophy and Opinions, I [1923]

[620] Hungry men have no respect for law, authority or human life.
Philosophy and Opinions, I [1923]

[621] To see your enemy and know him is part of the complete education of man.
Philosophy and Opinions, I [1923]

[622] Radicalism is a label that is always applied to people who are endeavoring to get freedom.
Philosophy and Opinions, I [1923]

[623] [On poverty]:

A hellish state to be in. It is no virtue. It is a crime.
Philosophy and Opinions, I [1923]

[624] Lift up yourselves . . . take yourselves out of the mire and hitch your hopes to the stars.
Philosophy and Opinions, I [1923]

[625] There has never been a movement where the leader has not suffered for the cause and not received the ingratitude of the people. I, like the rest, am prepared for the consequence.
Philosophy and Opinions, I [1923]

[626] If hell is what we are taught it is, then there will be more Christians there than days in all creation.
Philosophy and Opinions, I [1923]

[627]   There is only one thing to save the Negro, and that is an immediate
        realization of his own responsibilities.
                          Address, Carnegie Hall, New York City [August 1, 1924]

[628]   The white man has given us morals from his head and lies from his
        heart.
                          Address, Carnegie Hall, New York City [August 1, 1924]

[629]   The Negro must be up and doing if he will break down the prejudice
        of the rest of the world.
                          Philosophy and Opinions, II [1925]

[630]   The bones of injustice have a peculiar way of rising from the tombs to
        plague and mock the iniquitious.
                          Philosophy and Opinions, II [1925]

RENÉ MARAN

(1887 - 1960)   Fort de France, Martinique, West Indies

René Maran is perhaps best known for his novel Batouala *(1921), for which
he won the Grand Prix Broguette-Gonin. Although he wrote several novels,
few of Maran's works have been translated into English. The following
quotations from* Batouala *have been translated from the French.*

[631]   I shall never tire of cursing the wickedness of white men, especially
        their duplicity.
                          Batouala [1921]

[632]   Vengeance is not a food which is eaten hot.
        It is a good thing to hide your hatred under the most warm-
        hearted cordiality; cordiality being the ash with which you damp
        the fire, in order to allow it to hatch.
                          Batouala [1921]

[633]   Hatred is one long wait.
                          Batouala [1921]

[634]   Praised be the bush. Do people think it dead? It is alive, full of life,
        and only speaks to its children, and to them alone. It uses what
        language it pleases to talk to the wide spaces under its command;
        it uses smoke, sounds, smells, inanimate objects to address the
        spaces when trees grow and grass flourishes, and wild cattle graze.
             Praise to the bush! The bush of the *kagas* and the marshes,
        the bush of the forests and the plains!
                             Batouala [1921]

FENTON JOHNSON

(1888 - 1958)   Chicago, Illinois

Fenton Johnson, a well-know poet in Chicago's black literary circle during
the 1920s, published several volumes of poetry including A Little Dreaming
(1913) and Songs of the Soil *(1916).*

[635]   Let us go away,
            You and I,
        On a crimson ray,
            From the sky.
        Let us feel the blue
            Soft and clear
        And the golden hue,
            Be so near.
        For the morn is fair
            Where the stars lie,
        Let us two go there,
            You and I.
                     Let Us Go Away [1913]

[636]   Doan' you hyeah me preachin',
            Chillun in de valley?
        Doan' you hyeah me 'spoundin'
            Chillun in de valley?
        Freedom sh's a-comin'
        In de Savior's keeridge,
        Ah kin hyeah it shoutin'
        F'um de mouf ob cannons;
        Oh, de robes am whituh
        Dan de light ob mawnin'

Oh, de songs am sweetuh
Dan de banjo's tummin,
Mighty am de gethrin'
Ob de wounded chillun,
Mighty am de buhstin'
F'um de th'oats ob singuhs.
Git yo' clo's a-ready,
Cleah yo' cotton patches,
Set yo' feet a-dancin'
In de Gospel mannah,
Ah kin hyeah de blowin'
Ob de golden trumpets.
Freedom's hitched huh hosses
And she's drawin' nighuh.
Bury all yo' troubles,
Bury all yo' grievin's,
God hab hyeahed yo' prayin'—
Freedom's in de whirlwind,
An' we's in de valley.

Plantation Sermon [1914]

[637] My cobblestones are red with England's blood,
My parks are monuments of other days,
My battle cry the cry that right is might,
Humanity my God and mother love.
I blush when Justice cowers in the dust,
When once again we lead to Calvary
The Nazarene enwrapt in scarlet cloak.
I am the sister of the man oppressed,
The sword that flashed at primal Eden's gate,
"No man may enter save the pure in heart."
I sit at Plato's feet, and glean the gold
That drifts from such a rich eternal mind;
Good England's culture is my fading past,
Columbia the glory of my dreams.
O sisters mine, go sound your drums of gold,
Go build your monuments to Greed and Pelf,
For I would rather cherish martyrs' blood
Than all the wealth enshrined in Amsterdam,
And I would rather boast the motherhood
Of Attucks and of Shaw than rule the world.
O God of Winthrop, here I spread Thy couch,
For I have kept Thy faith despite the age.

The Soul of Boston [1915]

[638] The rose lay dying in the summer heat
       And longed to save her life so fair and brief
       A dryad, bathing in the noonday sun,
       Spied her and dropped a tear to show her grief
       The panting bloom drank deep the sweetening drop—
       And lived an hour to deck a singer's wreath.
                 The Dying Rose [1915]

[639] Honey tak' dat banjo f'om de wall!
       Play de chune you played in slav' tahm,—
       "Cuddle, cuddle to yo' lovah's breas'."
       Lawdy! but dat music's got a cha'm.
       Fifty yeahs, an' yet its meller, lak
       Moonlight streamin' on de cabin flo'.
       Hol' mah han', mah honey, sing de song
       While mah soul goes out de cabin do'.
              De Music Calls (s. 4) [1916]

ASA PHILIP RANDOLPH

(1889 - 1979)   Crescent City, Florida

Asa Philip Randolph, social activist and one of America's leading labor figures, was organizer and for many years president of the Brotherhood of Sleeping Car Porters. He was founder and co-editor, with Chandler Owen, of The Messenger, *and was an instrumental force in the establishment of the United States Fair Employment Practices Commission.*

[640] Make wars unprofitable and you make them impossible.
            The Cause and Remedy of Race Riots, The Messenger
            [September, 1919]

[641] In every truth, the beneficiaries of a system cannot be expected to
     destroy it.
            The Truth About Lynching [c. 1922]

[642] Violence seldom accomplishes permanent and desired results.
     Herein lies the futility of war.
            The Truth About Lynching [c. 1922]

[643] If the great laboring masses of people, black and white, are kept forever snarling over the question as to who is superior or inferior, they will . . . take a long time to combine for achievement of a common benefit.

Segregation in Public Schools, The Messenger [June, 1924]

[644] True liberation can be acquired and maintained only when the Negro people possess power: and power is the product and flower of organization . . . of the masses.

The Crisis of the Negro and the Constitution. Annual address, National Negro Congress, Philadelphia, Pennsylvania [October 15-17, 1937]

[645] If Negroes secure their goals, immediate and remote, they must win them, and to win them they must fight, sacrifice, suffer, go to jail and, if need be, die for them.

The Crisis of the Negro and the Constitution. Annual address, National Negro Congress, Philadelphia, Pennsylvania [October 15-17, 1937]

[646] In politics, as in other things, there is no such thing as one getting something for nothing. The payoff may involve compromises of various types that may strike at the ideals and principles one has held dear all his life.

Why I Can't Run for Congress on the Old Party Ticket, The Call [April 28, 1944]

[647] The concrete demands and just grievances of the Negro people . . . is a weapon that will circle the globe as a moral missile.

Address, Carnegie Hall, New York City [January 24, 1960]

[648] The Negro's patience has come to an end. We will not wait any longer.

New America [September 24, 1963]

BETTIOLA HELOISE FORTSON   ·
(born 1890)   Hopkinsville, Kentucky

Bettiola Fortson was an actress, dramatic reader, poet, and suffragette who owned and operated her own millinery business. A collection of her writings, Original Poems and Essays, *was published in 1915.*

[649] When Hannibal flashed his sword from its scabbard, the
           boundaries of Rome oscillated on the map. He was the archangel
           of war.

> *The Part Played by Negro Soldiers in the Wars of the World*
> [1915]

[650] You laugh because my skin is black
             And By What Right
       I am here as God's own choice;
       He made the color of my skin,
       He gave me this my voice
       And to you made me akin.

> *Duo Jure? (By What Right?)* [1915]

[651] Why do you black your face
       And imitate the Negro race?
       If I classed myself so high
       I wouldn't want you nigh.

       I don't care how you tried
       The secret you cannot hide:
       I know why you black your face,
       To rank in wit like my race.

> *"Found Out"* [1915]

CLAUDE McKAY

(1890 - 1948)   Sunnyville, Jamaica, West Indies

Poet and novelist Claude McKay was a major force in Afro-American literature and a dominant writer during the Harlem Renaissance. Among his best known works are Home to Harlem *(1928),* Banjo *(1929), and* Selected Poems, *published posthumously in 1953.*

[652]   If we must die—let it not be like hogs
        Hunted and penned in an inglorious spot,
        While round us bark the mad and hungry dogs,
        Making their mock at our accursed lot.
        If we must die, O let us nobly die,
        So that our precious blood may not be shed
        In vain; then even the monsters we defy
        Shall be constrained to honor us though dead!
        Oh, Kinsmen! We must meet the common foe!
        Though far outnumbered let us still be brave,
        And for their thousand blows deal one death blow!
        What though before us lies the open grave?
        Like men we'll face the murderous, cowardly pack,
        Pressed to the wall, dying, but fighting back!
                    If We Must Die [1917]

[653]   The sun sought thy dim bed and brought forth light,
        The sciences were sucklings at thy breast;
        When all the world was young in pregnant night
        Thy slaves toiled at thy monumental best.
        Thou ancient treasure-land, thou modern prize,
        New peoples marvel at thy pyramids!
        The years roll on, thy sphinx of riddle eyes
        Watches the mad world with immobile lids.
        The Hebrews humbled them at Pharoah's name.
        Cradle of Power! Yet all things were in vain!
        Honor and Glory, Arrogance and Fame!
        They went. The darkness swallowed thee again.
        Thou art the harlot, now thy time is done,
        Of all the mighty nations of the sun.
                    Africa [c. 1917]

[654]   For the dim regions whence my fathers came
        My spirit, bondaged by the body, longs.
        Words felt, but never heard, my lips would frame;

My soul would sing forgotten jungle songs.
I would go back to darkness and to peace,
But the great western world holds me in fee,
And I may never hope for full release
While to its alien gods I bend my knee.
Something in me is lost, forever lost,
Some vital thing has gone out of my heart,
And I must walk the way of life a ghost
Among the sons of earth, a thing apart;
For I was born, far from my native clime,
Under the white man's menace, out of time.

Outcast [c. 1918]

[655]   The world in silence nods, but my heart weeps:
See, willing to its lidless bleary eyes, pour
Forth heavily black drops of burning gore;
Each drop rolls on the earth's hard face then leaps
To heaven and fronts the idle guard that keeps
His useless watch before the august door.
My blood-tears, wrung in pain from my heart's core,
Accuse dumb heaven and curse a world that sleeps:
For yesterday I saw my flesh and blood
Dragged forth by pale-faced demons from his bed
Lashed, bruised and bleeding, to a piece of wood,
Oil poured in torrents on his sinless head.
The fierce flames drove me back from where I stood;
There is no God, Earth sleeps, my heart is dead.

J'Accuse [1919]

[656]   I shall return again; I shall return
To laugh and love and watch with wonder-eyes
At golden noon the forest fires burn,
Wafting their blue-black smoke to sapphire skies.
I shall return to loiter by the streams
That bathe the brown blades of the bending grasses,
And realize once more my thousand dreams
Of waters rushing down the mountain passes.
I shall return to hear the fiddle and fife
Of village dances, dear delicious tunes
That stir the hidden depths of native life,
Stray melodies of dim remembered runes.
I shall return, I shall return again,
To ease my mind of long, long years of pain.

I Shall Return [c. 1919]

[657]   For one brief moment rare like wine,
        The gracious city swept across the line:
        Oblivious of the color of my skin,
        Forgetting that I was an alien guest,
        She bent to me, my hostile heart to win,
        Caught me in passion to her pillowy breast;
        The great, proud city, seized with a strange love,
        Bowed down for one flame hour my price to prove.
                              The City's Love [c. 1920]

[658]   Negroes are like trees. They wear all colors naturally.
                              Home to Harlem [1928]

[659]   I ain't a big-headed nigger, but a white man has got to respect me,
        for when I address myself to him the vibration of brain magic
        that I turn on him is like an electric shock on the spring of his
        cranium.
                              Banjo [1929]

[660]   . . . if a man is not faithful to his own individuality, he cannot be
        loyal to anything.
                              A Long Way from Home [1937]

[661]   It is hell to belong to a suppressed minority. . . .
                              A Long Way from Home [1937]

JOMO MZEE KENYATTA

(1891 - 1978)   Ngenda, Kenya

*Jomo Kenyatta played a primary role in the struggle for Kenya's indepen-
dence from colonial rule. He was Kenya's first and only prime minister
until his death in 1978. A collection of Kenyatta's speeches,* Harambee!,
was published in 1964 and a biography, Kenyatta, *by Jeremy Brown, in
1972.*

[662]   Our children may learn about heroes of the past. Our task is to
        make ourselves architects of the future.
                    Address, Kenyatta Day, Nairobi, Kenya [October 20, 1947]

[663]   Unity cannot be taken for granted.
>   Address, Madarka Day, Nairobi, Kenya [June 1, 1965]

[664]   The vigor and quality of a nation depend on its capacity to renew itself each generation.
>   Address, Kenya Youth Festival, Nairobi, Kenya
>   [October 10, 1966]

[665]   . . . I have sometimes looked with wonder on the jargon of our times wherein those whose minds reside in the past are called "progressive" while those whose minds are vital enough to challenge and to mold the future are dubbed "reactionary."
>   *Suffering Without Bitterness* [1968]

[666]   . . . the world cannot exist without ladies. They are an important species.
>   Comment [Date Unknown]

WALTER FRANCIS WHITE

(1893 - 1955)   Atlanta, Georgia

Walter White, well known for his daring exposés of lynching, was a long-time executive secretary of the NAACP and writer of a syndicated newspaper column, fiction, and nonfiction works. White's autobiography, A Man Called White, *was published in 1949.*

[667]   Intolerance can grow only in the soil of ignorance; from its branches grow all manner of obstacles to human progress.
>   *The Rope and the Faggot* [1929]

[668]   I am a Negro. My skin is white, my eyes are blue, my hair is blond.
>   *A Man Called White* [1948]

[669]   Either we must attain freedom for the whole world or there will be no world left for any of us.
>   *Fifty Years of Fighting* [1950]

JACKIE "MOMS" MABLEY

(c. 1894 - 1975)   Brevard, North Carolina

Comedienne "Moms" Mabley, who performed for several decades in vaudeville, gained national recognition in the 1960s through recordings and television guest spots. She was featured in one film, "Amazing Grace" (1974).

[670] [On declining an invitation to appear on the Ed Sullivan Television Show]:

Mr. Sullivan didn't want to give me but four minutes. Honey, it takes Moms four minutes just to get out on stage.
Interview, *Newsday* [April 6, 1967]

[671] Them teenagers ain't all bad. I love 'em if nobody else does. There ain't nothin' wrong with young people. Jus' quit lyin' to 'em.
Interview, *Newsday* [April 6, 1967]

[672] If Elizabeth can run England, I can run America as president. What has she got that I didn't used to have, and can't get again?
Interview, *Black Stars* [May, 1973]

[673] Love is like playing checkers. You have to know which man to move.
Interview, *Black Stars* [May, 1973]

[674] I know a man so old, he has to use axle grease to keep his legs from creakin' when he walks.
Interview, *Black Stars* [May, 1973]

[675] Pollution is so bad in New York that I saw the Statue of Liberty holdin' her nose.
Interview, *Black Stars* [May, 1976]

[676] [Advice to children on crossing the street]:

Damn the lights. Watch the cars. The lights ain't never killed nobody.
Interview, *Newsday* [May 13, 1973]

[677] I'd rather pay a young man's fare to California than tell an ol' man the distance.
Interview, *Newsday* [May 13, 1973]

[678]   Don't let ol' folks tell you about the good ol' days. I was there.
        Where was they at?
                        Jet [January 3, 1974]

[679]   [On her early days in show business]:

        I don't care if you could stand on your eyebrows, if you was
        colored you couldn't get no work at all outside the black theater
        and nightclub circuits.
                        New York Post [July 31, 1974]

[680]   I used to work like a dog, and I never even knew what a one-
        hundred-dollar bill looked like until I had been in the business
        almost 50 years.
                        New York Post [July 31, 1974]

[681]   Show business taught me everything, and I'd do it again. And I tell
        everybody to travel and not get married too soon. Because if you
        do, you'll always find somebody in the next country you like
        better.
                        Washington Post [October 4, 1974]

[682]   There ain't nothin' an ol' man can do but bring me a message from
        a young one.
                        ''Moms' '' best known line

JEAN TOOMER

(1894 - 1967)   Washington, D.C.

*Novelist Jean Toomer, a graduate of the University of Wisconsin and City
College of New York, traveled widely both here and abroad. His single
novel,* Cane *(1923), which sold only five hundred copies upon publication,
is considered a classic work in Afro-American literature.*

[683]   African Guardian of Souls, Drunk with rum,
        Feasting on a strange cassava,
        Yielding to new words and a weak palabra
        Of a white-faced sardonic god—
        Grins, cries
        Amen,
        Shouts hosanna.
                        Conversion from *Cane* [1923]

[684] We have many reformers, few transformers.
               Definitions and Aphorisms [1931]

[685] We start with gifts. Merit comes from what we make of them.
               Definitions and Aphorisms, VI [1931]

[686] Let your doing be an exercise, not an exhibition.
               Definitions and Aphorisms, IX [1931]

[687] Man adjusts to what he should not; he is unable to adjust to what
         he should.
               Definitions and Aphorisms, XI [1931]

[688] Acceptance of prevailing standards often means we have no
         standards of our own.
               Definitions and Aphorisms, XII [1931]

[689] Fear is a noose that binds until it strangles.
               Definitions and Aphorisms, XVI [1931]

[690] Men are most active when evading real issues, most powerful when
         rejecting real values.
               Definitions and Aphorisms, XVIII [1931]

[691] Some people endure so little so well that they appear satisfied.
               Definitions and Aphorisms, XVIII [1931]

[692] Men try to run life according to their wishes; life runs itself
         according to necessity.
               Definitions and Aphorisms, XX [1931]

[693] In being I am equal.
               Definitions and Aphorisms, XXV [1931]

[694] One may receive the information but miss the teaching.
               Definitions and Aphorisms, XXXVII [1931]

[695] Most novices picture themselves as masters—and are content with
         the picture. This is why there are so few masters.
               Definitions and Aphorisms, XL [1931]

[696] People mistake their limitations for high standards.
               Definitions and Aphorisms, XL [1931]

[697] We learn the rope of life by untying its knots.
               Definitions and Aphorisms, LI [1931]

[698] Men do not make impressions; impressions make men.
Definitions and Aphorisms, LIV [1931]

[699] A man is not as much as he feels he is, but as much as he feels.
Definitions and Aphorisms, LV [1931]

[700] The realization of ignorance is the first act of knowing.
Definitions and Aphorisms, LXIII [1931]

[701] Man, if he so wills, can do much for man, but only in the natural and human orders. We can be men only if we help each other.
The Flavor of Man, Address, Annual Meeting, Young Friends Movement of Philadelphia, Pennsylvania [1949]

GEORGE SAMUEL SCHUYLER
(1895 - 1977)   Providence, Rhode Island

George S. Schuyler, a prominent journalist during the 1920s, was for many years an associate editor for the Pittsburgh Courier. *His articles were published in various periodicals including* American Mercury *and* The Messenger. *Schuyler's only novel,* Black No More *(1931), is a satire on America's color problem.*

[702] Morality is largely a matter of geography.
Lights and Shadows of the Underworld, The Messenger [August, 1923]

[703] Few people are able to face realities of life without a stimulant.
Lights and Shadows of the Underworld, The Messenger [August, 1923]

[704] The most deluded people are the so-called sophisticated who imagine they have no delusions.
Shafts and Darts, The Messenger [November, 1923]

[705] [On social service]:

A palliative invented by the upper-class, administered by the bright offspring of the middle-class to ease the pains of the working-class to keep them from ousting the upper-class.
Shafts and Darts, The Messenger [February, 1927]

[706]   [Act of God]:

A term applied to unexpected fires, wrecks, eruptions of volcanoes
and other catastrophies in which lives and property are
destroyed. This term is freely used as advertising for the church
by Christian clergymen and laymen, but was doubtless invented
by atheists as a libel on the Diety.
Shafts and Darts, The Messenger [February, 1927]

[707]   [Military casualty]:

The legalized murder or wounding of a uniformed wage slave of
one ruling class by that of another in time of war. Homicides
committed by wage slaves in time of peace usually net them "a
hot seat."
Shafts and Darts, The Messenger [February, 1927]

[708]   [Mourning]:

An advertisement of elegibility for another marriage; a bid for
sympathy and attention from the largely indifferent public; often
a public expression of sorrow for a feeling of secret relief.
Shafts and Darts, The Messenger [February, 1927]

[709]   The Negro . . . is a close student of the contradictory pretensions
and practices of the ofay gentry, and it is this that makes him
really intelligent in a republic of morons.
Our White Folks [1927]

[710]   When the Southern white man asks the liberal Caucasian, "Do you
want your daughter to marry a nigger?," he is probably hitting
the nail on the head, for that is the crux of the entire color
problem.
Our White Folks [1927]

[711]   This book is dedicated to all Caucasians in the great Republic who
can trace their ancestry back ten generations and confidently
assert that there are no black leaves on the family tree.
Preface, *Black No More* [1931]

[712]   Harlem! Praised. Reviled. Criticized. Ridiculed. Denounced. A
loveable hodge-podge of conflicting colors, contradictory
movements, extremes in everything, leavened by the saving grace
of the good old-fashioned belly laugh. A teeming international

city, a gridiron of brick cubicles rescued from obscurity by the blacks.

> *Harlem Tempo* [written November 10, 1936]

[713]   The talk about racial inferiority is nonsense on its face.

> *Physical Aspects of Harlem* [written c. 1938]

[714]   All revolutionary movements here trip on the color line.

> *How to Be Happy, Though Colored* [written 1939]

[715]   By and large . . . the Aframerican is not a particularly sadistic fellow, despite his long and intimate association with Caucasians.

> *How to be Happy, Though Colored*, "Thank You Fuehrer" [written 1939]

[716]   The colored brother is pleased, if sceptical, whenever white Christians practice Christianity. It happens so seldom.

> *How to Be Happy, Though Colored*, "Thank You Fuehrer" [written 1939]

[717]   Physical fusion, which continues despite futility of legal and illegal terror, is the best national insurance.

> *How to Be Happy, Though Colored*, "The Long View" [written 1939]

RUDOLPH FISHER

(1897 - 1934)   Washington, D.C.

Rudolph Fisher, a roentgenologist by profession, operated his own x-ray lab and contributed to leading medical journals before devoting full time to writing in 1924. He wrote plays, short stories, and two novels: The Walls of Jericho *(1928) and* The Conjure Man Dies *(1932).*

[718]   What an enormity, blackness!

> *High Yaller* [1925]

[719]   Angels rush in when fools is almost dead.

> *Blades of Steel* [1927]

[720]   Black triumph is always white tragedy.
        Walls of Jericho [1928]

[721]   'Taint the church that makes folks, its the folks that make the
        church. Only trouble with church is, folks ain' no count.
        Walls of Jericho [1928]

[722]   Horrible thing, prejudice . . . does you all up. Puffs you all out of
        shape.
        Dust [1931]

[723]   . . . whatever you do, do like a church steeple: aim high and go
        straight.
        Miss Cynthie [1933]

ELIJAH MUHAMMAD

(1897 - 1975)   Sandersville, Georgia

*Elijah Muhammad was founder and spiritual leader of the Black Muslims,
known today as the American Muslim Nation. During the 1960s the organization, under his guidance, exerted a religious and moral influence in Afro-
American communities across the nation. A collection of Muhammad's
essays are published as* Message to the Black Man in America *(1965).*

[724]   Love yourself and your kind.
        Message to the Black Man in America [1965]

[725]   The slave master will not teach you the knowledge of self, as there
        would not be a master-slave relationship any longer.
        Message to the Black Man in America [1965]

[726]   We are the originals. . . .
        Message to the Black Man in America [1965]

[727]   No nation respects a beggar.
        Message to the Black Man in America [1965]

ALBERT JOHN LUTHULI

(1898 - 1968)   Groutville, Natal, Republic of South Africa

*Albert Luthuli, a Zulu chieftain, was among the first blacks to openly
protest white racism in contemporary South Africa. Luthuli received the
Nobel Peace Prize in 1961.*

[728]   [On South Africa]:

It is a museum piece in our time, a hangover from the dark past of
mankind, a relic of an age which everywhere else is dead or
dying.

Nobel Peace Prize Acceptance Address, Stockholm,
Sweden [December 10, 1961]

PAUL ROBESON

(1898 - 1976)   Princeton, New Jersey

*Paul Robeson was an accomplished scholar, athlete, singer, linguist, and
actor. Harassment by the United States government for his political beliefs
drove Robeson abroad, where he lived for many years. Robeson published
his autobiography,* Here I Stand, *in 1958.*

[729]   [On spirituals]:

These songs are to Negro culture what the works of the great poets
are to English culture: they are the soul of the race made
manifest.

The Culture of the Negro, London Spectator [June 15, 1934]

[730]   . . . I defy any part of an insolent, dominating America, however
powerful; I defy any errand boys, Uncle Toms of the Negro people
to challenge my Americanism, because by word and deed I
challenge this vicious system to death; because I refuse to let my
personal success as part of a fraction of one percent of the Negro
people, to explain away the injustices to 14 million of my people;
because with all the energy at my command, I fight for the right
of Negro people and other oppressed, labor-driven Americans to
have decent homes, decent jobs, and the dignity that belongs to
every human being.

For Freedom and Peace, Address, Welcome Home Rally,
Rockland Palace, New York City [June 19, 1949]

[731]   My father was a slave, and my people died to build this country,
        and I am going to stay and have a piece of it just like you.
                        Statement made before the House Un-American Activities
                        Committee [June 12, 1956]

[732]   . . . I heard my people singing—in the glow of parlor coalstone and
        on summer porches sweet with lilac air, from choir loft and
        Sunday morning pews—and my soul was filled with their
        harmonies.
                        Here I Stand [1958]

[733]   Freedom is a hard-bought thing. . . .
                        Here I Stand [1958]

EDWARD KENNEDY "DUKE" ELLINGTON

(1899 - 1974)   Washington, D.C.

*Duke Ellington was a jazz musician without peer and a legend during his
lifetime. Ellington's innovative musical genius influenced many, and his
legacy is preserved in the hundreds of works he composed over a long and
productive career. Ellington completed his autobiography,* Music Is My
Mistress, *in 1973.*

[734]   Freedom is sweet, on the beat,
        Freedom is sweet to the reet complete.
        It's got zestness and bestness,
        Sugar and cream on the blessedness,
        No more pains, no more chains,
        To keep free from being free.
        Freedom is sweet fat, and that's for me.
                        It's Freedom from "Sacred Concert" [1965]

[735]   It's harder to defeat
        Than it is to spell,
        Revenge is not sweet,
        It's bitter as Hell.
                        *Don't Get Down on Your Knees to Pray Until You Have
                        Forgiven Everyone* from "Sacred Concert" [1965]

[736]   Nobody knows what a square is—it's just nobody wants to be one.
                        Music Is My Mistress [1973]

[737]   When face-to-face with one's self . . . there is no cop-out.
Music Is My Mistress [1973]

[738]   People do not retire. They are retired by others.
Music Is My Mistress [1973]

[739]   There is hardly any money interest in the realm of art, and music
will be here when money is gone.
Music Is My Mistress [1973]

[740]   Music is my mistress, and she plays second fiddle to no one.
Music Is My Mistress [1973]

[741]   Love is indescribable and unconditional. I could tell you a thousand
things that it is not, but not one that it is.
Music Is My Mistress [1973]

[742]   Gray skies are just clouds passing over.
Music Is My Mistress [1973]

[743]   You can't jive with the Almighty.
Comment [Date Unknown]

[744]   Love you madly.
Greeting to his audiences

LOUIS ARMSTRONG

(1900 - 1971)   New Orleans, Louisiana

*Louis Armstrong was one of the most influential and durable of all jazz
artists. His success as a soloist and entertainer helped establish jazz as a vital
musical force worldwide. His autobiography,* Satchmo: My Life in New
Orleans, *was published in 1954.*

[745]   [On playing trumpet with Joe Oliver]:

We never had to look at each other when we played, both thinkin'
the same thing.
Time [February 21, 1949]

[746]   Music is either good or bad, and it's got to be learned. You got to
have balance.
New York Post [December 17, 1952]

[747]   I worked on a coal wagon and, hell, I was singin' sellin' coal.
        "Stone coal, lady! Nickel a water bucket."
                            Interview, *Life* [April 15, 1956]

[748]   Before my time the name was levee camp music, then in New
        Orleans we called it ragtime. The fantastic music you hear on
        radio today—used to hear 'way back in the old sanctified
        churches where the sisters would shout till their petticoats fell
        down. Nothin' new. Old soup warmed over.
                            Interview, *Life* [April 15, 1956]

[749]   I've had some ovations in my time, had beautiful moments. But it
        seems like I was more content . . . growing up in New Orleans,
        just bein' around with the old timers. And the money we made
        then, I lived off of it. We were poor and everything like that, but
        music was all around you. Music kept you rollin'.
                            Interview, *Life* [April 15, 1956]

[750]   I don't let my mouth say nothin' my head can't stand.
                            Interview, *Life* [April 15, 1956]

[751]   . . . the main thing is to live for that audience. What you're there
        for is to please people the best way you can. Those few moments
        belong to them.
                            Interview, *Life* [April 15, 1956]

ARNA WENDELL BONTEMPS

(1902 - 1973)   Alexandria, Louisiana

Poet, novelist, dramatist, teacher, librarian, and scholar, Arna Bontemps
published numerous works, including historical works, anthologies, and
children's books. Among the most popular are God Sends Sunday *(1913),*
The Sad-Faced Boy *(1937), and* Drums at Dusk *(1939).*

[752]   Oh the brown leaves
        Fall in the bitter blast like tears
        From an aged widow . . . .
        And whispering winds
        Steal the violets' breath

And bury their leaves in snow . . . .
And the tides flow back
Like the ebbing years
Into cool immunity
But memory's voice
Like the music of waves,
Sings April tunes
    Forever
Spring Music [1925]

[753] A tree is more than a shadow
blurred against the sky
more than ink spilled on the fringe
of white clouds floating by.
A tree is more than an April design
or a blighted winter bough
where love and music used to be.
A tree is something in me,
very still and lonely now.
A Tree Design [c. 1963]

[754] Darkness brings the jungle to our room:
the throb of rain is the throb of muffled drums.
Darkness hangs our room with pendulums
of vine and in the gathering gloom
our walls recede into a denseness of
surrounding trees. This is a night of love
retained from those lost nights our fathers slept
in huts; this is a night that must not die.
Let us keep the dance of rain our fathers kept
and tread our dreams beneath the jungle sky.
The Return (s. 2) [c. 1963]

LANGSTON HUGHES

(1902 - 1967)   Joplin, Missouri

Writer Langston Hughes had a long, productive literary career. His huge output covered a wide range of prose, poetry, drama, music and journalism. Hughes' poetry is published in several collections: The Dream Keeper *(1932),* Shakespeare in Harlem *(1942), and* Ask Your Mama, 12 Moods for Jazz *(1961).*

[755]   The mills
        That grind and grind.
        And grind away the lives of men,—
        Their stacks
        Are great black silhouettes
        Against the sky.
        In the dawn
        They belch red fire.
        The mills,—
        Grinding out new steel,
        Old men.
                        Steel Mills [1916]

[756]   It is we who are liars:
        The Pretenders-to-be who are not
        And the Pretenders-to-be who are.
        If we who use words
        As screen for thoughts
        And weave dark garments
        To cover the naked body
        Of the too white Truth.
        It is we with the civilized souls
            Who are liars.
                        Liars [1925]

[757]   The younger Negro artists who create now intend to express our
        individual dark-skinned selves without fear or shame. If white
        people are pleased we are glad. If they are not, it doesn't matter.
        We know we are beautiful. And ugly, too. The tom-tom cries,
        and the tom-tom laughs. If colored people are pleased we are
        glad. If they are not, their displeasure doesn't matter either. We
        build our temples for tomorrow, strong as we know how, and we
        stand on top of the mountain free within ourselves.
                        The Negro Artist and the Racial Mountain, The Nation
                        [June 23, 1926]

[758]   Ever'thing there is but lovin' leaves a rust on yo' soul.
               Not Without Laughter [1930]

[759]   Well, son, I'll tell you:
          Life for me ain't been no crystal stair.
          It's had tacks in it,
          And splinters,
          And boards torn up,
          And places with no carpet on the floor—
          Bare.
          But all the time
          I'se been a-climbin' on,
          And reachin' landin's,
          And turnin' corners,
          And sometimes goin' in the dark
          Where there ain't been no light.
          So boy, don't you turn back.
          Don't you set down on the steps
          'Cause you find it's kinder hard.
          Don't you fall now—
          For I'se still goin', honey,
          I'se still climbin'
          And life for me ain't been no crystal stair.
               Mother To Son [1930]

[760]   I wish the rent
          Was heaven sent
               Little Lyric (of Great Importance) [1942]

[761]   If your reputation
          In the community is good
          Don't snub the other fellow—
          It might be misunderstood—
          Because a good reputation
          Can commit suicide
          By holding its head
          Too far to one side.
               Snob [1942]

[762]   Down on '33rd Street
          They cut you
          Every way they is.
               Statement [1942]

[763]   My old mule,
        He's got a grin on his face.
        He's been a mule so long
        He's forgot about his race.
        I'm an old mule—
        Black
        And don't give a damn!
        So you got to take me
        Like I am.
                              Me and the Mule [1942]

[764]   Tell all my mourners
        To mourn in red—
        Cause there ain't no sense
        In my bein' dead.
                              Wake [1942]

[765]   . . . I was born poor—and colored—and almost all the prettiest
        roses I have seen have been in rich people's yards, not in mine.
        That is why I cannot write exclusively about roses and moonlight
        —for sometimes in the moonlight my brothers see a fiery cross
        and a circle of Klansmen's hoods. Sometimes in the moonlight a
        dark body swings from a lynching tree, but for his funeral there
        are no roses.
                              My Adventures as a Social Poet, Phylon/Third Quarter,
                              [1947]

[766]   . . . when poems stop talking about the moon and begin to mention
        poverty, trade unions, color, color lines and colonies, somebody
        tells the police.
                              My Adventures as a Social Poet, Phylon/Third Quarter,
                              [1947]

[767]   She wears her morals like a loose garment.
                              Simply Heavenly, act I, scene iii [1957]

[768]   In this world . . . it's hard for man to live until he dies.
                              Simply Heavenly, act I, scene iv [1957]

[769]   Did you ever see ten Negroes
        weaving metal from two quarters
        into a cloth of dollars
        for a suit of good-time wearing?
        Weaving out of long-term credit
        interest beyond caring?
                              Show Fare, Please (s. 3) [1961]

COUNTEE CULLEN

(1903 - 1946)   Baltimore, Maryland

An outstanding poet of the Harlem Renaissance of the 1920s, Countee Cullen earned many honors and produced several volumes of poetry. Cullen's own selection of his best work was published posthumously in On These I Stand *(1947).*

[770]   I doubt not God is good, well meaning, kind,
     And did He stoop to quibble could tell why
     The little buried mole continues blind,
     Why flesh that mirrors Him must some day die
     Make plain the reason tortured Tantalus
     Is baited by the fickle fruit, declare
     If merely brute caprice dooms Sisyphus
     To struggle up a never-ending stair.
     Inscrutable His ways are, and immune
     To catechism by a mind too strewn
     With petty cares to slightly understand
     What awful brain compels His awful hand.
     Yet do I marvel at this curious thing:
     To make a poet black, and bid him sing!
                Yet Do I Marvel [c. 1921]

[771]   What is Africa to me:
     Copper sun or scarlet sea,
     Jungle star or jungle track,
     Strong bronzed men, or regal black
     Women from whose loins I sprang
     When the herds of Eden sang?
     One three centuries removed
     From the scenes his fathers loved,
     Spicy grove, cinnamon tree,
     What is Africa to me?
                Heritage (s. 1) [c. 1922]

[772]   His spirit smoke ascended to high heaven.
     His father, by the cruelest way of pain,
     Had bidden him to his bosom once again;
     The awful sin remained still unforgiven.
     All night a bright and solitary star
     (Perchance the one that ever guided him,
     Yet gave him up at last to Fate's wild whim)
     Hung pitifully o'er the swinging char.

Day dawned, and soon the mixed crowds came to view
The ghastly body swaying in the sun:
The women thronged to look but never a one
Showed sorrow in her eyes of steely blue;
And little lads, lynchers that were to be,
Danced round the dreadful thing in fiendish glee.

The Lynching [c. 1923]

[773] He wore his coffin for a hat,
         Calamity his cape,
     While on his face a death's-head sat
         And waved a bit of crepe.

For a Pessimist [c. 1924]

[774] She even thinks that up in heaven
         Her class lies late and snores.
     While poor black cherubs rise at seven
         To do celestial chores.

For a Lady I Know [c. 1924]

[775] I have wrapped my dreams in a silken cloth,
     And laid them away in a box of gold;
     Where long will cling the lips of the moth,
     I have wrapped my dreams in a silken cloth;
     I hide no hate, I am not even wroth
     Who found earth's breath so keen and cold;
     I have wrapped my dreams in a silken cloth,
     And laid them away in a box of gold.

For a Poet [c. 1924]

ZORA NEALE HURSTON

(1903 - 1960)   Eatonville, Florida

Zora Neale Hurston graduated from New York City's Barnard College with a degree in anthropology. As a specialist in Afro-American folklore she assembled one of the finest collections in the field. Among Hurston's works are Jonah's Gourd Vine *(1934) and* Dust Tracks on a Road *(1942).*

[776] Wese a mingled people.

Jonah's Gourd Vine [1934]

[777]   De brother in black don't fret to death. White man worry and kill
        hisself. Colored folks fret uh li'l while and gwan tuh sleep.
        Jonah's Gourd Vine [1934]

[778]   We black folks don't love our chillun. We couldn't do it when we
        wuz in slavery. We borned 'em but dat didn't make 'em ourn. . . .
        But we's free folks now. De big bell done rung! Us chillun is
        ourn. Ah doan know, mebbe hit'll take some of us generations,
        but us got tuh 'gin tuh practice on treasurin' our younguns. Ah
        loves dese heah already uh whole heap. Ah don't want 'em
        knocked and 'buked.
        Jonah's Gourd Vine [1934]

[779]   Over on the East Coast Ah used to have a road boss, and he was so
        mean and times was so hard till he laid off the hands of his
        watch.
        Mules and Men [1935]

[780]   Ah'm standin' in my tracks and steppin' back on my abstract.
        (I'm standing my ground.)
        Mules and Men [1935]

[781]   It was so hot dat I struck a match to light my pipe and set the lake
        afire. Burnt half of it, den took de water dat was left and put out
        de fire.
        Mules and Men [1935]

[782]   You know when it lightnings, de angels is peepin' in de lookin'
        glass; when it thunders, they's rollin' out de rain barrel; and
        when it rains, somebody done dropped a barrel or two and bust
        it.
        Mules and Men [1935]

[783]   My old man had some land dat was so rich dat our mule died and
        we buried him down in our bottom land, and de next mornin' he
        had done sprouted l'il jackasses.
        Mules and Men [1935]

[784]   She's so ugly she looks like the devil ground in pieces.
        Mules and Men [1935]

[785]   Ah seen a man so ugly till they spread a sheet over his head at night
        so sleep could slip up on him.
        Mules and Men [1935]

[786] She pulled in her horizon like a great fish net. Pulled it from around
       the waist of the world and dropped it over her shoulders. So much
       of life in its meshes! She called her soul to come and see.
                    Their Eyes Were Watching God [1937]

[787] There is something about poverty that smells like death. Dead
       dreams dropping off the heart like leaves in dry season and
       rotting around the feet; impulses smothered too long in the fetid
       air of underground caves. The soul lives in sickly air. People can
       be slaveships in shoes.
                    Dust Tracks on a Road [1942]

[788] Love, I find, is like singing. Everybody can do enough to satisfy
       themselves, though it may not impress the neighbors as being
       very much.
                    Dust Tracks on a Road [1942]

JEAN-JOSEPH RABEARIVELO

(1903 - 1937)   Antananarivo,
                                          Democratic Republic of Madagascar

*Jean-Joseph Rabearivelo founded a literary review and paved the way for
creation of a new Madagascan literature written in French. A series of
personal problems led to his suicide at the age of thirty-four. A selection of Rabearivelo's verse appears in* 24 Poems *(1962). The following
poems have been translated from the French.*

[789] Have you ever seen dawn marauding
       in the orchards of night?
       Behold her returning now
       on the footpaths of the East
       overgrown with flowering speargrass:
       she is entirely stained with milk
       like her children, raised of old by heifers;
       her hands that carry a torch
       are black and blue like the lips of a girl
       chewing ripe berries.

       The birds she caught in her net escape,
       They fly before her.
                    Birth of Day I [c. 1921]

[790]   A purple star
        evolved in the depth of the sky—
        a flower of blood unfolding on the prairie of night
        Evolve, evolve.
        Then become a kite, abandoned by a sleeping child,
        It appears to approach and at the same time withdraw.
        It loses its colour like a drooping flower,
        becomes cloud, turns white dissolves:
        is nothing now but a diamond point
        cutting across the blue mirror of sky
        which is reflecting now the glorious lure
        of the nubile morning.
                        Birth of Day I [c. 1921]

[791]   One hardly knows
        whether the first call
        has come from East or West
        But now
        the cocks
        in their coops pierced by stars
        and other spears of darkness
        they summon each other
        they breathe into sea shells
        they respond from all sides.
        And he returns
        he who went to sleep in the ocean,
        the skylark ascends
        and goes to meet him with songs
        imbibed with dew.
                        Birth of Day II [c. 1922]

[792]   On the edge of stagnant shadows
        on dams
        hard and naked like rocks
        but growing early grass
        countless fishermen range
        to cast their lines.

        Treetops grow bulbous
        like ripening fruit
        in the valleys that become larger and more watery
        than melons,
        flights of frightened birds are stirred up
        and drifts of blind light
        who also frighten them
        and prevent them from biting.

Unperturbed,
masters of their destiny,
the fishermen call each other with their shadow voices
to spread their nets;
and they return to the sea
the silver and purple fishes
that merge—beyond our reach—with the sky.
                    XXIV [c. 1923]

NNAMDI AZIKIWE

(1904 -   )   Onitsha, Nigeria

*African leader and diplomat Nnamdi Azikiwe played a primary role in the
early African liberation movement and was the first president of independent
in Nigeria.* A Life of Azikiwe, *by Kwatei A. B. Jones-Quartey was published
in 1965.*

[793]   Originality is the essence of true scholarship. Creativity is the soul
        of the true scholar.
                        Address, Methodist Boys' High School, Lagos, Nigeria
                        [November 11, 1934]

[794]   Blessed are the common people. God loves them, that is why he made
        millions of them.
                        Address, Annual Convention of National Council of Nigeria
                        and the Cameroons, Kaduna, Nigeria [April 5, 1948]

[795]   We must not betray the masses.
                        Address, Annual Convention of National Council of Nigeria
                        and the Cameroons, Kaduna, Nigeria [April 5, 1948]

[796]   We struggle towards the same ultimate objective: to revive the
        stature of man so that man's inhumanity to man shall cease.
        Your success shall be our success and your failure shall be our
        failure. In this basic unity lies the promise of great advancement
        for the black race throughout the entire world.
                        Address, Fiftieth Anniversary of the NAACP, New York,
                        New York [July 19, 1959]

NICOLÁS GUILLÉN

(1904 -   )   Camaguey, Cuba

Nicolás Guillén is one of the best known poets in Afro-Cuban literature. A two-volume Spanish edition of Guillén's complete works (Obra Poética), was published in 1974. A selection of Guillén's poems in English are found in Cuba Libre *(1948). The quotation from Guillén's address to the Cultural and Scientific Conference for World Peace was given in English.*

[797]   Negro
        in the cane fields.
        White man
        above the cane fields,
        Earth
        beneath the cane fields.
        Blood
        that flows from us.
                          Cane [1930]

[798]   Knife-toting sweet-man
        become a knife himself:
        whittling chips of the moon
        until the moon runs out,
        whittling chips of shadow
        until the shadow runs out,
        whittling chips of song
        until the song runs out—
        and then,
        sliver by sliver
        the dark body
        of his no-good gal.
                          Blade [1931]

[799]   Your fingernails drip
        from your hands
        in a bunch
        of ten purple grapes.

        Your skin, flesh of a burned tree trunk
        drowned in the depths of your mirror
        gives back
        smokily
        the timid sea-weed
        of your being.
                     Madrigal [1931]

[800] We've got Chinese, white, black and mixed;
       but remember that our colors are cheap,
       for after many years of contracts and tricks
       nobody's purity runs very deep.
                          West Indies Ltd. I (s. 2) [1934]

[801] How many ships, how many ships!
       How many Negroes, how many Negroes!
       What broad brilliance of sugar canes!
       What lashes of the slave trader!
       Blood? Blood. Tears? Tears . . .
       Half-opened veins and eyelids
       And empty daybreaks
       And sunsets at the mill
       And a great voice, a strong voice,
       Shattering the silence.
       How many ships, how many ships!
       How many Negroes!
                  Ballad of the Two Grandfathers (s. 5) [1934]

[802] I die if I don't work,
       and if I do, I die.
       Either way I die, I die,
       either way I die.
                          Blues (s. 1) [1934]

[803] Art . . . cannot be an egotistic activity engulfed in the limits of pure
       creation, free of all human contamination.
                          Address, Cultural and Scientific Conference for World
                          Peace, New York, New York [March 25-27, 1949]

DONALD JEFFREY HAYES

(1904 -   )   Raleigh, North Carolina

Donald Jeffrey Hayes currently lives in his hometown of Raleigh, North Carolina.

[804]   I do perceive that lesser gods exist
        On some near plane within the reach of those
        Who walk as through a valley filled with mist,
        Where faith, in step with doubt, both comes and goes!
        I do perceive anomaly to be
        At home with faith's unknown complexity—
        But Thou, O Lord, in patience over all,
        Wait for our spirit's answer to Thy call. . . .
        The lesser gods, in their own way, serve Thee,
        As might a roadside inn with open door,
        Above whose lintel, written plain to see,
        Is this: "LET ALL WHO PAUSE HERE—HIM ADORE!"
        So—in Thy glorious patience over all—
        Grant time for our respondence to Thy Call . . . !
                    Sonnet VII [Date Unknown]

[805]   Thinking of you brings thought of things unchanging
        Not transient beauties which fade overnight;
        Nor age to age all self plans rearranging,
        Like spectral change on prisms turned in light;
        Nor yet September—th'after thought of summer,
        With draining color and subsiding zest,
        Paced by the slowed beat of the heart's wise drummer
        Sounding retreat at promise's behest. . . .
        I would choose something free of grief's despair,
        Wherein Trust might ensconce your loveliness:
        A full sonata played on strings of air,
        With misty themes for woodwinds to confess. . . .
            Such would be food for thought and thought thus fed
            Might feed some dreamer's dream when we are dead . . . !
                    Sonnet XXXI [Date Unknown]

LEROY (SATCHEL) PAIGE

(c. 1904 -   )   Mobile, Alabama

Pitcher Satchel Paige did not make it to the major leagues until he was well past his prime in 1948—a year after Jackie Robinson broke the color barrier in organized baseball. He is now a member of the baseball Hall of Fame. Paige recounted his baseball days in Maybe I'll Pitch Forever *(1962).*

[806]   I may not be the bestest pitcher in the world, but I sure out-cutes
        'em.
                              Boston Globe [February 16, 1950]

[807]   Avoid fried meats, which angry up the blood.

        If your stomach disputes you, lie down and pacify it with cool
           thoughts.

        Keep the juices flowing by jangling around gently as you move.

        Go very light on the vices, such as carrying on in society. The social
           ramble ain't restful.

        Avoid running at all times.

        Don't look back. Something might be gaining on you.
                              Formula for Staying Young [1953]

[808]   . . . don't pray when it rains if you don't pray when the sun shines.
                              New York Post [October 4, 1959]

FRANK MARSHALL DAVIS

(1905 -   )   Arkansas City, Kansas

The articulate verses of Frank Marshall Davis, published primarily during the Depression years, never gained widespread popularity. Davis' poems are found in two of his collections: Black Man's Verse *(1935) and* I Am the American Negro *(1937).*

[809]   In the attic
        in the bottom of an old trunk
        I found a woman's soul
        tied with blue ribbon
        just so

in neat packages
6 by 3 by 3
and covered with gray dust
                    Finding [1935]

[810]   This room is an unscored symphony
        of colors and sounds
        People sit like geometric angels
        awaiting measurement
        Their talk is countless bubbles
        breaking against the ceiling
        Sharp scissors of a radio
        snip fancy cutouts in the thick noise
        Gray pigeons of tobacco smoke
        fly lazily in the air above
        Like a leafy tree in high winds
        the room moves its heads and hands
                    Mojo Mike's Beer Garden (s. 5) [1935]

[811]   Having attained success in business
        possessing three cars
        one wife and two mistresses
        a home and furniture
        talked of by the town
        and thrice ruler of the local Elks
        Robert Whitmore
        died of apoplexy
        when a stranger from Georgia
        mistook him
        for a former Macon waiter.
                    Robert Whitmore [1935]

[812]   I was a weaver of jagged words
        A warbler of garbled tunes
        A singer of savage songs
        I was bitter
        Yes
        Bitterly and sorely sad
        For when I wrote
        I dipped my pen
        In the crazy heart
        Of mad America
                    Frank Marshall Davis: Writer (s. 4) [1936]

[813] Peddling from door to door
       Night sells
       Black bags of peppermint stars
       Heaping cones of vanilla moon
       Until
       His wares are gone
       Then shuffles homeward
       Jingling the gray coins
       Of daybreak.
                        Four Glimpses of Night, III [1937]

JAY SAUNDERS REDDING

(1906 -   )   Wilmington, Delaware

Distinguished author and educator Saunders Redding has written several
criticisms of Afro-American literature, a novel, an autobiography, and
several volumes of history, including They Came in Chains *(1950).*

[814] Funny thing, but if you ain't got nothin' seems like there ain't
         nothin' you can do, an' if you got something, you's 'fraid to do
         anything. It ain't nobody's fault . . . but it sure looks like we'se
         in a poke.
                        No Day of Triumph [1942]

[815] While there is almost no religion operating in race relations, there is
         plenty of God.
                        On Being a Negro in America [1951]

LÉOPOLD SÉDAR SENGHOR
(1906 -   )   Joal, Senegal

Léopold Senghor, poet, philosopher, and politician, was the first and only president of independent Senegal until his resignation in January, 1981. Collections of his works available in English include Selected Poems *(1964) and* Prose and Poetry *(1954). The following quotations, with the exception of the address given in English at Fordham University, have been translated from the French.*

[816] Bless you mother.

Recognize your son by the look in his eyes, the authenticity
     of his heart his lineage.
Recognize his comrades recognize the fighter and salute in
     the red evening of your age.
The bright dawn of a new day.
                    On Appeal from the Race of Sheba—VII [1936]

[817] I must hide in the intimate depths of my veins
The Ancestors stir dark-skinned, shot with lightning
     and thunder
And my guardian animal, I must hide him
Lest I smash through the boom of scandal.
He is my faithful blood and demands fidelity
Protecting my naked pride against
Myself and all the insolence of lucky races.
                    Totem [1945]

[818] All day long along the long straight rails
(Unbending will on the listless sands)
Across the dryness of Cayor and Baol where
     the arms of the baobabs twist in anguish
All day long, all along the line
Through tiny stations, each exactly like the last,
     chattering little black girls uncaged from school
All day long, roughly shaken on the benches of
     the clanking, dust-covered wheezing antique train
I come seeking to forget Europe in the pastoral heart of Sine.
                    All Day Long [c. 1946]

[819] . . . the African woman does not need to be liberated. She has been
       free for many thousands of years.

> *Constructive Elements of Civilization of a Black African*
> *Inspiration* [1959]

[820] . . . the civilization of the twentieth century cannot be universal
       except by being a dynamic synthesis of all the cultural values of
       all civilizations. It will be monstrous unless it is seasoned with the
       salt of negritude. For it will be without the saviour of humanity.

> Address, Ghana Parliament [February, 1961]

[821] European reason is abstract mainly because it has willfully forsaken
       spiritual values.

> Address, Fordham University, New York, New York
> [November 2, 1961]

[822] Negritude is a fact: a culture.

> *The Problematics of Negritude*, Address, Dakar, Senegal
> [April, 1970]

EDWARD S. SILVERA

(1906 - 1937)   Florida

Little is known about Edward Silvera, who attended Lincoln University in
Pennsylvania. He wrote considerable poetry during his college years but
eventually decided on a career in medicine.

[823] Trees are tall black slaves
       Driven by the stinging whip
       Of the cruel north wind;
       And in the darkness of the night
       They sing sad soul songs
       Like I used to sing
       When I was a slave
       Driven by the whip
       Of the world.

> *Slaves* [1927]

[824] There is a coarseness
       In the songs of black men
       Coarse as the songs

Of the sea,
There is a weird strangeness
In the songs of black men
Which sounds not strange
To me.

There is beauty
In the faces of black women,
Jungle beauty
And mystery
Dark hidden beauty
In the faces of black women,
Which only black men
See.

Jungle Taste [1927]

ADAM CLAYTON POWELL, JR.

(1908 - 1972)   New Haven, Connecticut

Throughout his lifetime, Adam Clayton Powell, Jr., was active in the on-going battle for civil rights, both as pastor of Harlem's Abyssinian Baptist Church and as a United States Congressional representative for Harlem. Powell wrote two collections of essays, Marching Blacks *(1945) and* Keep the Faith, Baby *(1967), in addition to an autobiography,* Adam by Adam *(1971).*

[825] The Negro is a born anti-Fascist.
            Marching Blacks, "Civil War II" [1945]

[826] There is no future for a people who deny their past.
            Marching Blacks, "Civil War II" [1945]

[827] The Negro has always been a revolutionary, not because he is black
          but because he is a man.
            Marching Blacks, "Once Upon a Time" [1945]

[828] I was born to be a radical. . . .
            Marching Blacks, "Once Upon a Time" [1945]

[829] Innate racial differences do not exist.
            Marching Blacks, "Super Non-Aryans" [1945]

[830]   We must be willing to die at all times, full knowing that if enough people are so willing, no one will have to.
>   *Marching Blacks*, "Till the End of the War" [1945]

[831]   The white man has become the black man's burden.
>   *Marching Blacks*, "Black Man's Burden" [1945]

[832]   No one can say that Christianity has failed. It has never been tried.
>   *Marching Blacks*, "Black Man's Burden" [1945]

[833]   The world has not been conquered for Anglo-Saxon nations by might alone; the missionaries prepared the way.
>   *Marching Blacks*, "Black Man's Burden" [1945]

[834]   Mix a conviction with a man and something happens.
>   *Keep the Faith, Baby*, "Minimum Living—Minimum Religion" [1967]

[835]   Past evils are the cause of present chaos.
>   *Keep the Faith, Baby*, "The Courage to Repent" [1967]

[836]   Freedom is an internal achievement rather than an external adjustment.
>   *Keep the Faith, Baby*, "Man's Debt to God" [1967]

[837]   It's never the right time to take a particular stand.
>   *Keep the Faith, Baby*, "One Must Die for Many" [1967]

[838]   Black power is black responsibility.
>   *Keep the Faith, Baby*, "Black Power: A Form of Godly Power" [1967]

RICHARD WRIGHT

(1908 - 1960)   Natchez, Mississippi

Richard Wright is one of America's great authors and his works stand as citadels of the Afro-American experience. Wright made his home in Paris, France, where he continued to write until his death in 1960. Among Wright's best known works are Native Son *(1940) and* Black Boy *(1945).*

[839]   The white folks ain never gimme a chance!
        They ain never give no black man a chance!

There ain nothin in yo whole life yuh kin keep
from em! They take yo lan! They take yo
freedom! They take yo women! N then they take
yo life!
Long Black Song [1936]

[840] Seems like the black folks is jus los in one big white fog.
Long Black Song [1936]

[841] Freedom belongs t the strong.
Long Black Song [1936]

[842] Half the time I feel like I'm on the outside of the world peeping in
through a knot-hole in the fence.
Native Son [1940]

[843] . . . we are not what we seem.
Twelve Million Black Voices [1941]

[844] We are with the new tide. We stand at the crossroads. We watch
each new procession. The hot wires carry urgent appeals. Print
compels us. Voices are speaking. Men are moving! And we shall
be with them. . . .
Twelve Million Black Voices [1941]

[845] . . . no word that I had ever heard fall from the lips of southern
white men, had ever made me really doubt the worth of my own
humanity.
Black Boy [1945]

[846] . . . guilty folks is scared folks.
The Outsider [1953]

[847] Men copied the realities of their hearts when they built prisons.
The Outsider [1953]

[848] The world changes, but men are always the same.
The Outsider [1953]

[849] A nigger's a black man who don't know who he is.
The Long Dream [1958]

[850] Some folks have to go into business. The black man's born in
business.
The Long Dream [1958]

[851]   All black dreams ain't dead. . . . Some of 'em live and walk around,
        but they dead just the same.
                    The Long Dream [1958]

[852]   White folks see eleven inches on a foot rule; we black folks see the
        whole damn rule.
                    The Long Dream [1958]

[853]   Be proud of being black, son. Live black, die black, eat black, sleep
        black, buy black, sell black, and love black.
                    The Long Dream [1958]

CHESTER BOMAR HIMES

(1909 -   )   Jefferson City, Missouri

*Chester Himes began his career as a writer of popular fiction, but his later
works expanded to reflect the schizophrenia of Afro-American life. Himes
has written many novels and essays, and volume I of his autobiography,*
The Quality of Hurt, *was published in 1972.*

[854]   Martyrs are needed to create incidents. Incidents are needed to
        create revolutions. Revolutions are needed to create progress.
                    Negro Martyrs are Needed, Crisis [May, 1944]

[855]   The ruling class or race must share their freedom with everyone in
        order to preserve it; or they must give it up.
                    Negro Martyrs are Needed, Crisis [May, 1944]

[856]   Democracy is not tolerance. Democracy is a prescribed way of life
        erected on the premise that all men are created equal.
                    If You're Scared, Go Home! [1944]

[857]   Any man's a coward who won't die for what he believes.
                    If He Hollers Let Him Go [1945]

[858]   You'll never get anything from these goddam white people unless
        you fight them.
                    If He Hollers Let Him Go [1945]

[859]   In this goddamn world they's all kind of wars always going on and
people is getting kilt in all of them. They's the races fighting
'gainst each other. And they's the classes cutting each other's
throats. And they's every mother's son fighting for hisself, just
to keep on living. And they's the nigger at the bottom of it all,
being fit by everybody and kilt by everybody.
The Lonely Crusade [1945]

BAYARD RUSTIN

(1910 -   )   West Chester, Pennsylvania

*Active in the labor movement for many years, Bayard Rustin gained nation-
al prominence as principal organizer of the 1953 Montgomery, Alabama
bus boycott and planner of the 1963 March on Washington. Rustin's
collection of essays,* Down the Line, *was published in 1971.*

[860]   There is a strong moralistic strain in the civil rights movement that
would remind us that power corrupts, forgetting that the absence
of power also corrupts.
From Protest to Politics Commentary, [February, 1965]

[861]   [On bigotry]:

Its birthplace is the sinister back room of the mind where plots and
schemes are hatched for the persecution and oppression of other
human beings.
*The Premise of the Stereotype, New York
Amsterdam News* [April 8, 1967]

[862]   When you're wrong, you're wrong. But when you're right, you're
wrong anyhow.
Down the Line [1971]

GORDON PARKS

(1912 -   )   Fort Scott, Kansas

Photographer, writer, musician, and film director, Gordon Parks is a former award-winning photojournalist for Life. *His directorial credits include the popular "Shaft" series and "Leadbelly" (1976). Among Parks's published works are* A Choice of Weapons *(1965),* The Learning Tree *(1966), and several books of poetry.*

[863]   I had some kind of innate capability to turn the violence and
        bitterness inside me into work. . . . When I felt I couldn't say
        what was inside me in photography, I turned to music or poetry
        and the novel. Maybe the work gets it out of my system without
        bashing someone's head in.
                        Editorial, *Life* [May 13, 1963]

[864]   Until my mid-teens I lived in fear; fear of being shot, lynched or
        beaten to death—not for any wrong doing of my own. I could
        easily have been the victim of mistaken identity or an act of terror
        by hate-filled white men.
                        "The Long Search for Pride," *Life* [August 16, 1963]

[865]   I have learned that the subtle art of rejection used with finesse, can
        be every bit as abusive as a punch in the face.
                        "The Long Search for Pride," *Life* [August 16, 1963]

[866]   I feel sometimes, that finally I chose photography as a profession
        because it was something I could work at without white consent.
                        "The Long Search for Pride," *Life* [August 16, 1963]

[867]   We were poor, though I did not know it at the time; the rich soil
        surrounding our clapboard house had yielded food for the
        family. And the love of this family had eased the burden of being
        black.
                        A Choice of Weapons [1965]

[868]   What I want
        What I am
        What you force me to be
        is what you are.
                        "The Cycle of Despair," *Life*, [March 8, 1968]

AIMÉ CÉSAIRE

(1913 -   )   Fort de France, Martinique

Aimé Césaire is considered the foremost Caribbean poet utilizing the concept of negritude in his works. One of his best known epic poems is Return to My Native Land, *published in English translation from the French in 1968.*

[869]   . . . .

> voum rooh oh
> that may return the time of
> promises
> and the bird who knew my name
> and the woman who had a thousand names
> and the fountain of sun and of tears
> and her hair of minnows
> and her steps my climates
> and her eyes my seasons
> and the days without nuisance
> and the nights without offence
>   and the stars of confidence
> and the wind of complicity
> But who alters my voice? Who scratches
> my voice? Sticking in my throat a
> thousand fangs of bamboo. A thousand
> stakes of sea-urchin. It is you, dirty end
> of the world. Dirty end of dawn.
> It is you, dirty hatred. It is you, the lord
> of insults and a hundred years of whipping.
> It is a hundred years of my attempts
> at just staying alive.
> rooh oh

. . . .

from *Return to My Native Land* [1947]

ROMARE BEARDEN
(1914 -   )   Charlotte, North Carolina

One of America's most respected painters, Romare Bearden has received wide acclaim for his works, particularly in the medium of collage. He has had many one-man exhibitions, and has participated in group shows both here and abroad. The Art of Romare Bearden *was published in 1972.*

[870]   I create social images within the work so far as the human condition is social. I create racial identities so far as the subjects are Negro, but I have not created protest images because the world within the collage, if it is authentic, retains the right to speak for itself.
> Interview, *Art News* [October, 1964]

[871]   I am a man concerned with truth, not flattery, who shares a dual culture that is unwilling to deny the Harlem where I grew up or the Haarlem of the Dutch masters that contributed its element to my understanding of art.
> Interview, *Art News* [October, 1964]

[872]   I want to see how life can triumph.
> *Newsweek* [April 5, 1971]

[873]   The human heart is limited and only capable of loving and caring for but a few people. If this were not so, we'd all be saints and really take care of our brothers.
> Interview, *Encore* [October, 1972]

[874]   Black art has always existed. It just hasn't been looked for in the right places.
> Interview, *Encore* [October, 1972]

[875]   White people know doggone well there is Black art, and use it to make money.
> Interview, *Encore* [October, 1972]

[876]   Real knowledge, properly used, will help anyone.
> Interview, *Encore* [October, 1972]

[877]   Art is the soul of a people.
> Interview, *Encore* [October, 1972]

[878] I have chosen to paint the life of my people as I know and feel it—
passionately and dispassionately. It is important that the artist
identify with the self-reliance, hope and courage of the people
about him, for art must always go where energy is.
Interview, *Essence* [May, 1975]

[879] You can't regiment spirit, and it is the spirit that counts.
Interview, *Ebony* [November, 1975]

[880] The European traditions are not as interesting as before. Something
else is waiting to get born.
Interview, *Ebony* [November, 1975]

[881] We look too much to museums. The sun coming up in the morning
is enough.
Interview, *Ebony* [November, 1975]

[882] There are roads out of the secret places within us along which we
must all move as we go to touch others.
Notes [Date Unknown]

RALPH ELLISON

(1914 -   )   Oklahoma City, Oklahoma

Ralph Ellison was a college lecturer, a writer-in-residence at Rutgers University, and a visiting fellow at Yale University. His literary reputation rests primarily on his only novel, The Invisible Man *(1947).*

[883] . . . if the word has the potency to revive and make us free, it has
also the power to blind, imprison and destroy.
Twentieth-Century Fiction and the Black Mask of Humanity
[written 1946]

[884] Life is to be lived, not controlled, and humanity is won by
continuing to play in face of certain defeat.
The Invisible Man [1947]

[885] In going underground, I whipped it all except the mind. . . .
The Invisible Man [1947]

[886]   When we finally achieve the right of full participation in American
        life, what we make of it will depend upon our sense of cultural
        values and our creative use of freedom, not upon our racial
        identification.
                            Some Questions and Some Answers [1958]

[887]   If the writer exists for any social good, his role is that of preserving
        in art those human values which can endure by confronting
        change.
                            Interview, *That Same Pain, That Same Pleasure*
                            [December, 1961]

[888]   . . . the real death of the United States will come when everyone is
        just alike.
                            Interview, *That Same Pain, That Same Pleasure*
                            [December, 1961]

DUDLEY FELKER RANDALL

(1914 -   )   Washington, D.C.

*Librarian and poet Dudley Randall has devoted much of his time to pub-
lishing the works of promising young Afro-American poets through his own
company, Broadside Press.*

[889]   A critic advises
        not to write on controversial subjects
        like freedom or murder,
        but to treat universal themes
        and timeless symbols
        like the white unicorn.

        A white unicorn?
                            Black Poet, White Critic [1968]

[890]   not only crocus faces
        or fresh-snowfall faces,
        but driftwood faces,
        grooved by salt waters,
        gnarled by the winds,

chiselled by stones,
and so molded by tides
as to resound
antiphonies,—
such faces,
driftwood faces,
also
are beautiful.

Faces [1970]

BILLIE HOLIDAY

(1915 - 1959)   Baltimore, Maryland

Billie Holiday, a unique blues singer whose style became a model for those who followed in her footsteps, was also the lyricist of "God Bless the Child," a song that became her trademark. An autobiography, Lady Sings the Blues, *was published in 1956.*

[891] Money, you've got lots of friends
Crowding round your door
But when its done
And spending ends
They don't come no more
Rich relations give
Crust of bread and such
You can help yourself but don't take much
Mama may have
Papa may have
But God bless the child that's got his own
That's got his own.

God Bless the Child (s. 3) [1941]

[892] All dope can do for you is kill you . . . the long hard way. And it
can kill the people you love right along with you.

Lady Sings the Blues [1956]

JOHN HENRIK CLARKE

(1915 -   )   Union Springs, Alabama

Distinguished historian John Henrik Clarke is associate editor of Freedom ways, *and a professor in the Department of Black and Puerto Rican Studies, Hunter College, New York City. He is compiler and editor of* American Negro Short Stories *(1966),* William Styron's Nat Turner: 10 Black Writers Respond *(1968), and* Harlem: A Community in Transition *(1969).*

[893]   The final interpretation of African history is the responsibility of scholars of African descent.

> *A New Approach to African History*, Address, Regional Conference on Afro-American History, Detroit Federation of Teachers, University of Detroit, Detroit, Michigan [May 11-13, 1967]

[894]   You cannot subjugate a man and recognize his humanity, his history and his personality; so, systematically, you must take this away from him. You begin by telling lies about this man's role in history.

> Address, Jewish Currents Conference, New York, New York [February 15, 1969]

[895]   Nature created no races.

> Address, Jewish Currents Conference, New York, New York [February 15, 1969]

[896]   A good teacher, like a good entertainer first must hold his audience's attention. Then he can teach his lesson.

> *A Search for Identity, Social Casework* [May, 1970]

[897]   It is too often forgotten that when the Europeans gained enough maritime skill and gunpowder to conquer most of the world, they not only colonized the bulk of the world's people but they colonized the interpretation of history itself. Human history was rewritten to favor them at the expense of other people. The roots of modern racism can be traced to this conquest and colonization.

> *Race: An Evolving Issue in Western Thought. Journal of Human Relations* [Third Quarter, 1970]

[898]   The Christian Church was the handmaiden for the development of racism.

> *Race: An Evolving Issue in Western Thought. Journal of Human Relations* [Third Quarter, 1970]

[899]   We are telling time by somebody else's clock.
> Introductory remarks, Friends of Like It is Seminar, City
> College of New York [October 11, 1980]

[900]   Image is what colonizes the mind.
> Introductory remarks, Friends of Like It Is Seminar, City
> College of New York [October 11, 1980]

JOHN OLIVER KILLENS

(1916 -   )   Macon, Georgia

John Killens, whose literary career was launched in 1954 with the highly successful novel Youngblood, *has published articles and written for films and television. Other Killens novels include* And Then We Heard the Thunder *(1962),* Slaves *(1969), and* Cotillion *(1971).*

[901]   My fight is not to be a white man in a black skin, but to inject some
black blood, some black intelligence into the pallid mainstream
of American life, culturally, socially, psychologically,
philosophically.
> *Explanation of the Black Psyche, The New York Times*
> [June 7, 1964]

[902]   To the average white man, a courthouse even in Mississippi is a
place where justice is dispensed. To me, the black man, it is a
place where justice is dispensed with.
> *Explanation of the Black Psyche, The New York Times*
> [June 7, 1964]

[903]   . . . in the middle of the twentieth century the Negro is the new
white hope.
> *Explanation of the Black Psyche, The New York Times*
> [June 7, 1964]

[904]   Western man wrote his history as if it were the history of the entire
human race. I hope that colored men all over the world have not
watched Western man too long to commit the fatal folly of
writing history with a colored pencil.
> *Explanation of the Black Psyche, The New York Times*
> [June 7, 1964]

[905]   The Negro was invented in America.
        The Black Man's Burden [1965]

[906]   . . . a people must face its history squarely in order to transcend it.
        The Black Man's Burden [1965]

[907]   The "Negro problem" and the white man's burden are historical
        misnomers. The problem never was "Negro." The problem is
        . . . . Caucasian, Anglo-Saxon, European, white.
        The Black Man's Burden [1965]

FRANK YERBY

(1916 -   )   Augusta, Georgia

*Frank Yerby is probably the most commercially successful of any Afro-
American writer. He gained instant recognition with his first novel,* The
Foxes of Harrow *(1949). One of his most recent novels is* The Dahomean
(1971).

[908]   . . . an American Negro isn't a man—he's a walking defense
        mechanism.
        Speak Now [1969]

GWENDOLYN BROOKS

(1917 -   )   Topeka, Kansas

*Gwendolyn Brooks is the only Afro-American who has won the Pulitzer
Prize for poetry (1950). A collection of her poems,* The World of Gwendolyn
Brooks, *was published in 1971, and an autobiography,* Report from Part
One, *in 1972.*

[909]   Mrs. Coley's three-flat brick
        Isn't here any more.
        All done with seeing her fat little form
        Burst out of the basement door;
        And with seeing her African son-in-law
        (Rightful heir to the throne)
        With his great white strong cold squares of teeth
        And his little eyes of stone;
        And with seeing the squat fat daughter
        Letting in the men
        When majesty has gone for the day—
        And letting them out again.
        The Vacant Lot [1944]

[910]   The past of his ancestors lean against
        Him. Crowd him. Fog out his identity.
        Hundreds of hungers mingle with his own,
        Hundreds of voices advise so dexterously
        He quite considers his reactions his,
        Judges he walks most powerfully alone,
        That everything is—simply what it is.
                        The Sundays of Satin-Legs Smith (s. 19) [1944]

[911]   Being you, you cut your poetry from wood.
        The boiling of an egg is heavy art.
        You come upon it as an artist should,
        With rich-eyed passion, and with straining heart.
        We fools, we cut our poems out of air,
        Night color, wind soprano, and such stuff.
        And sometimes weightlessness is much to bear.
        You mock it, though, you name it Not Enough.
        The egg, spooned gently to the avid pan,
        And left strict three minutes, or the four,
        Is your Enough and art for any man.
        We fools give courteous ear—then cut some more,
        Shaping a gorgeous Nothingness from cloud.
        You watch us, eat your egg, and laugh aloud.
                        The Egg Boiler [written between 1945-48]

[912]   What shall I give my children
        Who are adjudged the leastwise of the land,
        Who are my sweetest lepers, who demand
        No velvet and no velvety velour;
        But who have begged me for a brisk contour
        Crying that they are quasi, contraband
        Because unfinished, graven by a hand
        Less than angelic, admirable or sure.
        My hand is stuffed with mode, design, device.
        But I lack access to my proper stone.
        And a plenitude of plan shall not suffice
        Nor grief nor love shall be enough alone
        To ratify my little halves who bear
        Across an autumn freezing everywhere.
                        Children of the Poor, 2 [written 1947-48]

[913]   My last defense
        Is the present tense

        It little hurts me now to know
        I shall not go

        Cathedral-hunting in Spain
        Nor cherrying in Michigan or Maine.
                                Old Mary [1958]

[914]   Build now your Church, my brothers, sisters. Build
        never with brick nor Corten nor with granite.
        Build with lithe love. With love like lion-eyes.
        With love like morningrise.
        With love like black, our black—
        luminously indiscreet;
        complete, continuous.
                        The Sermon on the Warpland (s. 4) [1967]

[915]   Hateful things sometimes befall the hateful
        but the hateful are not rendered lovable
            thereby
                        from *In the Mecca* [written 1967-68]

OSSIE DAVIS

(1917 -   )   Cogdell, Georgia

Ossie Davis is an actor, director, and playwright, and author of Purlie
Victorious *(1961), a play that was successfully adapted for films and the
Broadway stage. Davis also pioneered in helping to create better work-
ing opportunities for Afro-Americans in the film industry.*

[916]   . . . being colored can be a lotta fun when ain't nobody lookin'.
                        Purlie Victorious, act I, scene i [1961]

[917]   Some of the best pretending in the world is done in front of white
            folks.
                        Purlie Victorious, act I, scene i [1961]

[918]   College ain't so much where you been as how you talk when you get
        back.
                    Purlie Victorious, act I, scene i [1961]

[919]   I find, in being black, a thing of beauty: a joy; a strength; a secret
        cup of gladness—a native land in neither time nor place—a native
        land in every Negro face! Be loyal to yourselves: your skin; your
        hair; your lips, your southern speech, your laughing kindness—
        are Negro kingdoms, vast as any other.
                    Purlie Victorious, act III, Epilogue [1961]

[920]   Every black man dies first of all from being black. The other cause
        of death is barely worth putting down on the death certificate.
                    from Funeral Eulogy for Godfrey Cambridge
                    [December, 1976]

FANNIE LOU HAMER

(1917 - 1977)   Montgomery County, Mississippi

*Fannie Lou Hamer was a leader in the grass-roots sector of the contemporary
civil rights struggle. She organized the Mississippi Freedom Democratic
Party (MFDP), ran for Congress, and organized economic cooperatives in
Sunflower County, Mississippi.*

[921]   White Americans today don't know what in the world to do
        because when they put us *behind* them, that's where they made
        their mistake. If they had put us in front they wouldn't have let
        us look back. But they put us behind them, and we watched
        every move they made. . . .
                    The Special Plight of the Black Woman, Address, NAACP
                    Legal Defense Fund Institute, New York, New York
                    [May 7, 1971]

[922]   . . . I used to think that if I could go North and tell people about the
        plight of black folk in the state of Mississippi everything would
        be alright. But traveling around I found one thing for sure: it's
        up-South and down-South, and its no different.
                    The Special Plight of the Black Woman, Address, NAACP
                    Legal Defense Fund Institute, New York, New York
                    [May 7, 1971]

[923]   It's been a special plight for the black woman. I remember my
        uncles and some of my aunts—and that's why it really tickled me
        when you talk about integration. Because I'm very black, but I
        remember some of my aunts was as white as anybody here—and
        blue-eyed and some green-eyed—and my grandfather didn't do
        it, you know.

> *The Special Plight of the Black Woman*, Address, NAACP
> Legal Defense Fund Institute, New York, New York
> [May 7, 1971]

[924]   We get up there and sing O say can you see . . . so proudly we hail.
        I don't know what we've got to hail about when the MDFP and
        SNCC are fighting so hard to make this a great society.

> *The Worker* [July 13, 1975]

[925]   . . . if this is a Great Society, I'd hate to see a bad one.

> *The Worker* [July 13, 1975]

PEARL BAILEY

(1918 -   )   Newport News, Virginia

*Pearl Bailey, best known for her easy-going singing style, has starred on
Broadway, television, and in films. In 1975 she served as a special advisor to the
United States delegation to the United Nations. Bailey has published several
books, including an autobiography,* Talking to Myself *(1971),* Pearl's
Kitchen *(1973), and* Hurry Up America, and Spit *(1976).*

[926]   We're a great heart people.

> *New York Post* [April 27, 1965]

[927]   Many people worry, but they don't do anything about it.

> Interview, *The New York Times* [November 26, 1967]

[928]   People see God every day, they just don't recognize him.

> Interview, *The New York Times* [November 26, 1967]

[929]   [On audiences]:

        I see their souls, and I hold them in my hands, and because I love
        them they weigh nothing.

> Interview, *The New York Times* [November 26, 1967]

[930] Every man has a place in this world, but no man has the right to designate that place.
> Interview, *The New York Times* [November 26, 1967]

[931] There are two kinds of talent, man-made talent and God-given talent. With man-made talent you have to work very hard. With God-given talent, you just touch it up once in a while.
> *Newsweek* [December 4, 1967]

[932] The prejudiced people can't insult you because they're blinded by their own ignorance.
> *The Raw Pearl* [1968]

[933] No one can figure out your worth but you.
> *The Raw Pearl* [1968]

[934] Everybody wants to do something to help, but nobody wants to be first.
> *The Raw Pearl* [1968]

[935] It's hard to accept strength and goodness together in the same person.
> *The Raw Pearl* [1968]

[936] You never find yourself until you face the truth.
> *The Raw Pearl* [1968]

[937] We have to face the uglies to admit our errors, and even if we repeat them, we ought not to excuse them.
> *Hurry Up America, and Spit* [1976]

[938] There is a way to look at the past. Don't hide from it. It will not catch you if you don't repeat it.
> *Hurry Up America, and Spit* [1976]

[939] We look into mirrors but we only see the effects of our times on us—not our effects on others.
> *Hurry Up America, and Spit* [1976]

[940] We must change in order to survive.
> *Hurry Up America, and Spit* [1976]

GAMAL ABDEL NASSER
(1918 - 1970)   Alexandria, Egypt

Egyptian nationalist and revolutionary leader Gamal Abdel Nasser was the first president of the United Arab Republic and served until his death in 1970. A biography, Nasser, the Man and the Miracle, *was written by Dewan Berindranath in 1966.*

[941] Power is not merely shouting aloud. Power is to act positively with all the components of power.
> *The Philosophy of Revolution* [1959]

[942] Fate does not play jokes.
> *The Philosophy of Revolution* [1959]

[943] To eradicate racial discrimination and apartheid, it is not enough to brand them as a humiliation to mankind as a whole in this and every other age, but it is imperative that there should be a valiant resistance by all means and ways until we reach the weapon of total boycott by which we can change this state of affairs.
> Address, African Summit Conference, Addis Ababa, Ethiopia [May 24, 1963]

ALICE CHILDRESS
(1920 -   )   Charleston, South Carolina

Alice Childress began her career with the American Negro Theatre as an actress, writer, and director. Her play, Trouble in Mind *(1955), won an Obie award for the 1955-56 New York season. Childress' most recent novel is* A Short Walk *(1979).*

[944] I don't like to think . . . makes me fightin' mad.
> *Trouble in Mind* [1955]

[945] Domestic workers have done a awful lot of good things in this country besides clean up people's houses.
> *Like One of the Family* [1956]

[946]   . . . it's a poor kinda man that won't fight for his own freedom.
Like One of the Family [1956]

[947]   . . . I believe racism has killed more people than speed, heroin, or
cancer, and will continue to kill until it is no more.
Stagebill [May, 1972]

ALEX HALEY

(1921 -   )   Ithaca, New York

With the publication of Roots *(1976), Alex Haley became famous as the
first Afro-American to trace his lineage back to Africa. He assisted in the
preparation of* The Autobiography of Malcolm X *(1964) and has written both
newspaper and magazine articles.*

[948]   History is written by the winners.
Interview, *The David Frost Television Show* [April 20, 1972]

[949]   White folks tell you one of dem name Columbus discover dis place.
But if he foun' Injuns here, he ain't discover it, is he?
Roots [1976]

WHITNEY MOORE YOUNG, JR.

(1921 - 1972)   Lincoln Ridge, Kentucky

*Although he was a well known lecturer and author, Whitney Young was
perhaps most familiar in his role as executive director of the National Urban
League. Among Young's written works are* To Be Equal *(1964) and* Beyond
Racism *(1969).*

[950]   Our country is in dire jeopardy as long as it has within its body
politic a socially and economically deprived group of citizens,
whether they be actually enslaved or denied the full benefits of
equality and freedom by an insidious economic and
psychological slavery.
Minorities in a Changing World, The New York Times
[October 6, 1963]

[951]   . . . no law can make one person respect or love another.
To Be Equal [1964]

[952]   Our ability to create has outreached our ability to use wisely the products of our invention.
To Be Equal [1964]

[953]   We create an environment where it is alright to hate, to steal, to cheat, and to lie if we dress it up with symbols of respectability, dignity and love.
To Be Equal [1964]

[954]   The unhealthy gap between what we preach in America and what we often practice creates a moral dry rot that eats at the very foundation of our democratic ideals and values.
To Be Equal [1964]

[955]   We can't . . . sit and wait for somebody else. We must go ahead— alone if necessary, but together in the end.
To Be Equal [1964]

[956]   The Negro is the barometer of all America's institutions and values.
To Be Equal [1964]

AHMED SÉKOU TOURÉ

(1922 -   )   Faranah, Guinea

Ahmed Sékou Touré is currently president of Guinea. His philosophy and ideas are recorded in Guinean Revolution and Social Progress *(1963). The following quotation has been translated from the French.*

[957]   To take part in the African revolution it is not enough to write a revolutionary song: you must fashion the revolution with the people. And if you fashion it with the people, the songs will come by themselves.
Address, Second Congress of Black Writers and Artists, Rome, Italy [1959]

JAMES BALDWIN

(1924 -   )   New York, New York

James Baldwin's long essay The Fire Next Time *(1962) established him as a major American writer. His considerable literary output ranges from novels and plays to numerous magazine articles. His latest novel is* Just Above My Head *(1979).*

[958]   Anyone who has ever struggled with poverty knows how extremely expensive it is to be poor.
                    Fifth Avenue Uptown, Esquire [July 1960]

[959]   Where there is no vision, people perish.
                    Fifth Avenue Uptown, Esquire [July 1960]

[960]   Know from whence you came. If you know whence you came, there is really no limit to where you can go.
                    The Fire Next Time [1962]

[961]   To defend one's self against fear is simply to insure that one will, one day, be conquered by it; fears must be faced.
                    The Fire Next Time [1962]

[962]   Heavenly witnesses are a tricky lot, to be used by whoever is closest to Heaven at that time.
                    The Fire Next Time [1962]

[963]   It's a awful thing to think about, the way love never dies.
                    The Amen Corner, Act III [1965]

[964]   Until the moment comes when we, the Americans, are able to accept the fact that my ancestors are both black and white, that on that continent we are trying to forge a new identity, that we need each other, that I am not a ward of America, I am not an object of missionary, I am one of the people who built the country . . . there is scarcely any hope for the American dream. If the people are denied participation in it, by their very presence they will wreck it.
                    The American Dream Is At the Expense of the American Negro. Debate, Cambridge University, Cambridge, England [February, 1965]

[965]   If you're afraid to die, you will not be able to live.
                    Television Interview, *Assignment America* [May 13, 1975]

[966]   We have paid for this country.
                    Television Interview, *Assignment America* [May 13, 1975]

SHIRLEY CHISHOLM
(1924 -   )   Brooklyn, New York

Shirley Chisholm, a former public school teacher, began her political career in the 1960s. She served in the New York State Assembly, was elected United States congressional representative from Brooklyn (1968), and in 1972 became the first woman to actively run as a presidential candidate. Her autobiography, Unbought and Unbossed, *was published in 1970.*

[967]   The Negro has been a most patient man.
                New York Post [June 22, 1968]

[968]   I know I'll survive. I'm a fighter.
                New York Post [June 22, 1968]

[969]   It really takes guts to take a stand.
                New York Post [March 4, 1969]

[970]   Men don't like independent women.
                The New York Times [April 13, 1969]

[971]   We have to help black men, but not at the expense of our own
        personalities as women.
                The New York Times [April 13, 1969]

[972]   Women don't get hung up, making deals the way men do.
                The New York Times [April 13, 1969]

[973]   . . . laws will not eliminate prejudice from the hearts of human
        beings. But that is no reason to allow prejudice to continue to be
        enshrined in our laws to perpetuate injustice through inaction.
                *Congressional Record, Joint Resolution 264, 91st Congress,
                2nd Session* [August 10, 1970]

[974]   As there were no black Founding Fathers, there were no founding
        mothers—a great pity on both counts.
                *Congressional Record, Joint Resolution 264, 91st Congress,
                2nd Session* [August 10, 1970]

[975]   [On health]:

        Health is a human right, not a privilege to be purchased.
                *Congressional Record, Joint Resolution 264, 91st Congress,
                2nd Session* [August 10, 1970]

[976] Of my two "handicaps," being female put many more obstacles in
       my path than being black.
                          Unbought and Unbossed [1970]

[977] Some members of congress are the best actors in the world.
                          Unbought and Unbossed [1970]

[978] Everyone else is represented in Washington by a rich and powerful
       lobby, it seems. But there is no lobby for the people.
                          Unbought and Unbossed [1970]

[979] The liberals in the House strongly resemble liberals I have known
       through the last two decades in the civil rights conflict. When it
       comes time to show on which side they will be counted, they
       suddenly excuse themselves.
                          Unbought and Unbossed [1970]

[980] When morality comes up against profit, it is seldom that profit
       loses.
                          Unbought and Unbossed [1970]

[981] Brotherhood Week makes me sick. . . . I have seen too many racists
       serve on Brotherhood Week committees, pretending to be decent
       human beings for seven days.
                          Unbought and Unbossed [1970]

[982] Racism is so universal in this country, so widespread and deep-
       seated, that it is invisible because it is so normal.
                          Unbought and Unbossed [1970]

[983] Black people have freed themselves from the dead weight of the
       albatross of blackness that once hung around their neck. They
       have done it by picking it up in their arms and holding it out with
       pride for all the world to see. They have done it by embracing it—
       not in the dark of the moon but in the searing light of the white
       sun. They have said *Yes* to it and found that the skin that was
       once seen as symbolizing their shame is in reality their badge of
       honor.
                          Women Must Rebel [1970]

[984] White male America has always made decisions for everyone else
       . . . no women, no blacks, no Indians.
                          Family Circle [May, 1972]

[985] True leaders have to be totally free.
                          Interview, *New York Daily News* [June 8, 1980]

NIPSEY RUSSELL

(c. 1924 -   )   Atlanta, Georgia

Nipsey Russell, who began his career at the age of six, was one of the first stand-up comedians to utilize the contemporary racial situation as material for his act. In addition to nightclub performances, Russell has appeared on television and in films.

[986]   Everything's a milestone now. Pretty soon there'll be the first
         Negro that ever walked across Broadway with the sun shining,
         who parts his hair on the right.
                      Interview, *New York Post* [September 27, 1964]

[987]   My saving grace has been words. What did Lincoln wear? How did
         he feel? What did he eat? Nobody can tell you that. But they can
         tell you what he said.
                      Interview, *New York Post* [September 27, 1964]

[988]   He who turns the other cheek, gets hit with the other fist.
                      Address, Frederick Douglass Award Banquet,
                      New York City [May 11, 1972]

FRANTZ FANON

(1925 - 1961)   Fort de France, Martinique

Frantz Fanon was educated in France and received a medical degree, specializing in psychiatry. His work, both in practice and in writing, focused on the damaging effects of white colonization on the black psyche. Fanon's best known works are Black Skins, White Masks *(1952) and* The Wretched of the Earth *(1961). The following quotations have been translated from the French.*

[989]   I am black. I am the incarnation of a complete fusion with the
         world, an intuitive understanding of the earth, an abandonment of
         my ego in the heart of the cosmos, and no white man, no matter
         how intelligent he may be, can ever understand Louis Armstrong
         and the music of the Congo.
                      Black Skins, White Masks [1952]

[990]   I feel myself a soul as immense as the world, truly a soul as deep as
        the deepest rivers, my chest has the power to expand without
        limit. I am a master and I am advised to adopt the humility
        of the cripple. Yesterday, awakening to the world, I saw the sky
        turn upon itself utterly and wholly. I wanted to rise, but the
        disemboweled silence fell back upon me, its wings paralyzed.
        Without responsibility straddling Nothingness and Infinity, I
        began to weep.
                                    Black Skins, White Masks [1952]

[991]   O my body, make of me always a man who questions!
                                    Black Skins, White Masks [1952]

[992]   No attempt must be made to encase man, for it is his destiny to be
        set free.
                                    Black Skins, White Masks [1952]

[993]   Radicalism and hatred and resentment . . . cannot sustain a war of
        liberation.
                                    The Wretched of the Earth [1961]

[994]   Each generation must, out of relative obscurity, discover its
        mission, fulfill it, or betray it.
                                    The Wretched of the Earth [1961]

PATRICE EMERY LUMUMBA

(1925 - 1961)   Katako Kombe, Congo (Zaire)

*African revolutionary Patrice Lumumba spearheaded the Congolese freedom
movement that led to independence and the birth of Zaire in 1960. He was
assassinated a year later. Lumumba's works are published, translated from
the French in* Lumumba Speaks: The Speeches and Writings of Patrice
Lumumba *(1972)*

[995]   The period of racial monopolies is now at an end.
                                    Address, International Seminar, Ibadan, Nigeria
                                    [March 22, 1959]

[996] The shores of the great river, full of promises,
       Henceforth belong to you.
       This earth and all its riches
       Henceforth belong to you.
       And the fiery sun, high in a colorless sky,
       Will burn away your pain
       Its searing rays will forever dry
       The tears your forefathers shed
       Tormented by their tyrannical masters
       On this soil that you still cherish.
       And you will make the Congo a free and happy nation,
       In the heart of this giant Black Africa.
                            Weep, O Beloved Black Brother (ll. 43-54) [September, 1959]

[997] Neither brutal assaults, nor cruel mistreatment,
           nor torture have ever led me to beg for mercy, for I prefer to die
           with my head held high, unshakeable faith, and the greatest
           confidence in the destiny of my country rather than live in slavery
           and contempt for sacred principles. History will one day have its
           say; it will not be the history taught in the United Nations,
           Washington, Paris, or Brussels . . . but the history taught in the
           countries that have rid themselves of colonialism and its puppets.
                            Excerpt from a letter to his wife [January, 1961]

[998] When you civilize a man, you only civilize an individual; but when
           you civilize a woman, you civilize a whole people.
                            Congo, My Country [1961]

[999] It is easy enough to shout slogans, to sign manifestos, but it is quite
           a different matter to build, manage, command, spend days and
           nights seeking the solution of problems.
                            Congo, My Country [1961]

[1000] No one is perfect in this imperfect world. . . .
                            Congo, My Country [1961]

MALCOLM X
(1925 - 1965)   Omaha, Nebraska

One of the first contemporary Afro-American voices raised in the renewed struggle for equality was that of Malcolm X, who was a central figure in the early days of the Nation of Islam (now known as the American Muslim Nation). The Autobiography of Malcolm X *was published in 1964.*

[1001]   Revolutions are never peaceful. . . .
>   Address, New York, New York [December 1963]

[1002]   I am not an American. I am one of 22 million black people who are victims of Americanism.
>   *Ballot or the Bullet*, Address, Cory Methodist Church, Cleveland, Ohio [April 3, 1964]

[1003]   Truth is on the side of the oppressed.
>   Address, Militant Labor Forum Symposium, New York, New York [May 29, 1964]

[1004]   I believe there are some sincere white people. But I think they should prove it.
>   Address, Williams Institutional CME Church, Harlem, New York, New York [December 20, 1964]

[1005]   Learn to see . . . listen . . . and think for yourself.
>   *Malcolm X Talks to Young People*, Address, Hotel Theresa, New York, New York [December 31, 1964]

[1006]   . . . after you get your freedom, your enemy will respect you.
>   *Malcolm X Talks to Young People*, Address, Hotel Theresa, New York, New York [December 31, 1964]

[1007]   . . . you cannot separate peace from freedom, because no one can be at peace unless he has his freedom.
>   Address, Militant Labor Forum, New York, New York [January 7, 1965]

[1008]   The colleges and universities in the American education system are skillfully used to miseducate.
>   Interview, *Young Socialist* [January 18, 1965]

[1009]   I feel like a man who has been asleep somewhat and under someone else's control. Now I think with my own mind. . . .
>   Interview, *The New York Times* [February 22, 1965]

ALTHEA GIBSON DARBEN
(1927 -   )   Silver, South Carolina

Althea Gibson, who learned paddle tennis on the streets of Harlem, won the World's Women's Singles Tennis Championship at Wimbledon, England (1957), and was named to the Lawn Tennis Hall of Fame in 1971. She has written two books, I Always Wanted to Be Somebody *(1958) and* So Much to Live For *(1968).*

[1010]   In the field of sports you are more-or-less accepted for what you do
         rather than what you are.
                            New York Post [July 22, 1956]

[1011]   [On winning the Wimbledon trophy]:

         I was honored and elated to receive the trophy from the Queen, but
         I am just as happy, just as proud to come home to be greeted by
         my friends.
                            The New York Times [July 7, 1957]

[1012]   No matter what accomplishments you make, somebody helps you.
                            Time [August 26, 1957]

[1013]   I want my success to speak for itself as an advertisement for my
         race.
                            I Always Wanted to Be Somebody [1958]

[1014]   [On her retirement from tennis]:

         Being champion is all well and good, but you can't eat a crown.
                            So Much To Live For [1968]

[1015]   I sometimes think that most of us who aspire to be tops in our fields
         don't really consider the amount of work required to *stay* tops.
                            So Much To Live For [1968]

[1016]   . . . no matter how liberal, how well accepted into the white
         community, no matter how popular or famous, no matter how
         unprejudiced a Negro may be, most of us have to wear some sort
         of mask outside our own group, and it's a relief to be able to put
         that mask down from time to time when we're back with our own
         kind.
                            So Much To Live For [1968]

[1017]   Talent wins out.
                            Ms. Magazine [December, 1973]

DAVID MANDESSI DIOP
(1927 - 1960)   Bordeaux, France

David Diop, a brilliant young Senegalese poet, was killed in an airplane crash off Dakar in 1960. All his manuscripts were destroyed in the accident. His only collection of poetry, Coup de Pilons, *was published in 1956. The following selections have been translated from the French.*

[1018]   You who move like a battered old dream
         A dream transpierced by the blades of the mistral
         By what bitter ways
         By what muddy wanderings of accepted suffering
         By what caravels drawing from isle to isle
         The curtains of negro blood torn from Guinea
         Have you carried your old coat of thorns
         To the foreign cemetery where you read the sky . . .
                    Nigger Tramp (ll. 1-8) [1956]

[1019]   Africa my Africa
         Africa of proud warriors or ancestral savannahs
         Africa that my grandmother sings
         On the bank of her distant river
         I have never known you
         But my face is full of your blood
         Your beautiful black blood which waters the wide fields
                    Africa (s. 1) [1956]

[1020]   My brother you flash your teeth in response to every hypocrisy
         My brother with gold-rimmed glasses
         You give your master a blue-eyed faithful look
         My poor brother in immaculate evening dress
         Screaming and whispering and pleading in the parlours of
                   condescension
         We pity you
         Your country's burning sun is nothing but a shadow
         On your serene "civilized" brow
         And the thought of your grandmother's hut
         Brings blushes to your face that is bleached
         By years of humiliation and bad conscience
         And while you trample on the bitter red soil of Africa
         Let these words of anguish keep time with your restless step—
         Oh, I am so lonely here
                    The Renegade [1959]

LEONTYNE PRICE
(1927 -   )   Laurel, Mississippi

Leontyne Price, one of the world's great concert and opera singers, is an international performer. She has made several award-winning recordings and has appeared as a television guest artist. A biography, Leontyne Price: Highlights of a Prima Donna *(1973), was written by Hugh Lee Lyon.*

[1021] If you're not feeling good about you, what you're wearing outside
        doesn't mean a thing.
                              Interview, *Essence* [February, 1975]

[1022] We are positively a unique people. Breathtaking people. Anything
        we do, we do big! Despite attempts to stereotype us, we are crazy,
        individual and uncorral-able people.
                              Interview, *Essence* [February 1975]

[1023] The ultimate of being successful is the luxury of giving yourself the
        time to do what you want to do.
                              Interview, *Newsday* [February 1, 1976]

[1024] Who I am is the best I can be.
                              Television interview, *Go Tell It* [October 26, 1980]

LERONE BENNETT, JR.
(1928 -   )   Clarkesdale, Mississippi

Distinguished scholar and historian Lerone Bennett has lectured extensively and published several books on black history, including Before the May-flower *(1964) and* Pioneers in Protest *(1968).*

[1025] No group moves en masse to a predetermined goal. There are
        advances and retreats, brilliant victories and stunning defeats.
        The battle goes on for decades against rain and fire and storm
        and hate. There are mountains to climb and rivers to cross and
        enemies on all sides—and within. . . . Dark nights follow dark
        nights and the valley of the mind, where all great battles are
        fought, reverberates with the screams and groans of the dying and
        defeated. The people halt on a dry level place and regroup;
        stragglers drop out; the timid go over to the enemy; straws are
        clutched, dope or drink or God or sex, each man or woman
        clutching according to different lights.
                              Prologue, *Confrontation in Black and White* [1965]

MARTIN LUTHER KING, JR.

(1929 - 1968)   Atlanta, Georgia

Martin Luther King, Jr., won world-wide acclaim for his use of nonviolence as an instrument for social change in America. He was the youngest winner in history of the Nobel Peace Prize (1968). Among the biographies on King are What Manner of Man *(1968), by Lerone Bennett, and Davis L. Lewis'* Martin Luther King, Jr., A Critical Biography *(1978).*

[1026]   There is nothing more tragic than to find an individual bogged down in the length of life, devoid of breadth.
>   *The Measure of the Man* [1959]

[1027]   . . . everything that we see is a shadow cast by that which we do not see.
>   *The Measure of the Man* [1959]

[1028]   Nothing pains some people more than having to think.
>   *Strength to Love* [1963]

[1029]   A nation or civilization that continues to produce soft-minded men purchases its own spiritual death on the installment plan.
>   *Strength to Love* [1963]

[1030]   We are not makers of history. We are made by history.
>   *Strength to Love* [1963]

[1031]   Shallow understanding from people of goodwill is more frustrating than absolute misunderstanding from people of ill-will.
>   *Letter from a Birmingham Jail* [January 16, 1963]

[1032]   We will have to repent in this generation not merely for the vitriolic words and actions of the bad people, but for the appalling silence of the good people.
>   *Letter from a Birmingham Jail* [January 16, 1963]

[1033]   We must use time creatively . . . and forever realize that the time is always ripe to do right.
>   *Letter from a Birmingham Jail* [January 16, 1963]

[1034]   Oppressed people cannot remain oppressed forever.
>   *Letter from a Birmingham Jail* [January 16, 1963]

[1035]   War is a poor chisel to carve out tomorrows.
>   Television documentary [December, 1965]

LORRAINE HANSBERRY

(1930 - 1965)   Chicago, Illinois

Lorraine Hansberry was the first Afro-American to win the New York Drama Critics Circle Award. Her play, A Raisin in the Sun *(1959), was adapted for film and presented as a Broadway musical. Hansberry wrote two other plays:* A Sign in Sidney Brustein's Window *(1965), and* Les Blancs, *produced posthumously in 1970.*

[1036]   Seem like God don't see fit to give the black man nothing but dreams—but He did give us children to make them dreams seem worthwhile.
> *A Raisin in the Sun*, act I, scene i [1959]

[1037]   There ain't no causes—there ain't nothing but taking in this world, and he who takes most is smartest—and it don't make a damn bit of difference how.
> *A Raisin in the Sun*, act III [1959]

[1038]   The laws which force segregation do not presume the inferiority of a people; they assume an inherent equalness. It is the logic of the lawmakers that if a society does not erect artificial barriers between people at every point of contact, the people might fraternize and give their attention to the genuine, shared problems of the community.
> *A Matter of Color* [1965]

[1039]   I do not "hate" all white people—but I desperately wish I did. It would make things infinitely easier.
> *Les Blancs*, act I, scene iii [1970]

[1040]   Take away the violence and who will hear the man of peace?
> *Les Blancs*, act II, scene ii [1970]

RICHARD RIVE

(1931 -   )   Cape Town, Republic of South Africa

Poet and novelist Richard Rive was educated in Cape Town and has won various awards. His work has appeared in South African periodicals and has also been published in several foreign languages. A collection of his short stories, African Songs, *was published in 1963.*

[1041] Where the rainbow ends
        There's going to be a place, brother,
        Where the world can sing all sorts of songs,
        And we're going to sing together, brother,
        You and I, though you're white and I'm not.
        It's going to be a sad song, brother,
        Because we don't know the tune
        And it's a difficult tune to learn.
        But we can learn, brother, you and I.
        There's no such tune as a black tune.
        There's no such tune as a white tune.
        There's only music brother,
        Where the rainbow ends.
                Where the Rainbow Ends [1963]

DICK GREGORY

(1932 -   )   Saint Louis, Missouri

Dick Gregory, the first nationally recognized Afro-American comedian, is a popular college lecturer and has campaigned on behalf of the world's poor people. Among his most popular books are Nigger *(1964), and* What's Happening *(1965).*

[1042] This book is dedicated to Abraham Lincoln. If it wasn't for Abe,
        I'd still be on the open market.
            From the Back of the Bus [1962]

[1043] You remember Brotherhood Week? The only week in the year when
        you wanna take a Negro to lunch you gotta ask for a number?
            From the Back of the Bus [1962]

[1044]   You gotta say this for the white race—its self-confidence knows no
         bounds. Who else could go to a small island in the South Pacific
         where there's no poverty, no crime, no unemployment, no war
         and no worry, and call it a "primitive society?"
         From the Back of the Bus [1962]

[1045]   I never learned hate at home, or shame. I had to go to school for
         that.
         Nigger [1964]

[1046]   A scared Negro is one thing. A mad Negro is something else.
         Nigger [1964]

[1047]   The answer to the race problem is simple—it's give and take. If they
         don't give, we're going to take it.
         What's Happening [1965]

[1048]   America has put a tight shoe on the Negro and now he has a callous
         on his soul.
         The Shadow That Scares Me [1968]

FRANCIS ERNEST KOBINA PARKES

(1932 -   )   Korle Bu, Ghana

*Francis Kobina Parkes was a graduate of the school at Adisadel, Ghana. He
worked briefly as a newspaper journalist and was associated with Radio
Ghana. Parkes' poems have been published in anthologies.*

[1049]   How can I, who cannot control
         My own waking and dreaming, ever hope to make my voice
         heard in the wrangling for mankind's soul?
         Blind Steersman (s. 1) [1965]

[1050]   Give me black souls
         let them be black
         Or chocolate brown
         Or make them the
         Colour of dust
         Dustlike

Browner than sand
But if you can
Please keep them black
Black.

African Heaven (s. 1) [1965]

ANDREW YOUNG

(1932 -   )   New Orleans, Louisiana

Andrew Young was active with SCLC (Southern Christian Leadership Conference) in the 1960s and a close associate of Martin Luther King, Jr. He was congressional representative from Georgia (1973-1977), and was United States Ambassador to the United Nations from 1977 to 1979. A biography, Andrew Young *(1978), was written by Janice Clare Simpson.*

[1051] The people who are the most militant are often the ones who were least involved when things were tough and dangerous.
New York Magazine [July 12, 1976]

[1052] Northern blacks are Southern blacks. They just moved North.
New York Magazine [July 12, 1976]

[1053] Once the Xerox copier was invented, diplomacy died.
Interview, *Playboy* [July, 1977]

[1054] Black people have been hurt by white people so long they tend to keep testing a relationship, like a dog that's been kicked a whole lot.
Interview, *Playboy* [July, 1977]

[1055] Chaos occurs when human rights are not respected.
Interview, *Playboy* [July, 1977]

[1056] . . . its a blessing to die for a cause, because you can so easily die for nothing.
Interview, *Playboy* [July, 1977]

[1057] I've never been a moral leader. That is a term people used to try to sanctify the civil rights movement once we got successful.
Interview, *Playboy* [July, 1977]

[1058] I make people think. I make them mad. I make them argue with
        each other and with me, and I deny them the opportunity to be
        uninvolved in what's going on in the world.
                            Washington Post [July 21, 1978]

[1059] I won't let people be neutral.
                            Washington Post [July 21, 1978]

[1060] [On his resignation from the United Nations]:

        I really don't feel a bit sorry for a thing I have done. I have tried to
        interpret to our country some of the mood of the rest of the
        world. Unfortunately, but by birth, I come from the ranks of
        those who had known and identified with some level of
        oppression in the world. By choice I continue to identify with
        what would be called in biblical terms the least of these my
        brothers.

                    The New York Times [August 16, 1979]

ERNEST J. GAINES

(1933 -   )   Oscar, Louisiana

Ernest Gaines wrote two novels before The Autobiography of Miss Jane
Pittman *(1971) propelled him into the literary spotlight. A television film
version of the novel won an Emmy Award in 1974.*

[1061] Niggers hearts been broke ever since niggers been in this world.
                    The Autobiography of Miss Jane Pittman [1971]

[1062] That's another thing about a nigger: he knows everything. There
        ain't a thing on earth he don't know—till somebody with brains
        come along.
                    The Autobiography of Miss Jane Pittman [1971]

[1063] . . . I have a scar on my back I got when I was a slave. I'll carry it to
        my grave. You got people out there with this scar on their brains,
        and they will carry that scar to their grave. The mark of fear . . .
        is not easily removed.
                    The Autobiography of Miss Jane Pittman [1971]

[1064] Any person who's worth a goddamn must really struggle.
                    Interview, *Essence* [July, 1975]

FLIP WILSON
(1933 -   )   Jersey City, New Jersey

Comedian Flip Wilson gained nationwide success during the early 1970s as star of his own television variety series. Since that time he has performed in television specials and recorded several comedy albums. Wilson also appeared in the film, "Uptown Saturday Night" (1971).

[1065]   Violence is a tool of the ignorant.
>   Interview, *Ebony* [April, 1968]

[1066]   [Geraldine's line]:

What you see is what you get.
>   Interview, *Ebony* [December, 1970]

[1067]   [Geraldine's line]:

Don't you push me, honey. Don't you *ever, never* push me.
>   Interview, *Ebony* [December, 1970]

[1068]   Funny is an *attitude*.
>   Interview, *Black Stars* [February, 1973]

[1069]   Being your own man does not mean taking advantage of anyone
         else.
>   Interview, *Black Stars* [February, 1973]

[1070]   I never talk down to my audience.
>   Interview, *Black Stars* [February, 1973]

IMAMU AMIRI BARAKA

(1934 -   )   Newark, New Jersey

The talent of poet, novelist, and dramatist Imamu Baraka (formerly LeRoi Jones) blossomed during the 1960s. Two plays, The Slave *and* The Toilet, *were produced in 1965, and a collection of his poetry,* Black Magic: Sabotage, Target Study, Black Art, *was published in 1969.*

[1071]   Despair sits on this country in most places like a charm, but there is
             a special gray death that loiters in the streets of a Negro slum.
                           Cold, Hurt, and Sorrow [1962]

[1072]   Hope is delicate suffering.
                           Cold, Hurt, and Sorrow [1962]

[1073]   A man is either free or he is not. There cannot be any
             apprenticeship for freedom.
                           Tokenism: 300 Years for Five Cents [1962]

[1074]   We live in fragments
             like speech. Like fits
             of wind, shivering against
             the window.

             Pieces of meaning, pierced
             and strung together. The bright bead
             of the poem, the bright bead
             of your woman's laughter.
                           Tight Rope [written between 1961-63]

[1075]   Rising gate
             with disappearing locks.
             Then tingling wind. Sun engines
             picking up their whirrr, starling wheeling
             across oil and pulling it into clouds.
             Turning
             as a last measure, to scream. But too far away. The control
             is what lifts me. The sky is not open, but curves, in blue
             sinking tones.
             to send us back in the deep flesh of our own places.
                           Morning Purpose [written between 1961-63]

[1076]   Make some muscle
             in your head but, use the muscle in your heart.
                           Young Soul [written between 1963-65]

[1077]   We love to be here, which is why we don't die.
         Labor Management 2 (s. 3) [written between 1963-65]

[1078]   Morning uptown, quiet on the street,
         no matter the distinctions that can be
         made, quiet, very quiet, on the street.
         Sun's not even up, just some kid and me,
         amazed there is grace for us, without our
         having to smile too tough, or be very pleasant
         even to each other. Merely to be mere, ly
         to be.
         Song Form [written between 1963-65]

[1079]   We are beautiful people
         with african imaginations
         full of masks and dances and swelling chants
         with african eyes, and noses, and arms,
         though we sprawl in grey chains in a place
         full of winters, when what we want is sun.
         Ka 'Ba (s. 3) [written between 1963-65]

ARTHUR MITCHELL

(1934 -   )   New York, New York

*Arthur Mitchell, who began dancing as a teenager, had his debut as soloist
with the New York City Ballet in 1954. He left the company in 1969 to form
The Dance Theater of Harlem, the first Afro-American classical ballet
company, where he is choreographer and co-director with Karl Shook.*

[1080]   . . . we must carry the arts to the people, not wait for the people to
         come to the arts.
         Dance Magazine [March, 1970]

[1081]   We have to prove beyond the shadow of a doubt that it is talent and
         training, not color, that makes a ballet dancer.
         Dance Magazine [March, 1970]

[1082]   It's a very lonely thing to be one of the first.
         Interview, *New York Post* [January 2, 1971]

[1083]   I believe in helping people the best way you can; my way is through
          my art. But sometimes you need a splash of cold water in your
          face to make you see the right way to do it.
                              Interview, *New York Post* [January 2, 1971]

[1084]   There is no such thing that all blacks have rhythm. Its not that
          they're born with rhythm, but in black homes you always hear
          music. It becomes instinctive, a lot rubs off. But the thing we
          don't have is the uptightedness, the old Victorianism of not
          letting your feelings show. We never had a tradition of
          suppressing emotion and it was not considered wrong to cry, to
          laugh. We had to be able to show this emotion, because what
          black could afford a psychiatrist?
                              Interview, *New York Post* [January 2, 1971]

ELDRIDGE CLEAVER

(1935 -   )   Wabbeseka, Arkansas

*Eldridge Cleaver, who began writing while incarcerated in various California
prisons, was a decisive voice of protest during the 1960s and co-chairman of
the Black Panther Party. Cleaver's published works include* Soul on Ice
(1968) and Post-Prison Writings and Speeches *(1969).*

[1085]   We shall have our manhood.
                              Soul on Ice [1968]

[1086]   There is the America of the American dream, and there is the
          America of the American nightmare. I feel that I am a citizen of
          the American dream, that the revolutionary struggle of which I
          am a part is a struggle against the American nightmare, which is
          the present reality. It is the struggle to do away with this
          nightmare and to replace it with the American dream which
          should be the reality.
                              Conversation with Eldridge Cleaver [1970]

[1087]   I don't think you have to teach people how to be human. I think
          you have to teach them how to stop being inhumane.
                              Conversation with Eldridge Cleaver [1970]

BARBARA JORDAN

(1936 -   )   Houston, Texas

Barbara Jordan established strong political credentials in her home state of Texas, and was elected congressional representative in 1972. She served until 1978. Her autobiography, Barbara Jordan: A Self Portrait, *was published in 1978.*

[1088]   While, to be sure, we are students in a segregated institution, and while certainly we must work within the framework of the laws of our state, let it be realized by every student that the challenge facing us is not the defense of any system, be it segregated or integrated; the challenge facing us is to equip ourselves that we will be able to take our place wherever we are in the affairs of men.

Notes From a High School Debate [c. 1951]

[1089]   My faith in the constitution is whole.

Address, National Television [July 25, 1974]

[1090]   If you had to work in the environment of Washington, D.C. as I do, and watch those men who are so imprisoned and so confined by their 18th-century thought patterns, you would know that if anybody is going to be liberated, it's men who must be liberated in this country.

Address, International Women's Year Conference, Austin, Texas [November 10, 1975]

[1091]   The women of this world . . . must exercise leadership quality, dedication, concern, and commitment which is not going to be shattered by inanities and ignorance and idiots who would view our cause as one that is violative of the American dream of equal rights for everyone.

Address, International Women's Year Conference, Austin, Texas [November 10, 1975]

[1092]   What the people want is very simple. They want an America as good as its promise.

Address, Commencement, Harvard University [June 16, 1977]

[1093]   The stakes . . . are too high for government to be a spectator sport.
                    Address, Commencement, Harvard University
                    [June 16, 1977]

[1094]   When do any of us ever do enough?
                    Interview, *Senior Scholastic* [October, 1977]

BILL COSBY

(1937 -   )   Philadelphia, Pennsylvania

Comedian Bill Cosby began his career as a performer in the coffee houses of
Philadelphia, and has since expanded his talents in television, recordings,
writing, and education. He starred in the film hits "Uptown Saturday
Night" (1974) and "A Piece of the Action" (1977). Bill Cosby's Personal
Guide to Tennis Power *and* Fat Albert's Survival Kit *were published in 1975.*

[1095]   You can never give complete authority and over-all power to
                    anyone until trust can be proven.
                    Ebony [September, 1966]

[1096]   [On television]:

         We must realize that unless a show is an educational program out of
         black America, you're not going to find reality.
                    Ebony [September, 1966]

[1097]   Television is business, and business is America.
                    Ebony [September, 1966]

[1098]   The fact that I'm not trying to win converts bugs some people, but
                    I don't think an entertainer *can*. I've never known any white
                    bigot to pay to see a black man, unless the black man was being
                    hung.
                    Interview, *Playboy* [May, 1969]

[1099]   The greatest moment of an award . . . is when they announce your
                    name, the moment when you're expected to say thank you. Then
                    it's on to the next thing. You can't hang around bathing your
                    body in the reflection of a trophy.
                    Interview, *Playboy* [May, 1969]

[1100]   There can't be an argument over the fact that we should have
         equality in America. But the white man doesn't want us to have
         it, because then he'll be giving up a freedom of his—to reject us
         because of color.
                            Interview, *Playboy* [May, 1969]

[1101]   When the French, Poles and Czechs come off the boat, they're
         welcomed to America, "the land of the free, the home of the
         brave." The Statue of Liberty welcomes them, but it doesn't
         welcome the man who was born here—the black man. There's no
         lamp lit for him; so the black man has to climb up there and light
         it for himself.
                            Interview, *Playboy* [May, 1969]

[1102]   . . . it isn't a matter of black is beautiful as much as it is white is not
         all that's beautiful. . . .
                            Interview, *Playboy* [May, 1969]

[1103]   If white America chooses to withhold equality from the black man,
         the result is going to be a disaster for this country. But if whites
         allow the black man the same civil rights they themselves take for
         granted, then they're really in store for a shock; this country will
         turn into the coolest and grooviest society the world has ever
         seen.
                            Interview, *Playboy* [May, 1969]

[1104]   The serve was invented so that the net can play.
                            Bill Cosby's Personal Guide to Tennis Power [1975]

[1105]   People who live in glass houses shouldn't walk around in their
         underwear.
                            Fat Albert's Survival Kit [1975]

[1106]   A word to wise ain't necessary—it's the stupid ones who need
         the advice.
                            Fat Albert's Survival Kit [1975]

[1107]   If you itch, scratch. If you still itch, take a bath.
                            Fat Albert's Survival Kit [1975]

[1108]   I don't know the key to success, but the key to failure is trying to
         please everybody.
                            Ebony [June, 1977]

ELEANOR HOLMES NORTON
(1937 -   )   Washington, D.C.

Eleanor Holmes Norton has devoted her professional career to the on-going struggle of equal rights for all Americans. She was director of the New York City Commission on Human Rights (1970-1976) and headed the U.S. Equal Opportunity Commission (1977-1981).

[1109]   The only way to make sure people you agree with can speak is to support the rights of people you don't agree with.
New York Post [March 28, 1970]

[1110]   Being black has made me sensitive to any group who finds limitations put on it.
New York Post [March 28, 1970]

[1111]   This country would go bankrupt in a day if the Supreme Court suddenly ordered the powers that be to pay back wages to children of slaves and to the women who have worked all their lives for half wages or no pay.
McCall's [October, 1971]

[1112]   The essence of a free life is being able to choose the style of living you prefer free from exclusion and without the compulsion of conformity or law.
New York, Mecca or Menace, Commencement Address, Barnard College, New York, New York [June 6, 1972]

GEORGE LESTER JACKSON
(1941 - 1971)   Chicago, Illinois

George Jackson was one of the new breed of Afro-American revolutionaries spawned within the confines of America's prisons. He was killed in an alleged escape attempt from Soledad Prison in California. Soledad Brother, a collection of Jackson's letters written during his imprisonment, was published in 1970.

[1113]   The buffets and blows of this have and have-not society have engendered in me a flame that will live, will live to grow, until it either destroys my tormentor or myself.
Letter to His Father [March, 1965]

[1114]   The men of our group have developed as a result of living under a
         ruthless system, a set of mannerisms that numb the soul. We have
         been made the floor mat of the world. . . .
                        Letter to His Mother [March, 1966]

[1115]   . . . the monster they've engendered in me will return to torment its
         maker, from the grave, the pit, descent into hell won't turn me.
         I'll crawl back to dog his trail forever. They won't defeat my
         revenge, never, never. I'm part of a righteous people who anger
         slowly, but rage undammed. We gather at his door in such a
         number that the rumbling of our feet will make the earth tremble.
                        Letter to My Friend [March 24, 1970]

[1116]   They'll never count me among the broken men.
                        Letter to Fay [April, 1970]

JESSE JACKSON

(1941 -   )   Greenville, South Carolina

*Clergyman and civil rights leader Jesse Jackson was active with SCLC
(Southern Christian Leadership Conference) in the 1960s, and was national
director of Operation Breadbasket (1966-1971). He is currently executive
director of PUSH (People United To Save Humanity), and PUSH-Excel, an
educational program for black youth. A biography,* Jesse Jackson: the
Man, *by Barbara A. Reynolds was published in 1975.*

[1117]   Where big money stays, big decisions are made.
                        Time [March 1, 1968]

[1118]   The reason Joe Louis will always be respected in the black
         community is that at a time when other blacks couldn't even talk
         back to white people, Joe Louis was beating them up, knocking
         them down and making them bleed.
                        Interview, *Playboy* [November, 1969]

[1119]   I hear that melting pot stuff a lot, and all I can say is that we
         haven't melted.
                        Interview, *Playboy* [November, 1969]

[1120]   White folks don't want peace; they want quiet. The price you pay
         for peace is justice. Until there is justice, there will be no peace or
         quiet.
                                    Interview, *Playboy* [November, 1969]

[1121]   The burden of being black is that you have to be superior just to be
         equal. But the glory of it is that, once you achieve, you have
         achieved, indeed.
                            Interview, *Christian Science Monitor* [September 26, 1979]

[1122]   A lot of time people need more hope than help. Prophets give
         people direction and information and help. This is all people
         need.
                                    Interview, *Newsday* [September 28, 1980]

MUHAMMAD ALI

(1942 -   )   Louisville, Kentucky

*Three-time world heavyweight champion Muhammad Ali is considered the
greatest boxer in history. In addition to his ring career, Ali has appeared
frequently as a television guest artist, and was featured in the film "Freedom
Road" (1979). Ali's autobiography,* The Greatest: My Own Story, *was
published in 1976.*

[1123]   I don't have to be what you want me to be. I'm free to be who I
         want to be.
                                    The New York Times [October 25, 1964]

[1124]   Fame is no good. I can have no peace.
                                    New York Post [May 18, 1965]

[1125]   [On his fight with Floyd Patterson]:

         I'll beat him so bad he'll need a shoehorn to put his hat on.
                                    The New York Times [November 21, 1965]

[1126]   The real enemy of my people is right here.
                                    Daily Worker [April 25, 1967]

[1127]   Right now, in Louisville, Kentucky, my people are being clobbered
         and stoned . . . for simply demanding the right to live in the

neighborhood they choose. And they turn around and send us to war.

> Address, University of Chicago Anti-War Rally,
> Chicago, Illinois [May, 1967]

[1128] I believe I was born to help my people be free.

> *Newsweek* [April 7, 1969]

[1129] I'm one black man who got loose.

> *New York Daily News* [August 8, 1969]

[1130] Wars of nations are fought to change maps. But wars on poverty are fought to map changes.

> *The New York Times* [March 6, 1975]

[1131] I'm so fast I could hit you before God gets the news.

> *The New York Times* [June 29, 1975]

[1132] Christianity is a good philosophy if you live it, but it's controlled by white people who preach it but don't practice it. They just organize it and use it any which way they want to.

> Interview, *Playboy* [November, 1975]

[1133] The man who views the world at 50 the same as he did at 20 has wasted 30 years of his life.

> Interview, *Playboy* [November, 1975]

[1134] I know I got it made while the masses of black people are catchin' hell, but as long as they ain't free, I ain't free.

> Interview, *Playboy* [November, 1975]

[1135] There are no pleasures in a fight, but some of my fights have been a pleasure to win.

> Interview, *Playboy* [November, 1975]

[1136] [On boxing]:

It's just a job. Grass grows, birds fly, waves pound the sand. I beat people up.

> *The New York Times* [April 6, 1977]

[1137] [On Tarzan]:

An image used to brainwash the black world. It goes along with angels who are white, Jesus was white, Miss America is white,

Miss World is white, angel food cake is white, and devil's food cake is black.

The Village Voice [June 6, 1977]

[1138]   To be a great champion you must believe you are the best. If you're not, pretend you are.

Address, Dacca, Bangladesh [February 19, 1978]

[1139]   If there's one thing I know, it's how to sell the show.

City News [September 10, 1978]

[1140]   People will know you're serious when you produce.

Television interview with Dick Cavett [June 23, 1980]

HUBERT GEROLD (H. RAP) BROWN

(1943 -   )   Baton Rouge, Louisiana

H. Rap Brown was among the Afro-American radicals to surface during the 1960s. His experiences are recorded in Die, Nigger, Die! *(1969).*

[1141]   The liberation of oppressed people across the world depends upon the liberation of black people in this country.

Address, 19th anniversary of the *National Guardian*,
Hotel Americana, New York, New York [October 27, 1967]

[1142]   Aggression is the order of the day.

Letter from Jail [February 21, 1968]

[1143]   You cannot legislate an attitude. . . .

Die, Nigger, Die! [1969]

[1144]   Death is the price of revolution.

Die, Nigger, Die! [1969]

[1145]   I'd rather see a cat with a processed head and a natural mind than a natural head and a processed mind. It ain't what's on your head, it's what's in it.

Die, Nigger, Die! [1969]

[1146]   Violence is as American as cherry pie.

Die, Nigger, Die [1969]

ANGELA YVONNE DAVIS
(1944 -   )   Birmingham, Alabama

Social activist Angela Davis graduated with honors from Brandeis University, studied philosophy in Germany, taught briefly at U.C.L.A., and was once on the FBI's "Most Wanted" list. She is co-founder of the National Alliance Against Racist and Political Oppression, and has written an autobiography, Angela Davis *(1974).*

[1147] In the act of resistance the rudiments of freedom are already
          present.
> *Lectures on Liberation, I* [c. 1968]

[1148] The independence of the master is based on the dependence of the
          slave.
> *Lectures on Liberation, II* [c. 1968]

[1149] We have to talk about liberating minds as well as liberating society.
> Discussion between Angela Davis and Herbert Marcuse,
> University of California, Berkeley Campus
> [October 24, 1969]

[1150] . . . we have accumulated a wealth of historical experience which
          confirms our belief that the scales of American justice are out of
          balance.
> Statement to the Court, Marin County Courthouse, Marin
> County, California [January 5, 1971]

[1151] . . . racism cannot be separated from capitalism.
> *An Open Letter to High School Students*, written in Marin
> County Jail [March 23, 1971]

[1152] We know that the road to freedom has always been stalked by
          death.
> *Tribute to George Jackson, Daily World* [August 25, 1971]

[1153] . . . human beings cannot be willed and molded into non-existence.
> *Lessons: From Attica to Soledad, The New York Times*
> [October 8, 1971]

[1154]   The ruling circles are refusing to recognize that my freedom was
         won in the streets of this country and in the streets of the whole
         world.

> Address, rally in celebration of her court acquittal,
> Madison Square Garden, New York, New York
> [June 29, 1972]

[1155]   The struggle goes on.

> *People Before Profits*, Address, Harlem Rally,
> New York, New York [July 18, 1980]

NIKKI GIOVANNI

(1944 -   )   Knoxville, Tennessee

*Poet Nikki Giovanni was an honor graduate of Fisk University and gained
national prominence in the sixties when black protest was at its height.
Giovanni's poems are published in* Black Feeling, Black Talk, Black Judgment *(1970).*

[1156]   childhood remembrances are always a drag
         if you're Black
         you always remember things like living in Woodlawn
         with no inside toilet
         and if you become famous or something
         they never talk about how happy you were to have
         your mother
         all to yourself and
         how good the water felt when you got your bath
         from one of those
         big tubs that folk in chicago barbecue in
         and somehow when you talk about home
         it never gets across how much you
         understood their feelings
         as the whole family attended meetings about Hollydale
         and even though you remember
         your biographers never understand
         your father's pain as he sells his stock
         and another dream goes
         And though you're poor it isn't poverty that
         concerns you

and though they fought a lot
it isn't your father's drinking that makes any difference
but only that everybody is together and you
and your sister have happy birthdays and very good
Christmasses
and I really hope no white person ever has cause
to write about me
because they never understand
Black love is Black wealth and they'll
probably talk about my hard childhood
and never understand that
all the while I was quite happy
                    Nikki-Rosa [1968]

[1157]   As things/come
         let's destroy
         them we can destroy
         what we be/come
         let's build
         what we become
         when we dream
                    Word Poem (Perhaps Worth Considering) [c. 1968]

PROVERBS

Cameroon

DUALA

[1158]   A chattering bird builds no nest.

[1159]   Foresight spoils nothing.

[1160]   The stream won't be advised, therefore, its course is crooked.

Dahomey (Benin)/Togo/Ghana

EWE

[1161]   Distance suppresses the unpleasant.

[1162]   The gums best understand the teeth's affairs.

[1163]   When the snake is in the house, one need not discuss the matter at length.

[1164]   Crooked wood makes crooked ashes.

[1165]   Dirty water will also wash dirt.

Ghana

ACCRA

[1166]   Quarrel is not a food which is eaten.

[1167]   Whoever wants me as I am is content.

[1168]   Two ears, but they do not hear two stories.

[1169]   A river moves a river on.

[1170]   Hate has no medicine.

[1171]   It is the ear that troubles the mouth.

[1172]   If stretching were wealth, the cat would be rich.

[1173]   Winds have ears.

Ghana/Togo/Ivory Coast

ASHANTI

[1174] The monkey says that there is nothing like poverty for taking the conceit out of a man.

[1175] When you are a child, do not laugh at a short man.

[1176] An old man was in the world before a chief was born.

[1177] A slave's wisdom is in his master's head.

[1178] Even if your mother is not a good woman, she is your mother, nevertheless.

[1179] The white man lives in the castle; when he dies he lies in the ground.

[1180] When the fool is told a proverb, the meaning of it has to be explained to him.

[1181] When two men of equal wisdom play together, discord arises.

[1182] In truth there is no deceit.

[1183] One falsehood spoils a thousand truths.

[1184] Poverty is like honey. It is not peculiar to one place alone.

[1185] No one tests the depth of a river with both his feet.

[1186] He who is guilty is the one that has much to say.

[1187] Ancient things remain in the ears. (Tradition survives.)

TWI

[1188] Ingratitude is sooner or later fatal to its author.

[1189] Poverty makes a free man become a slave.

[1190] When the cat dies, the mice rejoice.

[1191] The eye envies, not the ear.

[1192] The slave does not choose his master.

[1193] When the occasion comes, the proverb comes.

Liberia

GREBO

[1194] The moon travelled at night until day overtook it.

JABO

[1195]   The fruit must have a stem before it grows.

[1196]   Leopard says: If man pushes you, then you push him.

[1197]   Buffalo says: Once you budge from your place, it's no longer your place.

[1198]   Evil deeds are like perfume—difficult to hide.

[1199]   Children are the wisdom of the nation.

[1200]   A grown-up who follows children is a fool.

[1201]   A beggar has no dignity.

[1202]   When it rains, the roof always drips the same way.

KRAHN

[1203]   Never try to catch a black cat at night.

VAI

[1204]   Your food is close to your stomach, but you must put it in your mouth first.

[1205]   When one man has his stomach full, it cannot satisfy every man.

[1206]   Do not look where you fell, but where you slipped.

Mali/Senegal/Gambia/Ivory Coast/Guinea/ Upper Volta/Ghana/Sierre Leone/Liberia

BAMBARA

[1207]   Each thing has its moment.

[1208]   Today's hunger does not share itself with tomorrow's hunger.

[1209]   One does not give a gift without motive.

[1210]   The word of the old man is a benediction.

[1211]   God gives nothing to those who keep their arms crossed.

[1212]   The desires of the lazy are too great for their labors.

[1213]   He who tells the truth is not well liked.

MALINKE

[1214]   Everybody loves a fool, but nobody wants him for a son.

[1215]   One is stopped not for what he thinks but for what he says.

[1216] If you wait for tomorrow, tomorrow comes. If you don't wait for tomorrow, tomorrow comes.

[1217] Nothing is achieved in a dream.

[1218] Better a refusal than deception.

[1219] News does not have wings. Yet it can cross the seven seas.

[1220] Wisdom comes with age.

Nigeria

EFIK

[1221] A knot in the tree spoils the axe; famine spoils friendship.

[1222] His heart lies quiet like limpid water.

[1223] The cricket cries, the year changes.

[1224] Time causes remembrance.

[1225] His wealth is superior to him.

[1226] God creates dreams.

[1227] Thought breaks the heart.

HAUSA

[1228] One who has never had a flogging will not pay any attention when you merely tell him to stop.

[1229] If you are not going to drink the pap, stop stirring it.

[1230] A big head is a big load.

[1231] The one in front has reached there, the one behind only hears about it.

[1232] As useless as a blind man turning around to look.

[1233] Hit a child and quarrel with its mother.

[1234] A war without headquarters is an expedition.

[1235] A multitude of words cloaks a lie.

[1236] May God preserve us from "if I had known."

[1237] Two is a pile, the third falls down.

[1238] Don't look for speed in a cheap horse; be content if it neighs.

[1239] Whoever spurns what is short, has not trodden on a scorpion.

[1240] For news of the heart, ask the face.

[1241] Profit is profit, even in Mecca.

IBO

[1242] All is never said.

[1243] A man's deeds are his life.

[1244] The proverb is the leaf that they use to eat a word.

[1245] Taking thought is strength.

NUPE

[1246] Force will never be without a place to sit down.

[1247] Money kills more people than a club.

Nigeria/Dahomey (Benin)/Sudan/Senegal/Guinea/Ivory Coast/ Mali/Upper Volta/Niger/Cameroon

FULFULDE

[1248] The one-eyed man doesn't thank God until he sees a blind man.

[1249] Borrowing is the first-born of poverty.

[1250] Silence is also speech.

[1251] Going slowly does not stop one from arriving.

[1252] No one is without knowledge except him who asks no questions.

[1253] Yesterday's cold has gone with yesterday's firewood.

[1254] Mosquitoes work, bite, then sing.

[1255] It is not what you wish that you will get but what is wished for you.

[1256] A dark night brings fear, but man still more.

[1257] An enemy slaughters, a friend distributes.

[1258] Be the town ever so far, there is another beyond it.

[1259] Guile excels strength.

[1260] Whoever cooks the food of malice, remnants will stick to his pocket.

Nigeria/Niger/Chad

KANURI

[1261] Wisdom is not in the eye, but in the head.

[1262] At the bottom of patience is heaven.

[1263] Property is the prop of life.

[1264] Hold a true friend with both thy hands.

[1265] The dawn has cut through. (Daybreak)

[1266] Hope is the pillar of the world.

Nigeria/Dahomey (Benin)/Togo

YORUBA

[1267] The thoughtless strong man is the chief among lazy men.

[1268] The dove finds everywhere comfortable.

[1269] There is no idol as expensive as the stomach; it receives offerings every day.

[1270] Truth came to market and could not be sold; we buy lies with ready cash.

[1271] Those killed by lack of wisdom are numerous. Those killed by wisdom do not amount to anything.

[1272] Poverty is "Who knows you?"; prosperity is "I am your relative."

[1273] Children are the clothes of men.

[1274] The white man made the pencil; he also made the eraser.

[1275] When hunger gets inside you, nothing else can.

[1276] However far the stream flows, it never forgets its source.

[1277] If you throw a stone in the market, you are liable to kill your kinsman.

[1278] Work is the medicine for poverty.

[1279] Covetousness is the father of unsatisfied desires.

[1280] Self-conceit deprives the wasp of honey.

[1281] Respect the elders; they are our fathers.

[1282] Perseverance is everything.

[1283] When the fox dies, the fowls never mourn; for the fox never rears a chicken.

[1284] The young cannot teach tradition to the old.

Senegal/Gambia

WOLOF

[1285] Lies, though many, will be caught by the truth as soon as she rises up.

[1286] The sky is the king of sheds.

[1287] The teeth serve as a fence to the mouth.

[1288] Not to know is bad; not to wish to know is worse.

[1289] Before one replies one must be present.

[1290] Without fingers the hand would be a spoon.

[1291] He who runs away and escapes is clever.

[1292] Before healing others, heal thyself.

[1293] Before proceeding, one must reach.

[1294] The split tree still grows.

[1295] He who can do nothing, does nothing.

[1296] Before eating, open thy mouth.

[1297] If you know the beginning, the end will not trouble you.

[1298] If the stars were loaves, many people would sleep out.

EAST AFRICA

Ethiopia

AMHARIC

[1299] The custom of a country embarrasses the king.

[1300] A toga that one drapes while running, also comes untied while one is running.

[1301] A powerful friend becomes a powerful enemy.

[1302] He who shames his parents stinks.

[1303] Honor is remote to those who tell lies.

[1304] Man begins, God finishes.

[1305] Who touches a father touches the son.

[1306] Wisdom enclosed in the heart is like a light in a jug.

[1307] Truth and morning become light with time.

Kenya

BONDEI

[1308] A heavy burden does not kill on the day it is carried.

[1309] The journey of folly has to be travelled a second time.

[1310] Today's satiety is tomorrow's hunger.

[1311] Sticks in a bundle are unbreakable.

[1312] A traveller with a tongue does not lose his way.

[1313] The man who goes ahead stumbles, that the man who follows may
        have his wits about him.

GIRYAMA

[1314] Tellers there are, listeners there are not.

KIKUYU

[1315] Necessities never end.

[1316] Nobody walks with another man's gait.

[1317] On the way to one's beloved there are no hills.

[1318] Self-defense is not fear.

Tanzania/Somalia/Zaire/Uganda/Kenya

SWAHILI

[1319] After distress, solace.

[1320] The cultivator is one; the eaters are many.

[1321] Being of use does no harm.

[1322] Aiming isn't hitting.

[1323] Standing is still going.

[1324] Bitter truth is better than sweet falsehood.

[1325] God created no man evil.

[1326] Fear a silent man; he has drums of the lips.

[1327] Truth-teller makes no mistake.

[1328] The soul has no price.

[1329] A man who has absolutely nothing doesn't know what poverty means.

[1330] A good thing sells itself; a bad thing advertises itself for sale.

[1331] A slave has no choice.

NORTH AFRICA

Egypt

[1332] The opinion of the intelligent is better than certainty of the ignorant.

[1333] Dine and recline if for two minutes; sup and walk if for two paces.

[1334] A sultan without the spirit of justice is like a river without water.

[1335] If there were no fault there would be no pardon.

[1336] In hell there are no fans.

[1337] No darkness like ignorance.

[1338] He who is lame visits the one who breaks his foot.

[1339] Poverty without debt is real wealth.

[1340] The fool can no more taste the sweetness of wisdom than the man with a cold can appreciate the scent of a rose.

[1341] Truth is the porter of God.

[1342] The tyrant is only the slave turned inside out.

[1343] There are two kinds of insatiable men: the scientist and the money-man.

[1344] Learn politeness from the impolite.

[1345] Equality in injustice is justice.

[1346] No friendship except after enmity.

[1347] Moderation is a tree with roots of contentment, and fruits of tranquility and peace.

[1348] He who chatters with you will chatter of you.

[1349]   Patience opens the door of rest.

[1350]   If you are ugly, be winsome.

[1351]   Your relations are your scorpions.

Libya/Algeria/Morocco/Tunisia

BERBER

[1352]   An intelligent enemy is better than an ignorant friend.

[1353]   However high the slanderer may rise, he will find the truth above
         him.

[1354]   He who does not travel will not know the value of men.

[1355]   The mouse in his hole is king.

[1356]   He who sows thorns must walk on them barefoot.

[1357]   In the gate of patience there is no crowding.

[1358]   Compete, don't envy.

[1359]   The true believer begins with himself.

[1360]   Little with health is better than much with sickness.

[1361]   Endurance pierces marble.

[1362]   The other world is a dwelling place of which this world is the
         vestibule.

[1363]   Silence is the door of consent.

[1364]   Instruction in youth is like engraving in stones.

[1365]   The man who is not jealous in love, does not love.

[1366]   One survives all wounds except those of a critic.

[1367]   A neighbor close by is better than a brother far away.

CENTRAL AFRICA

Uganda

GANDA

[1368]   Caution is not cowardice; even the ants marched armed.

[1369]   He who takes hold slowly goes a long way.

[1370]   Brethren love each other when they are equally rich.

[1371]   Resting isn't getting there.

[1372]   Even a wise man makes a mistake; the ears do not perceive a smell.

[1373]   Words are easy, friendship hard.

NYORO

[1374]   Too much confidence lost the frog its tail.

[1375]   The flute of old age chafes the lips.

Zaire

CONGO

[1376]   Those who inherit fortunes are often more troublesome than those
         who make them.

[1377]   Justice becomes injustice when it makes two wounds on a head that
         deserves one.

[1378]   Pride only goes the length one can spit.

[1379]   Thirst cannot be quenched by proxy.

MONGO

[1380]   The irritator harrasses; the whites torment us.

[1381]   "I know, I know" surpasses everything.

[1382]   He who cries like a parrot is a parrot.

[1383]   Rivalry is better than envy.

[1384]   War ends nothing.

[1385]   He who is proud of his clothing is not rich.

[1386]   Make conversation with one who surpasses you, not with one who
         quarrels with you.

[1387]   A small party; a big affair.

SOUTHERN AFRICA

Botswana

CHUANA

[1388]   An ant once made an errand boy of an elephant.

[1389]   Never follow a beast into its lair.

[1390]   Comrades in plunder know each other.

[1391]   Sleep, the near relative of death.

[1392]   Getting the better of a man is not finishing him.

[1393]   Ears usually witness a matter without invitation.

[1394]   A fool is a treasure to the wise.

[1395]   God is not partial.

[1396]   Love paralyzes the joints.

[1397]   Not her face, but her heart is comely.

[1398]   Wealth and poverty lie together.

Lesotho/Botswana/Republic of South Africa

SOTHO

[1399]   Hit one ring and the whole chain will resound.

[1400]   May your feet go softly all your days, and may your face be as the
           morning sun. (Blessing)

[1401]   We are people because of other people.

[1402]   If you wound your enemy with a two-pointed assegai, it hurts you
           also.

[1403]   Break not your heart; sorrow will roll away the mists at sunrise.

[1404]   It is not a person; it is only the grave of one.

[1405]   Woman is king.

Mozambique/Republic of South Africa/Swaziland/Zimbabwe

RONGA

[1406]   A master of a fool does not laugh at him.

[1407]   Shame has watchmen.

Republic of South Africa/Mozambique/Zambia/Zimbabwe

XHOSA

[1408]   One does not become great by claiming greatness.

[1409]   One fly does not provide for another.

[1410]   A spy for both. (Tattletale)

[1411] There is no beast that does not roar in its own den.

[1412] The sun never sets without fresh news.

ZULU

[1413] One man, no man.

[1414] He who hates, hates himself.

[1415] Responsibility rests not with the messenger but with the one who sent him.

[1416] He who installs a king never rules with him.

[1417] Equals have met.

[1418] Hope does not kill.

[1419] A mother is a mother, ye Zulus!

[1420] Death has no modesty.

[1421] Loneliness will wipe you out.

CAPE VERDE ISLANDS

[1422] A man without a wife is like a vase without flowers.

[1423] Fate conquers the coward.

[1424] To whom God gives wounds he will give ointment.

[1425] Every week has its Friday.

[1426] However early you rise, day breaks no earlier.

[1427] On account of one, all pay.

DEMOCRATIC REPUBLIC OF MADAGASCAR

MALAGASY

[1428] The discreet man knows how to hold his tongue.

[1429] The rifle is the son of a cannon; the voice of the father is the voice of the son.

[1430] Parents honor parents.

[1431] One doesn't notice his own faults, or one doesn't want to admit them.

[1432]   Poverty is an orphan abandoned for money and riches.

[1433]   To die in the flower of age is a life offered in sacrifice.

[1434]   Justice is like fire; if one covers it with a veil, it still burns.

[1435]   The lazy and those who want favors, work hard when they are
         being watched.

THE CARIBBEAN

Bahama Islands

[1436]   When han' full him hab plenty company.

[1437]   Big blanket make man sleep late.

[1438]   Misfortune nebber t'row cloud.

[1439]   Cunning better dan strong.

[1440]   Ev'ry day fishin' day, but no ev'ry day catch fish.

[1441]   Follow fashion break monkey' neck.

[1442]   When eye no see, mout' no talk.

[1443]   Hog run for him life; dog run for him character.

[1444]   Man can't whistle and smoke one time.

[1445]   Cockroach nebber so drunk, he no cross fowl yard.

[1446]   Rain nebber fall on one man' door.

[1447]   Sleep have no massa.

[1448]   No t'row away dirty water befo' you hab clean.

[1449]   You shake man han', you no shake him heart.

[1450]   Time longer dan rope.

Cuba

[1451]   Believe only half of what you see.

[1452]   Every head is a world.

[1453]   The new pleases and the old satisfies.

[1454]   Rolling stones meet each other.

[1455]   He who sows wind reaps a tempest.

Guadeloupe

[1456]   Honesty is reflected in the face.

[1457]   Near to church, near to hell.

[1458]   It is the first word that counts.

[1459]   A small cloud is useful to a big boat.

[1460]   A day of disputes; a day of insults.

[1461]   To enter is nothing; it is the leaving that counts.

Haiti

[1462]   Shoes alone know if the stockings have holes.

[1463]   All food is good to eat, but all words are not fit to speak.

[1464]   The sun sets, misfortunes never.

[1465]   The dog has four feet, but he does not walk them in four roads.

[1466]   The empty bag cannot stand up. (A hungry slave's reply when scolded for idleness.)

[1467]   The good white man dies; the bad remains.

[1468]   Let him who wishes to hatch sit on his own eggs.

[1469]   Poor people entertain with heart.

[1470]   All that you do not know is greater than you.

[1471]   The fish trusts the water, and it is in the water that it is cooked.

[1472]   Little by little the bird makes its nest.

[1473]   When a cockroach is giving a dance he never invites a chicken.

[1474]   Every vein affects the heart.

[1475]   It is because the crab has so much heart that he has no head.

[1476]   Beyond the mountains there are more mountains again.

Jamaica

[1477]   No put yourself in a barrel when match box can hol' you.

[1478]   "Come see me" is one t'ing, but "come lib wid me" is another.

[1479]   Good fren' better dan money in a pocket.

[1480] Before you married keep you' two eye open; after you married shut one.

[1481] De more you look de less you see.

[1482] Dem say a so a no so, dem say a no so a so.

[1483] Do more, talk less.

[1484] Every man no dribe dem donkey same way.

[1485] Finger nebber say "look yah," him say, "look yondah."

[1486] Handsome-to-pieces. (Superlative)

[1487] Man dat carry straw no fe fool wid fire.

[1488] Nearer to church, farder from God.

[1489] *Nyanga* (pride) mek crab go sideways.

[1490] When cow tail cut off, God-a-mighty brush fly.

[1491] Studeration beat education.

[1492] When mischief-maker meet, de devil go to dinner.

[1493] Sweet tongue hide bad heart.

[1494] When chicken tie up, cockroach want explanation.

[1495] Patient man ride jackass.

[1496] When man drunk, him walk and stagger; when 'ooman drunk, him sit down an' consider.

[1497] Clothes cover character.

[1498] When man dead, him done.

[1499] Sun cool, you call him afternoon.

Trinidad

[1500] Good fortune is never hunchbacked.

[1501] Conversation is food for the ears.

[1502] The drum makes a great fuss because it is empty inside.

[1503] Mouth open, story jump out.

[1504] The belly has no ears.

[1505] Fair words (sweet mouth) buy horses on credit.

[1506] It is the frog's own tongue that betrays him.

[1507] Mothers beget children but not their hearts.

[1508] The monkey knows which tree to climb.

[1509] Words have no color.

[1510] A penny will buy trouble which pounds cannot cure.

SOUTH AMERICA

Brazil

[1511] The shadow of the white man is the same as the Negro's.

[1512] The happiness of the poor man lasts only a day.

[1513] The white man dancing, the Negro playing.

[1514] The flesh of the white man also smells.

[1515] The flesh of the Negro supports the plantation.

[1516] In a quarrel with the white man, the Negro doesn't win.

[1517] A black chicken lays a white egg.

[1518] Judas was white and sold Christ.

[1519] The Negro is crying, the Negro is joking.

[1520] The Negro woman is the pepper, and everyone receives
        nourishment from her.

Guyana

[1521] Devil tempt but he no force.

[1522] "Don't care" keep might big house.

[1523] Promise get friend; perform keep him.

Surinam

[1524] The bones, before being thrown into the street, were on the
        master's table.

[1525] One has two ears but one never hears the words twice.

UNITED STATES

[1526] Rooster makes mo' racket dan de hen w'at de aig.

[1527] Licker talks mighty loud w'en it git loose fum de jug.

[1528] One-eyed mule can't be handled on de blind side.

[1529] Cockroach can never justify himself to a hungry chicken.

[1530] Don't chain your dog with sausages.

[1531] Whoever heard of a mouse making a nest in a cat's ear.

[1532] Poverty ain't no screw, but it's a very big nail. (Creole)

[1533] It don't take a prophet to recollect bad luck.

[1534] De church bells sometimes do better work dan de sermon.

[1535] De price of yo' hat ain't de measure of yo' brain.

[1536] De graveyard is de cheapes' boardin' house.

[1537] Buyin' on credit is robbin' next year's crop.

[1538] A mule can tote so much goodnes in his face that he don't have none left for his hind legs.

[1539] Man who gits hurt workin' oughta show de scars.

[1540] De noise of de wheels don't measure de load in de wagon.

[1541] Every man for hisself and God for we all. (Geechee)

[1542] Live, learn, die, and forget all. (Geechee)

[1543] Day is short as ever; time's as long as it has been. (Geechee)

[1544] Yestiddy din take keer ob itse'f.

[1545] When de fros' sen' you wud by de norf win', you better git de punkins.

[1546] 'Tis dangersome to let some folks food wid a gun—ef de gun's any count.

[1547] Oberseer used to reggerlate de daybreak.

[1548] Perliteness floats 'round loose on 'lection day.

[1549] Tain't much diffunce 'twist a hornit an' a yaller-jacket when dey bofe git under your clo'es.

[1550] You can't hurry up good times by waitin' for 'em.

[1551] A man dat pets a live catfish ain't crowded wid brains.

[1552] De people dat stirs up de mos' racket in de meetin' house ain't always de bes' Christians.

[1553]   Life is short and full of blisters.

[1554]   In God we trust, all others cash.

[1555]   De crawfish in a hurry look like he trying to git dar yesterday.

[1556]   He drinks so much whiskey that he staggers in his sleep.

[1557]   Time flies, but teks its own time in doin' it.

[1558]   It's de late worm dat gits caught by de early bird.

[1559]   If you can fool half the people all the time, that's enough—don't
         be a hog.

[1560]   The blacker the berry the sweeter the juice.

AUTHOR INDEX

SUBJECT
AND KEY WORD INDEX

ABILITY, race is not measured by its A to condemn (Washington) [398]
   had I the A and could I reach the nation's ear (Douglass) [218]
   initiative is the A to do the right thing (Miller) [443]
   our A to create (W. M. Young) [952]
   to thrive and live (Chestnutt) [408]
ABLE, few people are A to face the realities (Schuyler) [703]
   I have never been A to discover (B. Williams) [558]
ABOLITION is the dawn of liberty (de Assis) [316]
ABOMINATIONS, evil of gross and monstrous A (Crummell) [239]
ABSOLUTE truth is incompatible (de Assis) [303]
ABSTRACT, European reason is A (Senghor) [821]
ABUNDANT, when a thing is A (Tertullian) [31]
ABUSE us as you will (Langston) [279]
ACCELERATES, revolution A evolution (K. Miller) [447]
ACCEPT, hard to A strength and goodness (Bailey) [935]
ACCEPTANCE of prevailing standards (Toomer) [688]
ACCOMPANIMENTS of the slave system (Douglass) [215]
ACCOMPLISH, no race can A anything (Washington) [400]
ACCOMPLISHMENTS, no matter what A you make (Darben) [1012]
ACCOUNT, on A of one all pay (P) [1427]
ACCUSE, men who A women without reason (Ines de la Cruz) [60]
ACCUSED, I know the bitterness of being A and harrassed (J. Johnson) [575]
ACHIEVE, when we finally A full participation (Ellison) [886]
ACHIEVED, nothing is A in a dream (P) [1217]
ACHIEVEMENT, freedom is an internal A (Powell) [836]
ACHILLES, Tethys stretched out the waves for her A (Latino) [59]
ACQUIRED, true liberation can be A (Randolph) [664]
ACT of resistance (A. Davis) [1147]
ACTIVE, men are most A when evading real issues (Toomer) [690]
ACTIVITY, art cannot be an egotistic A (Guillén) [803]
   men of A and affluence (Cugoano) [95]
ACTS committed daily upon slave women (W. W. Brown) [202]
ADAPTABILITY of the Negro (Gibbs) [256]
ADGITATIN', I go fur A (Truth) [128]
ADJUSTMENTS, greatest handicaps to our mutual A (Pickens) [590]
ADJUSTS, man A to what he should not (Toomer) [687]
ADVERTISEMENT of eligibility (Schuyler) [708]
ADVISED, stream won't be A (P) [1160]
ADVISES, a critic A (Randall) [889]
ADVOCATES of liberty should conceive the idea (J. Forten) [110]
AFFAIR, a small party a big A (P) [1387]
AFFAIRS, gums best understand the teeth's A (P) [1162]

I defy any part of A (Robeson) [730]
if white A chooses to withhold equality (Cosby) [1103]
lynchers of A (Pickens) [598]
the Negro was invented in A (Killens) [905]
there is the A of the American dream (Cleaver) [1086]
white male A (Chisholm) [984]
AMERICAN, cheapness characterizes donations of the A people (Crummell) [248]
colleges and universities in A system (Malcolm X) [1008]
I am not A (Malcolm X) [1008]
I'm perfectly satisfied to be an A Negro (Fauset) [606]
Negro isn't a man (Yerby) [908]
Negro's temporary farewell to A Congress (G. H. White) [362]
religion and wrong (Redmond) [178]
strip A democracy and religion of its verbiage (Rogers) [581]
the A Negro must remake his past (Schomburg) [555]
there is the America of the A dream (Cleaver) [1086]
violence is as A as cherry pie (H. G. Brown) [1146]
AMERICANS, colored A in their fight for equality (Pickens) [601]
remember A (D. Walker) [117]
say we are ungrateful (D. Walker) [115]
white A cannot stand as idle spectators (Langston) [276]
white A today don't know (Hamer) [921]
AMONG men all things are common (Terence) [22]
the multitude of public prints (Sancho) [77]
ANCESTORS, the past of his A (G. Brooks) [910]
ANCIENT things remain in the ears (P) [1187]
ANGEL, an A robed in spotless white (Dunbar) [531]
too much liberty corrupts an A (Terence) [25]
ANGELS rush in when fools is almost dead (Fisher) [719]
ANGLO-SAXON, the Negro was here before the A evolved (Chestnutt) [409]
world has not been conquered for A nations (Powell) [833]
ANOMALY, a nation within a nation is an A (Douglass) [228]
ANOTHER, no race can speak for A (K. Miller) [454]
we cannot see the dreams of one A (de Assis) [320]
while one man leans against A (Langston) [277]
ANSWER to the race problem (Gregory) [1047]
ANT, made an errand boy of an elephant (P) [1388]
ANTAGONISM, race prejudice and race A (Ransom) [439]
ANTIPATHY, prejudice is not . . . dependent upon A (Ruggles) [180]
ANYBODY who believes the meek shall inherit the earth (Du Bois) [492]
ANYONE may become evil (Tertullian) [33]
who has struggled with poverty (Baldwin) [958]
ANYTHING, no race can accomplish A (Washington) [400]
nobody cares A for a man (Washington) [389]
you'll never get A from white people (Himes) [858]
APARTHEID, to eradicate racial discrimination and A (Nasser) [943]
APPEAL to the white man's pocket (Barnett) [440]
APPLIED, term A to unexpected fires (Schuyler) [706]
APRIL, end of A (Beckwourth) [142]
ARBITRARY power exacts usury (Saint Cyprian) [40]
ARE they not part (Anderson) [280]
ARGUMENT, there can't be an A (Cosby) [1100]

BRETHREN love each other (P) [1370]
BRICK, Mrs. Coley's three-flat B (G. Brooks) [909]
BRIEF, for one B golden moment rare like wine (McKay) [657]
   give very long legs to very B ideas (de Assis) [310]
BRIGHT, sun that B swan (ibn Sa'id) [56]
   we live where the B God of day (F. Williams) [62]
BROKE, niggers hearts been B (Gaines) [1061]
BROKEN, they'll never count me among the B men (G. Jackson) [1116]
BROOMS, he used to make B and husk mats (A. Smith) [297]
BROTHER, colored B is pleased (Schuyler) [716]
   in black don't fret to death (Hurston) [777]
   judge not thy B (Martin) [422]
   my brother you flash your teeth at every hypocrisy (Diop) [1020]
BROTHERHOOD week makes me sick (Chisholm) [981]
   you remember B Week (Gregory) [1043]
BROTHERS, build now your church my B sisters (G. Brooks) [914]
   come rouse ye B rouse (Reason) [236]
BROUGHT, God's tender mercy B thee here (Hammon) [63]
BROWN, oh the B leaves (Bontemps) [752]
BRUTAL, neither B assaults nor cruel mistreatment (Lumumba) [997]
BUDGE, buffalo says once you B from your place (P) [1197]
BUFFALO says once you budge from your place (P) [1197]
BUFFETS and blows of this have and have-not society (G. Jackson) [1113]
BUILD now your church my brothers sisters (G. Brooks) [914]
BUILDS, a chattering bird B no nest (P) [1158]
   love B (Bethune) [565]
BUNDLE, sticks in a B (P) [1311]
BURDEN, a heavy B does not kill (P) [1308]
   of being black (J. Jackson) [1121]
   we ask not that others bear our B (Ransom) [435]
   white man has become black man's B (Powell) [831]
BURIED, omniscience may visit the mistakes of B sires (Vernon) [525]
BURNING, what a B shame it is (Redmond) [177]
   white man stop lynching and B (Mason) [460]
BURNS, noonday B beneath the terrible light (Heredia) [159]
   truth B up error (Truth) [136]
BURY, we will sooner B ourselves (Christophe) [112]
BUSH, praised be the B (Maran) [634]
BUSINESS, having attained success in B (F. M. Davis) [811]
   pays philanthropy begs (Du Bois) [490]
   show B taught me everything (Mabley) [681]
   some folks have to go into B (Wright) [850]
   television is B (Cosby) [1097]
BUTTER, a man's bread and B (Garvey) [614]
BUY, fair words B horses on credit (P) [1505]
   penny will B trouble (P) [1510]
   never B wit (Terence) [24]
BY thee man liveth (Akhenaton) [8]

CABIN dance the banjo and the song (Whitman) [354]
CAGED, I know why the C bird sings (Dunbar) [537]

near to C (P) [1457]
nearer to C farder from God (P) [1488]
tain't the C that makes folks (Fisher) [721]
to her great charge untrue (Reason) [237]
whatever you do do like a C steeple (Fisher) [723]
CIRCLES, ruling C refusing to recognize my freedom was won (A. Davis) [1154]
CIVILIZATION, no C can become world-wide and enduring (Roman) [464]
    of the twentieth century (Senghor) [820]
      our C is a veneer (Chestnutt) [414]
      since return to C (Henson) [477]
      white man's C is a misnomer (K. Miller) [442]
CIVILIZATIONS, old C die hard (Crogman) [329]
CIVILIZE, when you C a man (Lumumba) [998]
CLASS, ruling C or race (Himes) [855]
CLIMB, monkey knows which tree to C (P) [1508]
CLOAKS, a multitude of words C a lie (P) [1235]
CLOSE, food is C to your stomach (P) [1204]
    neighbor C by (P) [1367]
CLOSE, when time shall C the door unto the house (Braithwaite) [574]
CLOSING, only by C the ears of the soul (Crummell) [249]
CLOTH, I have wrapped my dreams in a silken C (Cullen) [775]
CLOTHED, when fleecy skies have C the ground (Banneker) [82]
CLOTHES, children are C of men (P) [1273]
    cover character (P) [1497]
CLOTHING, he who is proud of C (P) [1385]
CLOUD, misfortune nebber t'row C (P) [1438]
    small C useful to big boat (P) [1459]
CLOUDS, gray skies are just C passing over (Ellington) [742]
CLUB, money kills more people than a C (P) [1247]
COAL, I worked on a C wagon (Armstrong) [747]
COARSENESS in the songs of black men (Silvera) [824]
COAST, over on the East C (Hurston) [779]
COBBLESTONES, my C are red with England's blood (F. Johnson) [637]
COCKROACH can never justify himself (P) [1529]
    nebber so drunk (P) [1445]
    when C is giving a dance (P) [1473]
COFFIN, he wore his C for a hat (Cullen) [773]
COLD, yesterday's C has gone (P) [1253]
COLLEGE ain't so much where you been (O. Davis) [918]
COLLEGES and universities in American system (Malcolm X) [1008]
COLONY of Santo Domingo (Toussaint L'Ouverture) [90]
COLOR, free people of C have succeeded (Rock) [273]
    never have I been tempted to cross the C line (Terrell) [457]
    no prejudice against C among the slaveholders (Rock) [275]
    of the skin (Banneker) [81]
    punish guilty man of C (J. Forten) [109]
    stimulus ever presented to the man of C (Russwurm) [149]
    words have no C (P) [1509]
COLORED, Americans in their fight for equality (Pickens) [601]
    anything disgraceful in being a C man (B. Williams) [555]
    being C can be fun (O. Davis) [916]

DELICATE, hope is D suffering (Baraka) [1072]
DELUDED, most D people are the sophisticated (Schuyler) [704]
DEMANDS and grievances of the Negro (Randolph) [647]
DEMOCRACY cannot long endure with the head of a God (Yates) [363]
   is not tolerance (Himes) [856]
   strip American D of its religion and verbiage (Rogers) [581]
DEMOCRATIC, if this nation is not truly D (Crummell) [246]
DEMON the spirit of Negro hate is (Ward) [235]
DEPRIVES, self-conceit D the wasp of honey (P) [1280]
DEPTH, a purple star evolved in the D of the sky (Rabearivelo) [790]
   length and breadth the height D of prejudice (W. Allen) [262]
   no one tests D of river (P) [1185]
DEPTHS, I must hide in the intimate D of my veins (Senghor) [817]
DESCENDANTS of Africans (Christophe) [114]
DESCRIPTIVE, if there were no other fact D of slavery (Douglass) [216]
DESIGNS, how excellent are thy D (Akhenaton) [7]
DESIRES, covetousness is the father of unsatisfied D (P) [1279]
   of the lazy (P) [1212]
DESPAIR sits on this country (Baraka) [1071]
DESPAIRS, youth never D (Dumas, père) [151]
DESPISE, do not D or hate your neighbor (Vernon) [518]
DESTINY is not only a dramatist (de Assis) [311]
DETERMINE, no man can D his own force of mind (Blyden) [282]
DEVELOPED, men of our group have D (G. Jackson) [1114]
DEVIL, black is suppose to symbolize the D (Turner) [288]
   diligence outdoes the D (Terence) [26]
   race prejudice is the D unchained (Chestnutt) [411]
   tempt but he no force (P) [1521]
   when the D speaks the truth (Origen) [38]
DIAMOND, Saint Louis woman wid her D rings (Handy) [550]
DICK, name of Deadwood D (Love) [371]
DIE, blessing to D for a cause (A. Young) [1056]
   I D if I don't work (Guillén) [802]
   if I D tomorrow (Montejo) [428]
   if we must D (McKay) [652]
   if you're afraid to D (Baldwin) [965]
   in the flower of age (P) [1433]
   live learn D (P) [1542]
   old civilizations D hard (Crogman) [329]
   rather D free men (Garnet) [206]
   we must be willing to D (Powell) [830]
DIED, many a man have D (Corrothers) [508]
DIES, every black man D (O. Davis) [920]
   good white man D (P) [1467]
   it's hard for a man to live until he D (Hughes) [768]
   when the cat D (P) [1190]
   when the fox D fowls never mourn (P) [1283]
DIFFERENCE between a hornet and a yellow jacket (P) [1549]
   if God or nature intended D (K. Miller) [444]
DIFFERENCES, innate racial D (Powell) [829]
DIGNIFIER, money is a great D (Dunbar) [534]

DIGNITY, a beggar has no D (P) [1201]
DILIGENCE outdoes the devil (Terence) [26]
DIM, for the dim regions whence my fathers came (McKay) [654]
 sun sought thy D bed (McKay) [653]
DINE and recline if for two minutes (P) [1333]
DIRT, dirty water will also wash D (P) [1165]
DIRTY, no t'row away D water (P) [1448]
DISAPPEARING, rising gate with D locks (Baraka) [1075]
DISC, sun a translucent D of glass (Darío) [480]
DISCHARGE, I heard the D from a gun (Banneker) [80]
DISCIPLINE, peoples need to pass through a period of D (Blyden) [281]
DISCOURAGED, we must not become D (Washington) [403]
DISCOVER, each generation must D its mission (Fanon) [994]
 I have never been able to D (B. Williams) [558]
DISCREET man knows how to hold his tongue (P) [1428]
DISCRIMINATION, to eradicate apartheid and racial D (Nasser) [943]
DISGRACEFUL, anything D in being a colored man (B. Williams) [555]
DISGUSTING, nothing is more D (Ruggles) [182]
DISHONEST in their hostility (al-Jahiz) [54]
DISPUTES, day of D (P) [1460]
DISTANCE suppresses the unpleasant (P) [1161]
DISTINCTION, human law may know no D among men (Douglass) [223]
DISTRESS, after D solace (P) [1319]
DO a common thing in an uncommon way (Washington) [394]
 as your master bids (Ptah-hotep) [3]
 de other fellow befo' he D you (Corrothers) [506]
 everybody wants to D something (Bailey) [934]
 good man will neither speak nor D (Cugoano) [93]
 he who can D nothing (P) [1295]
 more talk less (P) [1483]
 not deceive yourselves (Carter) [478]
 not despise or hate your neighbor (Vernon) [518]
 not look where you fell (P) [1206]
 whatever you D do with all your might (Aesop) [12]
 when do we D enough (Jordan) [1094]
DOG, don't chain your D with sausages (P) [1530]
 every D has his day (Terence) [19]
 has four feet (P) [1465]
 I used to work like a D (Mabley) [680]
DOING, let your D be an exercise (Toomer) [686]
 the Negro must be up and D (Garvey) [629]
DOLLARS not only count but rule (C. T. Walker) [419]
DOMESTIC workers have done a awful lot (Childress) [945]
DONATIONS, cheapness characterizes . . . D of the American people (Crummell) [248]
DONE, when man dead him D (P) [1498]
DONKEY, every man no dribe dem D same way (P) [1484]
DOOR, patience opens the D of rest (P) [1349]
 peddling from D to door (F.M. Davis) [813]
 rain nebber fall on one man' D (P) [1446]
 silence is the D of consent (P) [1363]
 when time shall close unto the D of the house (Braithwaite) [574]
DOPE, all D can do for you is kill you (Holiday) [892]

EVERYTHING, perseverance is E (P) [1282]
  show business taught me E (Mabley) [681]
  there is but loving (Hughes) [758]
  we see is a shadow (King) [1027]
EVERYWHERE, all things are silent even homes E (Vilaire) [548]
  dove finds E comfortable (P) [1268]
EVIL, anyone may become E (Tertullian) [33]
  communications corrupt good manners (Banneker) [83]
  deeds are like perfume (P) [1198]
  God created no man E (P) [1325]
  of gross and monstrous abominations (Crummell) [239]
  those who set in motion the forces of E (Chestnutt) [412]
EVILS, past E the cause of present chaos (Powell) [835]
EVOLUTION, revolution accelerates E (K. Miller) [447]
EVOLVED, a purple star E in the depths of the sky (Rabearivelo) [790]
  the Negro was here before the Anglo-Saxon E (Chestnutt) [409]
EXACERBATED forever be this wretched slavery (W. Allen) [263]
EXAMPLES, torments of a few are E for all (Saint Cyprian) [41]
EXCELLENT, how E are thy designs (Akhenaton) [7]
EXCELS, guile E strength (P) [1259]
EXCUSE, only E for pride in individuals or races (Douglass) [227]
EXECUTE, if men . . . dare . . . to E their hatred (J. Forten) [111]
EXERCISE, let your doing be an E (Toomer) [686]
EXHAUSTION, peace is the E of strife (Gibbs) [255]
EXIST, could slavery E long (Harper) [264]
  I do perceive that lesser Gods E (Hayes) [804]
  world cannot E without ladies (Kenyatta) [666]
EXISTED, black art has always E (Bearden) [874]
EXISTS, if a writer E for social good (Ellison) [887]
  prejudice against the Negro E (Washington) [395]
EXPENSIVE, no idol as E as the stomach (P) [1269]
EXPERIENCE, man who lacks E (Ptah-hotep) [2]
  we have accumulated a wealth of E (A. Davis) [1150]
EXPRESSION, mob law is the most forcible E (Fortune) [380]
EYE, before you married keep you' two eye open (P) [1480]
  envies not the ear (P) [1191]
  when E no see (P) [1442]
  wisdom is not in the E (P) [1261]
EYES, ye whose E with pity doth run o'er (Whitman) [355]

FACE, a people must F its history squarely (Killens) [906]
  few people are able to F the realities of life (Schuyler) [703]
  honesty reflected in the F (P) [1456]
  mule can tote so much goodness in his F (P) [1538]
  not her F (P) [1397]
  we have to F the uglies (Bailey) [937]
  when F-to-face with one's self (Ellington) [737]
  why do you black your F (Fortson) [651]
FACES, not only crocus F (Randall) [890]
FACILE, courts of this land are F instruments (Griggs) [543]
FACT, negritude is a F (Senghor) [822]
  if there were no other F descriptive of slavery (Douglass) [216]

one does not become G (P) [1408]
shores of the G river full of promises (Lumumba) [996]
to be a G champion (Ali) [1138]
GREEN, water pale light-flash across dark G (Vilaire) [549]
GRIEVANCES, demands and G of the Negro (Randolph) [647]
GRIND, mills that G and grind (Hughes) [755]
GROSS, evil of G and monstrous abominations (Crummell) [239]
GROUND, old flag never touched the G (Carney) [322]
when fleecy skies have cloth'd the G (Banneker) [82]
GROUP, men of our G have developed (G. Jackson) [1114]
no G moves en masse (Bennett) [1025]
GROW, intolerance can grow (W. White) [667]
GROWN-UP who follows children is a fool (P) [1200]
GROWS, split tree still G (P) [1294]
GUARDIAN, African G of souls (Toomer) [683]
GUIDED, best men are well G by love (Saint Augustine) [47]
GUILE excels strength (P) [1259]
GUILTY folks is scared folks (Wright) [846]
he who is G (P) [1186]
punish G man of color (J. Forten) [109]
GUMS best understand the teeth's affairs (P) [1162]
GUN, I heard the discharge from a G (Banneker) [80]
'tis dangersome to let some folks fool wid a G (P) [1546]
GUTS, it takes G to take a stand (Chisholm) [969]

HABITS acquired in a state of servitude (R. Allen) [105]
HABITUAL use of the superlative (de Assis) [309]
HALF, believe only H of what you see (P) [1451]
if you can fool H the people all the time (P) [1559]
life is H insanity (Margetson) [569]
HALLUCINATION, human passion is the H (Whipper) [158]
HAND, I see now near at H (Ransom) [438]
time touches all things with a destroying H (Chestnutt) [405]
tradition is the dead H of human progress (K. Miller) [448]
when H full (P) [1436]
without fingers the H would be a spoon (P) [1290]
you shake man H (P) [1449]
HANDICAP, a white woman has one H to overcome (Terrell) [456]
HANDICAPS, greatest H to our mutual adjustment (Pickens) [590]
of my two H (Chisholm) [976]
HANDLED, one-eyed mule can't be H on de blind side (P) [1528]
HANDMAIDEN, Christian Church was H (Clarke) [898]
HANDS, hold a true friend with both thy H (P) [1264]
we are puppets in the H of Fate (Chestnutt) [413]
your fingernails drip from your H (Guillén) [799]
HANDSOME to pieces (P) [1486]
HANNIBAL, when H flashed his sword (Fortson) [649]
HAPPINESS, let no one trust the H of the moment (de Assis) [298]
of poor man (P) [1512]
white man's H (Douglass) [214]
HARD, it is a H thing to live (Du Bois) [485]
it's H for a man to live until he dies (Hughes) [768]

HUNDRED, I have had the pleasure of helping six H persons (Ruggles) [183]
   three H long ships with strident beaks (Latino) [58]
HUNGER, today's H does not share itself (P) [1208]
   today's satiety is tomorrow's H (P) [1310]
   when H gets inside you (P) [1275]
HUNGRY, give a H man a stone (Douglass) [209]
   make a good Christian out of a H man (Washington) [396]
   men have no respect for law (Garvey) [620]
HURRY, crawfish in a H (P) [1555]
   you can't H up good times (P) [1550]
HURT, black people H by white people (A. Young [1054]
   man who gets H working (P) [1539]
HUSK, he used to make brooms and H mats (A. Smith) [297]
HYPOCRISY, my brother you flash your teeth at every H (Diop) [1020]

I ain't a big-headed nigger (McKay) [659]
   ain't no w'ite folks nigger (Chestnutt) [410]
   am a man concerned with truth (Bearden) [871]
   am a Negro (W. White) [668]
   am black (Fanon) [989]
   am glad daylong for the gift of song (Braithwaite) [571]
   am my mother's daughter (Bethune) [563]
   am not a man concerned with truth (Bearden) [871]
   am not an American (Malcolm X) [1002]
   am not trying to win converts (Cosby) [1098]
   am one black man (Ali) [1129]
   am so fast (Ali) [1131]
   am well in both body and mind (Copeland) [290]
   am your fellow-man (Douglass) [210]
   believe in helping people (Mitchell) [1083]
   believe in pride of race and lineage (Du Bois) [484]
   believe racism has killed more people (Childress) [947]
   called you master (Pennington) [166]
   can't read a book (Truth) [129]
   create social images (Bearden) [870]
   chose photography (Parks) [866]
   defy any part of America (Robeson) [730]
   die if I don't work (Guillén) [802]
   do not believe that whatever is is right (Bowen) [372]
   do not hate all white people (Hansberry) [1039]
   do not wish to be free (Hammon) [64]
   do perceive that lesser gods exist (Hayes) [804]
   don't feel sorry (A. Young) [1060]
   don't have to be (Ali) [1123]
   don't let my mouth say nothin' (Armstrong) [750]
   don't like to think (Childress) [944]
   doubt not God is good (Cullen) [770]
   elect to stay on the soil (Purvis) [175]
   feel like a man who has been asleep (Malcolm X) [1009]
   feel like I'm on the outside (Wright) [842]
   feel myself a soul (Fanon) [990]

IMPOLITE, learn politeness from the I (P) [1344]
IMPOSSIBLE, beautiful night makes sleep I (Martí) [366]
    to raise and educate a race (Bowen) [375]
    when reform becomes I (K. Miller) [450]
IMPRESSIONS, men do not make I (Toomer) [698]
IN all things pure and social (Washington) [391]
    being I am equal (Toomer) [693]
    God we trust (P) [1554]
    hell there are no fans (P) [1336]
    morning part of the day (Banneker) [84]
    our day mens is awful plentiful wid us (Jasper) [190]
    politics (Randolph) [646]
    the attic (F. M. Davis) [809]
    the evening by the moonlight (Bland) [369]
    the middle of the twentieth century (Killens) [903]
    the twilight of time (Smyth) [333]
INCHES, white folks see eleven I on a foot rule (Wright) [852]
INCIDENTS, martyrs needed to create I (Himes) [854]
INCOMPATIBLE, absolute truth is I (de Assis) [303]
INDELIBLE, fact worthy of I record (Whipper) [157]
INDEPENDENCE of the master (A. Davis) [1148]
INDEPENDENT men don't like I women (Chisholm) [970]
INDESCRIBABLE, love is I (Ellington) [741]
INDIFFERENCE, nothing so monstrously vast as our I (de Assis) [299]
INDIVIDUAL, every I and race that has succeeded (Washington) [397]
INDIVIDUALS, only excuse for pride in I or races (Douglass) [227]
INFERIORITY, talk about racial I (Schuyler) [713]
INFORMATION, one may receive the I (Toomer) [694]
INGRATITUDE is fatal to its author (P) [1188]
    kindness is rewarded with I (de Assis) [302]
INHERIT, anybody who believes the meek shall I the earth (Du Bois) [492]
    those who I fortunes (P) [1376]
INITIATIVE is the ability to do the right thing (K. Miller) [443]
INJUSTICE, bones of I (Garvey) [630]
    equality in I is justice (P) [1345]
    justice becomes I (P) [1377]
    of this world is great (Martí) [365]
INNATE, I had I capability (Parks) [863]
INSANITY is a matter of degree (de Assis) [307]
    life is half I (Margetson) [569]
INSATIABLE, two kinds of I men (P) [1343]
INSECT, no sound of I or of plundering bee (Heredia) [161]
INSIDE, tyrant is the slave turned I out (P) [1342]
    when hunger gets I you (P) [1275]
INSPIRATION of the race (Blyden) [285]
INSTINCT, human I to heed cry of the oppressed (K. Miller) [455]
INSTITUTION, we are students in a segregated I (Jordan) [1088]
INSTRUCTION in youth (P) [1364]
INSTRUMENTS, courts of the land are facile I (Griggs) [543]
    social sciences used as I (Du Bois) [501]
INSULT, prejudiced people can't I you (Bailey) [932]

LEANS, while one man L against another (Langston) [277]
LEAP, look before you L (Aesop) [17]
LEARN about politeness from the impolite (P) [1344]
    live L die (P) [1542]
    our children may L about heroes of the past (Kenyatta) [662]
    pray L first what 'tis to live (Terence) [27]
    to see listen and think for yourself (Malcolm X) [1005]
    we L the rope of life (Toomer) [697]
LEARNED, among other good trades I L (Bibb) [197]
    I have L that the art of rejection (Parks) [865]
    I never L to hate at home (Gregory) [1045]
    if I have L much from things (Washington) [401]
    I've L of life this bitter truth (G. D. Johnson) [612]
LEARNING, a little L indeed may be a dangerous thing (Douglass) [231]
LEAVE, I L you love (Bethune) [564]
LEAVES, oh the brown L (Bontemps) [752]
LEGALIZED murder or wounding of wage slave (Schuyler) [707]
LEGISLATE, you cannot L an attitude (H. G. Brown) [1143]
LEGS, give very long L to very brief ideas (de Assis) [310]
LENGTH and breadth the height and depth of prejudice (W. Allen) [262]
    pride only goes the L one can spit (P) [1378]
LESS, do more talk L (P) [1483]
    more you look de L you see (P) [1481]
LET him who wishes to hatch (P) [1468]
    love between us so divided be (Bedri) [429]
    no one trust the happiness of the moment (de Assis) [298]
    the history of the past be spread (Fortune) [378]
    us come together by the thousands (Bibb) [196]
    us go away (F. Johnson) [635]
    us hold up our heads (Washington) [399]
    us swear to the entire universe (Dessalines) [97]
    your doing be an exercise (Toomer) [686]
LEVEE, name was L camp music (Armstrong) [748]
LEVEL, men's minds are raised to the L of women (Dumas, père) [153]
LEVITY, man of L often errs (Sancho) [75]
LIARS, it is we who are L (Hughes)[756]
LIBERAL, when southern white man asks L Caucasian (Schuyler) [710]
LIBERALS in the House (Chisholm) [979]
LIBERATE, we have to L ourselves (Garvey) [618]
LIBERATED, African woman does not need to be L (Senghor) [819]
LIBERATION of oppressed people (H. G. Brown) [1141]
    true L can be acquired (Randolph) [644]
LIBERTY, abolition is the dawn of L (de Assis) [316]
    advocates of L should conceive the idea (J. Forten) [110]
    all men deprived of their L (Russwurm) [147]
    all our L ends (Vernon) [522]
    freedom and L are synonyms (J. M. Smith) [194]
    government that can give L (Douglass) [225]
    price of L is eternal vigilance (Douglass) [230]
    too much L corrupts an angel (Terence) [25]
LIBRARIES, you may ransack the L of the world (A. H. Grimké) [341]
LICKER talks mighty loud (P) [1527]

NECESSITY has no law (Terence) [20]
  is the mother of invention (Aesop) [9]
NECK, follow fashion break monkey' N (P) [1441]
NEED, knowledge is the prime N of the hour (Bethune) [566]
NEGRITUDE is a fact (Senghor) [822]
NEGRO, a question about what the N is capable of (Ward) [234]
  a scared N is one thing (Gregory) [1046]
  adaptability of the N (Gibbs) [256]
  America has put a tight shoe on the N (Gregory) [1048]
  American N isn't a man (Yerby) [908]
  demands and grievances of the N (Randolph) [647]
  demon the spirit of N hate is (Ward) [235]
  effort to make a case against the N (Ransom) [436]
  fear of N supremacy (T. Miller) [342]
  flesh of the N (P) [1515]
  God is a N (Turner) [289]
  grateful to friends (Roman) [469]
  I am a N (W. White) [668]
  I love being a N woman (Spencer) [607]
  if the N succeeds (Capponi) [335]
  I'm perfectly satisfied to be an American N (Fauset) [606]
  in the cane fields (Guillén) [797]
  no matter how accepted a N may be (Darben) [1016]
  one thing to save the N (Garvey) [627]
  prejudice against the N exists (Washington) [395]
  quartets and choruses (Robeson) [602]
  runaway N was the vanguard (Pickens) [585]
  struggle of the N (Pickens) [592]
  the American N must remake his past (Schomburg) [555]
  the N has always been a revolutionary (Powell) [827]
  the N has been a patient man (Chisholm) [967]
  the N has the field to himself (Rogers) [583]
  the N is a born anti-Fascist (Powell) [825]
  the N is a student of contradictory pretensions (Schuyler) [709]
  the N is bound to get his rights (F. J. Grimké) [346]
  the N is crying (P) [1519]
  the N is no longer running (F. J. Grimké) [348]
  the N is seldom frank (Pickens) [591]
  the N is the barometer (W. M. Young) [956]
  the N is the junior race of the world (Turner) [287]
  the N must be up and doing (Garvey) [629]
  the N problem (Killens) [907]
  the N was here before the Anglo-Saxon evolved (Chestnutt) [409]
  the N was invented in America (Killens) [905]
  the N who lives on the patronage (Garvey) [616]
  the N woman is the pepper (P) [1520]
  these songs are to N culture (Robeson) [729]
  to be a N in a day like this (Corrothers) [510]
  what a joy it is to investigate the N (Du Bois) [497]
  when the N gained his freedom (Mason) [459]
  younger N artists (Hughes) [757]

NOT her face (P) [1397]
  only crocus faces (Randall) [890]
  to know is bad (P) [1288]
NOTHING, ain't N an ol' man can do (Mabley) [682]
  foresight spoils N (P) [1159]
  God don't see fit to give the black man N (Hansberry) [1036]
  God gives N (P) [1211]
  he who can do N (P) [1295]
  if you ain't got N (Redding) [814]
  is achieved in a dream (P) [1217]
  is more disgusting (Ruggles) [182]
  is stable (Hall) [86]
  it N profits to show virtue in words (Saint Cyprian) [42]
  like poverty (P) [1174]
  man who has N (P) [1329]
  more tragic (King) [1026]
  pains people more than having to think (King) [1028]
  so monstrously vast as our indifference (de Assis) [299]
  talk without effort is N (Stewart) [164]
  to enter is N (P) [1461]
  war ends N (P) [1384]
NOTICE, one doesn't N his own faults (P) [1431]
NOTORIETY is often mistaken for fame (Aesop) [15]
NOVICES, most N picture themselves as masters (Toomer) [695]
NOW when the hopes and joys are dead (Whitfield) [253]
NYANGA make crab go sideways (P) [1489]

O my body (Fanon) [991]
  sovereign night (Martin) [421]
OBJECT of English navigators (Sancho) [73]
OBJECTIVE, we struggle toward the same O (Azikiwe) [796]
OBERSEER used to reggerlate daybreak (P) [1547]
OCCASION, it's the O that makes the revolution (de Assis) [318]
  when the O comes (P) [1193]
OCCUR, when God wills that an event will O (Bedri) [430]
OH, voum rooh O (Césaire) [869]
OLD, an O man was in the world (P) [1176]
  ain't nothin' an ol' man can do (Mabley) [682]
  carry me back to O Virginny (Bland) [367]
  civilizations die hard (Crogman) [329]
  flag never touched the ground (Carney) [322]
  flute of O age chafes the lips (P) [1375]
  good O days (Mabley) [678]
  I had ter sell dis O body (Griggs) [545]
  I know a man so O (Mabley) [674]
  my O man (Hurston) [783]
  my O mule (Hughes) [763]
  we are not O enough (Bowen) [376]
  word of O man (P) [1210]
  you who move like a battered O dream (Diop) [1018]
  young cannot teach tradition to the O (P) [1284]

PLOWED, black man has P hoed chopped cooked (Capponi) [334]
PLUNDER, comrades in P (P) [1390]
POCKET, appeal to the white man's P (Barnett) [440]
  good frien' better dan money in P (P) [1479]
POEM, a P is something sacred (Martí) [364]
POEMS, when P stop talking about the moon (Hughes) [766]
POETRY, being you, you cut your P from wood (G. Brooks) [911]
POINT, colored people are at a P (Fauset) [605]
  no man can P to any law (Douglass) [229]
POLES, when the French P Czechs come off boat (Cosby) [1101]
POLICY of those who proscribe any people (Delaney) [186]
POLITENESS floats 'round loose (P) [1548]
  learn P from the impolite (P) [1344]
POLITICS, in P (Randolph) [646]
POLLUTION so bad in New York (Mabley) [675]
POOR, happiness of P man (P) [1512]
  I was born P and colored (Hughes) [765]
  it's a P man who won't fight (Childress) [946]
  it's a P rule that won't work both ways (Douglass) [211]
  people entertain with heart (P) [1469]
  to be a P man is hard (Du Bois) [487]
  war is a P chisel to carve out tomorrows (King) [1035]
  we were P (Parks) [867]
PORTER, truth is the P of God (P) [1341]
POSSESSION of muscular strength (J. Johnson) [576]
POT, I hear melting P stuff a lot (J. Jackson) [1119]
POTENCY, if the word has P to revive (Ellison) [883]
POVERTY ain't no screw (P) [1532]
  anyone who has struggled with P (Baldwin) [958]
  borrowing is the first-born of P (P) [1249]
  is an orphan (P) [1432]
  is like honey (P) [1184]
  is who knows you (P) [1272]
  makes a free man become a slave (P) [1189]
  nothing like P (P) [1174]
  there is something about P (Hurston) [787]
  wealth and P lie together (P) [1398]
  without debt (P) [1339]
  work medicine for P (P) [1278]
POWER, arbitrary P exacts usury (Saint Cyprian) [40]
  black P is black responsibility (Powell) [838]
  is not merely shouting aloud (Nasser) [941]
  men like to hold onto P (Crummell) [238]
  such P has love (Fortune) [385]
POWERFUL, a P friend becomes a powerful enemy (P) [1301]
PRACTICED, philosophy is best P by the easy and affluent (Sancho) [68]
PRACTICES, so it P the profession (J. M. Valdés) [107]
PRAISE, men P what they know (Tertullian) [29]
PRAISED be the bush (Maran) [634]
  Harlem P reviled criticized ridiculed (Schuyler) [712]
PRAY, don't P when it rains (Paige) [808]

learn first what 'tis to live (Terence) [27]
we do not P not to be tempted (Origen) [36]
PREACH, unhealthy gap between what we P (W. M. Young) [954]
PREACHERS, today's listeners surpass yesterday's P (Vernon) [524]
PREACHING, doan' you hear me P (F. Johnson) [636]
PREFER, I P to see slavery go down peaceably (Harper) [268]
PREJUDICE against the Negro exists (Washington) [395]
  horrible thing P (Fisher) [722]
  I have no P against man or woman (Smyth) [330]
  if P could reason (Pickens) [588]
  is not dependent upon antipathy (Ruggles) [180]
  laws will not eliminate P (Chisholm) [973]
  length and breadth the height and depth of P (W. Allen) [262]
  no P against color among the slaveholders (Rock) [275]
  race P can't be talked down (F. J. Grimké) [351]
  race P is the devil unchained (Chestnutt) [411]
PREJUDICED people can't insult you (Bailey) [932]
  the ignorant are always P (Roman) [465]
PRESENT, past evils the cause of P chaos (Powell) [835]
PRESERVE, may God P us (P) [1236]
PRESSED, so often hast thou to thy bosom P (J. W. Johnson) [513]
PRETENDING, some of the best P (O. Davis) [917]
PRETENSIONS, the Negro is a student of contradictory P (Schuyler) [709]
PREVAILING, acceptance of P standards (Toomer) [688]
PRICE, death is the P of revolution (H. G. Brown) [1144]
  of liberty is eternal vigilance (Douglass) [230]
  of yo' hat (P) [1535]
  right kin' o' P allus pays (Dunbar) [536]
  soul has no P (P) [1328]
PRIDE, envy and P (Marrant) [101]
  I believe in P of race and lineage (Du Bois) [484]
  mek crab go sideways (P) [1489]
  of race (Schomburg) [556]
  only excuse for P in individuals or races (Douglass) [227]
  only goes the length one can spit (P) [1378]
PRIMARY motive of the black man (Pickens) [589]
PRIME, knowledge is the P need of the hour (Bethune) [566]
PRINCIPLE, self-love without P (Sancho) [70]
PRINCIPLES, humanity returning to first P (Vernon) [529]
PRINTS, among the multitude of public P (Sancho) [77]
PROBLEM, answer to the race P (Gregory) [1047]
  of the twentieth century (Du Bois) [488]
  one P thoroughly understood (Washington) [386]
  race P is a moral one (Crummell) [244]
  solve your own P (Capponi) [338]
  the Negro P (Killens) [907]
PROCEEDING, before P one must reach (P) [1293]
PROCESSED, I'd rather see a cat with a P head (H. G. Brown) [1145]
PRODUCE, a nation that continues to P soft-minded men (King) [1029]
PROFESSION, so it practices the P (J. M. Valdés) [107]
PROFIT is P (P) [1241]

people P by a preliminary dose of fear or force (Saint Augustine) [46]
    when morality comes up against P (Chisholm) [980]
PROFITS, it nothing P to show virtue in words (Saint Cyprian) [42]
PROGRESS goes forward ever backward never (Fortune) [381]
    tradition is the dead hand of human P (K. Miller) [448]
PROMISE get friend (P) [1523]
PROMISES, if the unemployed could eat plans and P (Du Bois) [495]
    shores of the great river full of P (Lumumba) [996]
PROP, property is the P of life (P) [1263]
PROPAGANDA, he who has a message and no P (Rogers) [582]
PROPERTY, a question of P in human flesh (Ransom) [434]
    I was regarded as P (Bibb) [199]
    is the prop of life (P) [1263]
PROPHET, it don't take a P (P) [1533]
PROPRIETY, she is a proverb of P (Dumas, fils) [259]
PROSCRIBE, policy of those who P any people (Delaney) [186]
PROSPER, no race can P (Washington) [390]
PROSPERITY, faith essential to P (Cotter) [432]
PROTEST, I will always P (Terrell) [458]
PROUD, be P of being black (Wright) [853]
PROVE, we have to P (Mitchell) [1081]
PROVERB is the leaf (P) [1244]
    she is a P of propriety (Dumas, fils) [259]
    when the fool is told a P (P) [1180]
PROVIDE, one fly doesn't P for another (P) [1409]
PROXY, thirst cannot be quenched by P (P) [1379]
PUBLIC, among the multitude of P prints (Sancho) [77]
PULLED, she P her horizon in like a fish net (Hurston) [786]
PUNISH the guilty man of colour (J. Forten) [109]
PUPPETS, we are P in the hands of Fate (Chestnutt) [413]
PURE, in all things P and social (Washington) [391]
PURGATORY is a pawnshop (de Assis) [313]
PURITY of woman is the P of the family (Bowen) [373]
PURPLE, a P star evolved in the depth of the sky (Rabearivelo) [790]
PUSH, don't you P me (Wilson) [1067]
PUSHES, if man P you (P) [1196]

QUALITY, vigor and Q of a nation (Kenyatta) [664]
QUARREL, hit a child and Q with its mother (P) [1233]
    is not a food which is eaten (P) [1166]
    with white man (P) [1516]
QUARTETS, Negro Q and choruses (Pickens) [602]
QUEEN, America cannot always sit as a Q (Douglass) [212]
QUENCHED, thirst cannot be Q by proxy (P) [1379]
QUESTION, a Q about what the Negro is capable of (Ward) [234]
    a Q of property in human flesh (Ransom) [434]
QUICK, error moves with Q feet (Crummell) [241]
QUICKSANDS, we are still surrounded by Q (Christophe) [113]
QUIET, his heart lies Q like limpid water (P) [1222]
    morning uptown on the Q street (Baraka) [1078]
    shaft of ridicule (Scarborough) [358]
    such is the Q bliss of soul (Horton) [119]

RACE, a R that does not read (Griggs) [547]
  answer to the R problem (Gregory) [1047]
  cultivate R love (Smyth) [332]
  every individual and every R that has succeeded (Washington) [397]
  first a R then part of a nation (Smyth) [331]
  I believe in pride of R and lineage (Du Bois) [484]
  I used to be a hater of white R (Washington) [402]
  impossible to raise and educate a R (Bowen) [375]
  in the R of fortune (Sancho) [74]
  inspiration of the R (Blyden) [285]
  is as the man (Pickens) [587]
  is but a date in history (Pickens) [597]
  locality nationality R sex religion may differ (Gibbs) [254]
  must make a common cause (Scarborough) [359]
  no R can accomplish anything (Washington) [400]
  no R can prosper (Washington) [390]
  no R can speak for another (K. Miller) [454]
  no R can wrong another race (Washington) [392]
  no R rises above its average man (Roman) [475]
  no religion operating in R relations (Redding) [815]
  not measured by its ability to condemn (Washington) [398]
  prejudice and R antagonism (Ransom) [439]
  prejudice can't be talked down (F. J. Grimké) [351]
  prejudice is the devil unchained (Chestnutt) [411]
  pride of R (Schomburg) [556]
  problem is a moral one (Crummell) [244]
  ruling class or R (Himes) [855]
  son of the land whose swarthy R late known (Aldridge) [173]
  the Negro is the junior R of the world (Turner) [287]
  to think unmoved of millions of our R (Manzano) [140]
  you gotta say this for the white R (Gregory) [1044]
RACES, I see the opening day of the darker R (Ransom) [438]
  modern science has not done away with R (Pickens) [593]
  nature created no R (Clarke) [895]
  only excuse for pride in individuals or R (Douglass) [227]
RACIAL, innate R differences (Powell) [829]
  period of R monopolies is at an end (Lumumba) [995]
  solidarity and not amalgamation is the goal (Roman) [461]
  talk about R inferiority (Schuyler) [713]
  to eliminate R discrimination and apartheid (Nasser) [943]
RACISM cannot be separated from capitalism (A. Davis) [1151]
  I believe R has killed more people (Childress) [947]
  is so universal in this country (Chisholm) [982]
RACKET, people dat stirs up de mos' R (P) [1552]
  rooster makes mo' R (P) [1526]
RADICAL, I was born to be a R (Powell) [828]

RADICALISM hatred and resentment (Fanon) [993]
  is a label (Garvey) [622]
  we need more R among us (Redmond) [176]

RAGGED, we are a R set (Stewart) [163]

RAILROAD, I was conductor of the Underground R (Tubman) [250]

Christians take R not from declarations of Christ (Marrant) [102]
good test of a man's R (F. J. Grimké) [350]
I never had R enough (Bibb) [198]
locality nationality race sex R may differ (Gibbs) [254]
man will be without R (Pickens) [594]
no R operating in race relations (Redding) [815]
one ounce of practical R (Sancho) [69]
strip American democracy and R of its verbiage (Rogers) [581]
without humanity (Truth) [133]
REMAIN, ancient things R in the ears (P) [1187]
men R in ignorance (Tertullian) [28]
REMAKE, the American Negro must R his past (Schomburg) [555]
REMEMBER Americans (D. Walker) [117]
you R Brotherhood Week (Gregory) [1043]
REMEMBRANCE, time causes R (P) [1224]
REMEMBRANCES, childhood R are always a drag (Giovanni) [1156]
REMINDED, every age is R by what it hears (Saint Cyprian) [39]
REMOTE, honor is R (P) [1303]
REMOVED, when we shall be R from the struggles (Bowen) [377]
RENT, I wish the R was heaven sent (Hughes) [760]
REPENT, we will have to R in this generation (King) [1032]
REPLIES, before one R (P) [1289]
REPRESENTED, everyone else R by lobby (Chisholm) [978]
REPUTATION, if your R in the community is good (Hughes) [761]
REQUIRES courage to read some books (Griggs) [546]
RESENTMENT, radicalism hatred and R (Fanon) [993]
RESISTANCE, act of R (A. Davis) [1147]
let your motto be R (Garnet) [205]
simplest trues often meet the sternest R (Douglass) [222]
RESPECT bought by gold (Harper) [266]
hungry men have no R for law (Garvey) [620]
no law can make one person love or R another (W. M. Young) [951]
the elders (P) [1281]
RESPECTABILITY, grade of work that determines the R (F. J. Grimké) [352]
RESPECTS, no nation R a beggar (Muhammad) [727]
true chivalry R all womanhood (Barnett) [441]
RESPONSIBILITY, black power is black R (Powell) [838]
rests not with the messenger (P) [1415]
REST, patience opens the door of R (P) [1349]
RESTING isn't getting there (P) [1371]
RESTORE, history must R what slavery took away (Schomburg) [557]
RESTS, responsibility R not with the messenger (P) [1415]
RESULTS, violence seldom accomplishes permanent R (Randolph) [642]
RETIRE, people do not R (Ellington) [738]
RETURN, I shall R again (McKay) [656]
since R to civilization (Henson) [477]
REVILED, Harlem praised R criticized ridiculed (Schuyler) [712]
REVIVE, if the word has the potency to R (Ellison) [883]
REVOLUTION accelerates evolution (K. Miller) [447]
death is the price of R (H. G. Brown) [1144]
it's the occasion that makes the R (de Assis) [318]
to take part in an African R (Touré) [957]

RULE, dollars not only count but R (C. T. Walker) [419]
   it's a poor R that won't work both ways (Douglass) [211]
   white folks see eleven inches on a foot R (K. Wright) [852]
   white man boasts of right to R (K. Miller) [446]
RULERS, God ordains kings and R (Jasper) [188]
RULES, if majority R (Roman) [466]
   majority R (Truth) [130]
RULING circles refuse to recognize my freedom was won (A. Davis) [1154]
   class or race (Himes) [855]
RUN, him dat fights an' R away (Corrothers) [509]
   hog R for him life (P) [1443]
   men try to R life (Toomer) [692]
   whole world is R on bluff (Garvey) [615]
   ye whose eyes with pity doth R o'er (Whitman) [355]
RUNAWAY, I was a R (Montejo) [424]
   Negro was the vanguard (Pickens) [585]
RUNNING, the Negro is no longer R (F. J. Grimké) [348]
   toga one drapes while R (P) [1300]
RUSH, angels R in when fools is almost dead (Fisher) [719]

SABBATH, I love to walk on the S (C. Forten) [292]
SACRED, a poem is something S (Martí) [364]
   I sincerely believe the S writ (Sancho) [72]
SAD, it is a S reflection (Crummell) [247]
SADISTIC, Aframerican not S (Schuyler) [715]
SAID, all is never S (P) [1242]
SAINT Louis woman wid her diamon' rings (Handy) [550]
SAME, we struggle towards the S objective (Azikiwe) [796]
   world changes men are the S (Wright) [848]
SANTO DOMINGO, colony of S (Toussaint L'Ouverture) [90]
SASS, blue bird S de robin (Dunbar) [541]
SATIETY, today's S is tomorrow's hunger (P) [1310]
SATISFIED, I'm perfectly S to be an American Negro (Fauset) [606]
SAUSAGES, don't chain your dog with S (P) [1530]
SAVE, one thing to S the Negro (Garvey) [627]
SAY, no one can S that Christianity has failed (Powell) [832]
   them S a so a no so (P) [1482]
   you S that I am a thief (Loguen) [193]
SCAR, I have a S on my back (Gaines) [1063]
SCARED, a S Negro is one thing (Gregory) [1046]
   guilty folks is S folks (Wright) [846]
SCHOOL, tomorrow S commences (C. Forten) [293]
SCIENCE, modern S has not done away with races (Pickens) [593]
SCIENCES, social S used as instruments (Du Bois) [501]
SCHOLARSHIP, originality is the essence of S (Azikiwe) [793]
SCORPIONS, your relations are your S (P) [1351]
SCRATCH, if you itch S (Cosby) [1107]
SCREW, poverty ain't no S (P) [1532]
SEA, between the sunlight and the S (Braithwaite) [573]
   one day we had a smooth S (Equiano) [91]
SEAS, over the S tonight love (Braithwaite) [572]

force will never be without a place to S down (P) [1246]
  we can't S and wait (W. M. Young) [955]
SITS, despair S on this country (Baraka) [1071]
SKIES, gray S are just clouds passing over (Ellington) [742]
  grey trees grey S and not a star (A. W. Grimké) [577]
  when fleecy S have cloth'd the ground (Banneker) [82]
SKILL, when Europeans gained maritime S (Clarke) [897]
SKILLFUL, to make a slave S (Crogman) [328]
SKIN, color of the S (Banneker) [81]
  my fight is not to be a white man in a black S (Killens) [901]
  you laugh because my S is black (Fortson) [650]
SKY, a purple star evolved in the depth of the S (Rabearivelo) [790]
  beneath S of her own native land (Pushkin) [145]
  is the king of sheds (P) [1286]
  midnight S and the silent stars (Douglass) [221]
SLANDERER, however high the S may rise (P) [1353]
SLATE, blue glaciers peaks of marble and of S (Heredia) [162]
SLAUGHTERS, an enemy S (P) [1257]
SLAVE, a S has no choice (P) [1331]
  accompaniments of the S system (Douglass) [215]
  acts committed daily upon S women (W. W. Brown) [202]
  if a S has a bad master (Douglass) [207]
  legalized murder or wounding of a wage S (Schuyler) [707]
  let the iron that enters into the soul of the S (Ruggles) [179]
  make a S skillful (Crogman) [328]
  master will not teach you knowledge of self (Muhammad) [725]
  my father was a S (Robeson) [731]
  poverty makes free man become a S (P) [1189]
  the slave does not choose his master (P) [1192]
  to make a contented S (Douglass) [219]
  to make a S skillful (Crogman) [328]
  tyrant is the S turned inside out (P) [1342]
SLAVEHOLDER, it is not the fault of the S (Northrup) [169]
SLAVERY, children born in S (C. Forten) [296]
  could S exist long (Harper) [264]
  exacerbated forever be this wretched S (W. Allen) [263]
  history must restore what S took away (Schomburg) [557]
  I . . . prefer to see S go down peaceably (Harper) [268]
  if there were no other fact descriptive of S (Douglass) [216]
  is a breeding bed (A. H. Grimké) [340]
  is gone (F. J. Grimké) [347]
  long way from S to freedom (Roman) [470]
  new-born babes . . . added to the victims of S (Harper) [265]
  not one feature of S (Pennington) [168]
  one sin that S committed against me (Pennington) [167]
SLAVE'S wisdom is in his master's head (P) [1177]
SLAVES, some of the S like us had kind masters (Love) [370]
  trees are tall black S (Silvera) [823]
SLEEP, beautiful night makes S impossible (Martí) [366]
  big blanket make man S late (P) [1437]
  have no massa (P) [1447]
  near relative of death (P) [1391]

spirit is reflection of S (Montejo) [427]
  such is the quiet bliss of S (Horton) [119]
  what is written upon the S of man (F. J. Grimké) [349]
SOULS, African guardian of S (Toomer) [683]
  give me black S (Parkes) [1050]
  I see their S (Bailey) [929]
SOUND, no S of insect or of plundering bee (Heredia) [161]
SOUTHERN, Northern blacks are S blacks (A. Young) [1052]
  this was a S auction (W. W. Brown) [203]
  when S white man asks liberal Caucasian (Schuyler) [710]
SOVEREIGN, O S night (Martin) [421]
SOWS, he who S thorns (P) [1356]
  he who S wind (P) [1455]
SPEAK, good man will neither S nor do (Cugoano) [93]
  I want my success to S (Darben) [1013]
  no race can S for another (K. Miller) [454]
SPEAKS, when the devil S the truth (Origen) [38]
SPECIAL plight for the black woman (Hamer) [923]
SPECTATORS, white Americans cannot stand as idle S (Langston) [276]
SPEECH, silence is also S (P) [1250]
SPEED don't look for S (P) [1238]
SPIRIT, demon the S of Negro hate is (Ward) [235]
  his S smoke ascended to high heaven (Cullen) [772]
  is reflection of soul (Montejo) [427]
  it is the S that knows beauty (Du Bois) [498]
  of war (Whipper) [155]
  sultan without S of justice (P) [1334]
  you can't regiment S (Bearden) [879]
SPIT, pride only goes the length one can S (P) [1378]
SPLIT tree still grows (P) [1294]
SPOILS, foresight S nothing (P) [1159]
  one falsehood S a thousand truths (P) [1183]
SPOON, without fingers the hand would be a S (P) [1290]
SPORTS, in the field of S (Darben) [1010]
SPOTLESS, an angel robed in S white (Dunbar) [531]
SPREAD, let the history of the past be S (Fortune) [378]
SPY, a S for both (P) [1410]
SQUARE, nobody knows what a S is (Ellington) [736]
STABLE, nothing is S (Hall) [86]
STAGNANT, on the edge of S shadows (Rabearivelo) [792]
STAIR, life for me ain't been no crystal S (Hughes) [759]
STAKES are high (Jordan) [1093]
STAND, the empty bag cannot S up (P) [1466]
  good run's better 'n' a bad S (Corrothers) [507]
  it takes guts to take a S (Chisholm) [969]
  right time to take a S (Powell) [837]
  sinner where will you S (J. W. Johnson) [514]
  white Americans cannot S as idle spectators (Langston) [276]
STANDARDS, acceptance of prevailing S (Toomer) [688]
  some people mistake their limitations for high S (Toomer) [696]
STANDING, I'm S in my tracks (Hurston) [780]
  is still going (P) [1323]

STAR, a purple S evolved in the depth of the sky (Rabearivelo) [790]
   grey trees grey skies and not a S (A. W. Grimké) [577]
STARS are foam-flecks (ibn Sa'id) [57]
   if S were loaves (P) [1298]
   midnight sky and the silent S (Douglass) [221]
START, we S with gifts (Toomer) [685]
STATE, a hellish S to be in (Garvey) [623]
   black man although reduced to the most abject S (R. Allen) [104]
   habits acquired in a S of servitude (R. Allen) [105]
STATUES, temples fall S decay mausoleums perish (Vernon) [515]
STAY, I elect to S on the soil (Purvis) [175]
STEAL, man of genius does not S (Dumas, père) [154]
STEEPLE, whatever you do do like a church S (Fisher) [723]
STEM, fruit must have S (P) [1195]
STERNEST, simplest trues often meet the S resistance (Douglass) [222]
STICKS in a bundle (P) [1311]
STIMULUS ever presented to the man of color (Russwurm) [149]
STIR about colored men getting their rights (Truth) [127]
STIRS, people dat S up de mos' racket (P) [1552]
STOCKINGS, shoes alone know if S have holes (P) [1462]
STOMACH, no idol as expensive as the S (P) [1269]
   when food is close to your stomach (P) [1204]
   when one man has his S full (P) [1205]
STONE, give a hungry man a S (Douglass) [209]
   throw S in market (P) [1277]
STONES, rolling S meet each other (P) [1454]
STOP, fiddlin' man jes' S his fiddlin' (Dunbar) [532]
   going slowly does not S one from arriving (P) [1251]
   underdog does not S to philosophize (Dunbar) [540]
   when poems S talking about moon (Hughes) [766]
STOPPED, one is S not for what he thinks (P) [1215]
STORIES, two ears do not hear two S (P) [1168]
STORY, mouth open S jump out (P) [1503]
STRAIGHT, though once S and tall (V. Smith) [79]
STRAIN, strong moralistic S (Rustin) [860]
STRANGE, human heart is a S mystery (Dumas, fils) [260]
STRANGLES, noose is a fear that binds until it S (Toomer) [689]
STRAW, man that carry S (P) [1487]
STREAM, however far the S flows (P) [1276]
   won't be advised (P) [1160]
STREAMS, rain S down like harp strings (Dunbar) [538]
STREET, bones before being thrown in the S (P) [1524]
   down on '33rd S (Hughes) [762]
   morning uptown quiet on the S (Baraka) [1078]
STRENGTH, guile excels S (P) [1259]
   hard to accept S and goodness (Bailey) [935]
   no S in a union that enfeebles (Fortune) [379]
   possession of muscular S (J. Johnson) [576]
   taking thought is S (P) [1245]
   union is S (Aesop) [10]
STRETCHING, if S were wealth (P) [1172]
STRIDENT, three hundred long ships with S beaks (Latino) [58]

STRIFE, peace is the exhaustion of S (Gibbs) [255]
STRINGS, rain streams down like harp S (Dunbar) [538]
STRIP American democracy and religion of its verbiage (Rogers) [581]
STRIVE to make something of yourselves (Crummell) [242]
STRONG, cunning better dan S (P) [1439]
  freedom belong to the S (Wright) [841]
  moralistic strain (Rustin) [860]
  thoughtless S man is chief (P) [1267]
STRUGGLE, in S for human rights (Pickens) [599]
  goes on (A. Davis) [1155]
  of the Negro (Pickens) [592]
  we S towards the same objective (Azikiwe) [796]
STRUGGLED, anyone who has S with poverty (Baldwin) [958]
STRUGGLES, when we shall be removed from the S (Bowen) [377]
STUDENT, the Negro is a S of contradictory pretensions (Schuyler) [709]
STUDENTS, we are S in a segregated institution (Jordan) [1088]
STUDERATION beat education (P) [1491]
STUDY, they who S mankind with a whip (Douglass) [220]
STUFF, I hear melting pot S a lot (J. Jackson) [1119]
STUMBLES, man who goes ahead S (P) [1313]
STUPIDITY, universal human S (Roman) [468]
SUBJUGATE, you cannot S a man (Clarke) [894]
SUCCEEDED, every individual and every race that has S (Washington) [397]
  free people of color have S (Rock) [273]
SUCCEEDS, if the Negro S (Capponi) [335]
  man who S (Pickens) [584]
SUCCESS, having attained S in business (F. M. Davis) [811]
  I want my S to speak (Darben) [1013]
  key to S (Cosby) [1108]
SUCCESSFUL, ultimate of being S (Price) [1023]
SUCH power has love (Fortune) [385]
SUFFERING, hope is delicate S (Baraka) [1072]
SUFFICE, if words S not (Aesop) [16]
SULLIVAN, Mr. S. didn't want to give me but four minutes (Mabley) [670]
SULTAN without spirit of justice (P) [1334]
SUN a disc of translucent glass (Darío) [480]
  cool you call him afternoon (P) [1499]
  never sets (P) [1412]
  sets misfortunes never (P) [1464]
  sought thy dim bed (McKay) [653]
  that bright swan (ibn Sa'id) [56]
SUNG, we've S sorry songs (Vernon) [527]
SUNLIGHT, between the S and the sea (Braithwaite) [573]
SUPERIOR, his wealth is S to him (P) [1225]
SUPERIORITY, men's S over the brute creation (Whipper) [156]
SUPERLATIVE, habitual use of the S (de Assis) [309]
SUPREMACY, fear of negro S (T. Miller) [342]
SUPPRESSED, hell to belong to S minority (McKay) [661]
  leaders of any S people (K. Miller) [449]
SUPPRESSES, distance S the unpleasant (P) [1161]
SURPASS, today's listener's S yesterday's preachers (Vernon) [524]

as T come (Giovanni) [1157]
for knowledge about all the T (Saint Augustine) [45]
hateful T sometimes befall the hateful (G. Brooks) [915]
if I have learned much from T (Washington) [401]
in all T pure and social (Washington) [391]
one of two T I had a right to (Tubman) [251]
people like to condemn T (Origen) [35]
time touches all T with destroying hand (Chestnutt) [405]
we must consider not only by whom all T were created (Tertullian) [30]
THINK, I don't like to T (Childress) [944]
I make people T (A. Young) [1058]
it's a awful thing to T about (Baldwin) [963]
learn to see listen and T for yourself (Malcolm X) [1005]
nothing pains people more than having to T (King) [1028]
to T unmoved of millions of our race (Manzano) [140]
THINKING, I was T about honors (B. Williams) [561]
of you (Hayes) [805]
THINKS, every age T it is perfect (Pickens) [596]
one is stopped not for what he T (P) [1215]
she even T that up in heaven (Cullen) [774]
THIRST cannot be quenched by proxy (P) [1379]
THIRTY-THIRD, down on T street (Hughes) [762]
THIS book is dedicated to all Caucasians (Schuyler) [711]
is called the land of the free (W. W. Brown) [200]
is the native rampart (Margetson) [570]
is the red man's country (Purvis) [174]
room is an unscored symphony (Davis) [810]
was a southern auction (W. W. Brown) [203]
THORNS, he who sows T (P) [1356]
journey of life is beset with T (Dumas, fils) [257]
THOSE, I know there are T who ask (Darío) [481]
killed by the lack of wisdom are numerous (P) [1271]
who are agitated must be chastened (Saint Augustine) [49]
who believe in ghosts (Roman) [474]
who inherit fortunes (P) [1376]
THOU knowest dear Florence (Manzano) [141]
THOUGHT breaks the heart (P) [1227]
only reconstruction worthwhile is of T (K. Miller) [453]
taking T is strength (P) [1245]
while with just T to know she lives (Martin) [423]
THOUGHTLESS strong man is chief (P) [1267]
THOUGHTS, what a plague of one's T (Saint Cyprian) [44]
THOUSANDS, let us come together by the T (Bibb) [196]
one falsehood spoils a T truths (P) [1183]
THREE, Mrs. Coley's T flat brick (G. Brooks) [909]
THRIVE, ability to T and live (Chestnutt) [408]
THROW a stone in market (P) [1277]
misfortune nebber T cloud (P) [1438]
no T away dirty water (P) [1448]
THROWN, bones before being T into the street (P) [1524]
THYSELF, before healing others heal T (P) [1292]

folks don't want peace (J. Jackson) [1120]
folks has their troubles (Chestnutt) [406]
folks see eleven inches on a foot rule (Wright) [852]
folks tell you (Haley) [949]
good W man dies (P) [1467]
I ain' no W folks nigger (Chestnutt) [410]
I do not hate all W people (Hansberry) [1039]
I used to be a hater of the W race (Washington) [402]
if W America chooses to withhold equality (Cosby) [1103]
Judas was W (P) [1518]
Lise however my mother was W (Durand) [323]
male America (Chisholm) [984]
man boasts of right to rule (K. Miller) [446]
man dancing (P) [1513]
man has become black man's burden (Powell) [831]
man has given us morals from his head (Garvey) [628]
man held onto us (Ransom) [437]
man lives in the castle (P) [1179]
man made pencil (P) [1274]
man stop lynching and burning (Mason) [460]
man's civilization a misnomer (K. Miller) [442]
man's happiness (Douglass) [214]
my fight is not to be a W man in a black skin (Killens) [901]
people know there is black art (Bearden) [875]
quarrel with W man (P) [1516]
shadow of W man (P) [1511]
sincere W people (Malcolm X) [1004]
to the average W man (Killens) [902]
we've got Chinese W black mixed (Guillén) [800]
when southern W man asks liberal Caucasian (Schuyler) [710]
woman has one handicap to overcome (Terrell) [456]
world has its jibes and cruel caricatures (Du Bois) [499]
you gotta say this for the W race (Gregory) [1044]
you'll never get anything from W people (Himes) [858]
WHITES, unfriendly W (Stewart) [165]
WHO I am (Price) [1024]
  poverty is W knows you (P) [1272]
  touches the father (P) [1305]
WHOEVER cooks the food of malice (P) [1260]
  heard of a mouse making a nest (P) [1531]
  spent the night on an estate (Manzano) [137]
  spurns what is short (P) [1239]
  wants me as I am is content (P) [1167]
WHOLE, it is better to be part of a great W (Douglass) [226]
  world is run on bluff (Garvey) [615]
WHY do you black your face (Fortson) [651]
  I know W the caged bird sings (Dunbar) [537]
WIFE, a man without a W (P) [1422]
WILL, abuse us as you W (Langston) [279]
  shallow understanding from people of good W (King) [1031]
WIN, I am not trying to W converts (Cosby) [1098]
  in the race of fortune knaves often W the prize (Sancho) [74]

ABOUT THE COMPILER AND EDITOR

ANITA KING is a freelance editor, writer, and researcher. Her articles have appeared in *ESSENCE* and *TUESDAY MAGAZINE*.